I was always comfortable relying on Ms. Assad's exceptional substantive expertise and commitment to her colleagues and our mission when we served together in an overseas war zone. Ms. Assad's deeply introspective account of her CIA career, faith, and humanitarian work is an exciting read with firsthand insightful observations of the war-torn Middle East and valuable lessons learned, which readers will cherish.

DANIEL HOFFMAN
Retired senior CIA officer

Michele Rigby Assad's *Breaking Cover* is an absolutely amazing read! It will grab your attention on every single page as you follow Michele's remarkable journey working as a spy for the CIA. Even as someone who spent three years undercover for the FBI at a Fortune 500 company during the investigation of one of the largest white-collar crime cases in US history, I was amazed at Michele's courage and perseverance as she fought terrorism in the most dangerous part of the world, the Middle East. I was especially touched at how she inspires us all. Michele Rigby Assad is a modern-day hero! Her book will inspire you to do more for your community, your country, and your society, and to live a life of significance.

MARK WHITACRE, PhD
Subject of the Warner Brothers movie *The Informant!,* starring Matt Damon as Mark Whitacre

The first time I met Michele, I was struck by her fashionista style, her quick wit, bright smile, and immense knowledge of the Middle East. She quickly proved herself to be a hard worker, a savvy ops officer, and an outside-of-the-box thinker. Her vivid descriptions of her life and travels with the CIA are very authentic, very personal, and a great read. The day Michele told me she was leaving the Agency, she explained that she felt a calling to do something impactful for women, and though she didn't know what that was going to be, she knew it would be significant. Her story is a riveting one. Although I can neither confirm nor deny that I worked with Michele, I can tell you she is a great patriot with a great faith who will continue to blaze trails wherever she goes.

FORMER COWORKER

Breaking Cover is an authentic and honest look into a world that operates all around us, but to which most are oblivious. Michele Rigby Assad masterfully shares the soul-baring tale of her life, from small-town Southern girl to fierce intelligence operative challenging evil face-to-face. This story is not a simple autobiography, but a story of how one individual—walking in humility and faith, recognizing that life is not about her, and willing to risk it all to serve her fellow man—changed and saved an untold number of lives. One thing is certain: *Breaking Cover* is just the beginning of Assad's story. The best is yet to come.

SUSAN RICHMOND JOHNSON
Managing principal, The Ashcroft Group LLC; former chief of staff for management, US Department of Homeland Security

Bold, beautiful, and brave, Michele Rigby Assad's *Breaking Cover* is a must-read. She grants readers rare access into what it's like to spend over a decade as an undercover officer in the CIA through riveting accounts of navigating life and work as a woman in war zones across the Middle East. Michele also lets us in on a bigger secret: She never felt like she was the secret agent type. Her courageous stories of resilience, faith, and grace will inspire millions of women (and men) to press on despite self-doubt, and to keep moving forward even in the face of fear.

JENNY BLAKE
Author of *Pivot: The Only Move That Matters Is Your Next One*

BREAKING COVER

★ ★ ★

MICHELE RIGBY ASSAD

BREAKING COVER

MY SECRET LIFE IN THE CIA
and WHAT IT TAUGHT ME *about*
WHAT'S WORTH FIGHTING FOR

TYNDALE
MOMENTUM™

The nonfiction imprint of
Tyndale House Publishers, Inc.

Visit Tyndale online at www.tyndale.com.

Visit Tyndale Momentum online at www.tyndalemomentum.com.

TYNDALE, *Tyndale Momentum*, and Tyndale's quill logo are registered trademarks of Tyndale House Publishers, Inc. The Tyndale Momentum logo is a trademark of Tyndale House Publishers, Inc. Tyndale Momentum is the nonfiction imprint of Tyndale House Publishers, Inc., Carol Stream, Illinois.

Breaking Cover: My Secret Life in the CIA and What It Taught Me about What's Worth Fighting For

Designed by Dean H. Renninger

Published in association with the literary agency of The Fedd Agency, Inc., P.O. Box 341973, Austin, TX 78734.

All Scripture quotations, unless otherwise indicated, are taken from the Holy Bible, *New International Version*,® *NIV.*® Copyright © 1973, 1978, 1984, 2011 by Biblica, Inc.® Used by permission. All rights reserved worldwide.

The Scripture quotation on page 216 is taken from the New King James Version,® copyright © 1982 by Thomas Nelson, Inc. Used by permission. All rights reserved.

For information about special discounts for bulk purchases, please contact Tyndale House Publishers at csresponse@tyndale.com, or call 1-800-323-9400.

This does not constitute an official release of CIA information. All statements of fact, opinion, or analysis expressed are those of the author and do not reflect the official positions or views of the Central Intelligence Agency (CIA) or any other U.S. Government agency. Nothing in the contents should be construed as asserting or implying U.S. Government authentication of information or CIA endorsement of the author's views. This material has been reviewed solely for classification.

ISBN 978-1-4964-1959-0

Printed in the United States of America

24	23	22	21	20	19	18
7	6	5	4	3	2	1

To my husband, Joseph: I wouldn't have done any of this without you by my side. Thank you for being my biggest advocate and believing in me when I didn't believe in myself. Thank you for teaching me so much about the world and pushing me to write this book—I wish that every woman would have that kind of champion urging her onward and upward.

To my sister, Julie Clow, an amazingly gifted woman who is not only the coolest and most intelligent person I know, but my best friend from birth. I couldn't have gotten through this life or written this book without your constant encouragement. You inspire me daily.

To my parents, Judy Morris and Art and Crystal Rigby, who taught me the power of positive thinking from a tender age, prayed for me through the darkest of hours, and rejoiced with me in the best of times. You never held me back from pursuing my dreams, even when they took me to places far from home.

CONTENTS

★   ★   ★

AUTHOR'S NOTE

★ ★ ★

A number of names and biographical details in this book have been altered to protect the identities of CIA sources, agency officers, and others who could be adversely affected by being associated with former CIA intelligence officers. Though the specifics of operations have been blurred, I have done my best to retain the details of my experiences, while changing enough information to protect sources, locations, and methods.

Thankfully, I documented many of my overseas adventures for personal as well as work purposes. During my first deployment in 2003, I started keeping a journal and shared many of those stories with a small group of family and friends. Regarding the evacuation, I kept notes on the interviews conducted at Mar Elia Church in Erbil, Iraq. Furthermore, I was able to refer back to a bevy of e-mails and cell phone texts to remember dates and specifics of that effort. The names and some identifying details of the potential evacuees we interviewed at Mar Elia have been changed to protect their privacy.

CIA operations included in the book were initially captured in agency cables in which I documented meeting dynamics, intelligence acquisition, and counterintelligence flags, as well as my findings and assessments. Since I am no longer employed by the CIA, I do not have access to those files and have had to recall those situations from memory. As a former employee, I obtained CIA clearance of the manuscript to ensure that no equities, such as sources or methods, would be harmed through the publication of this material.

PROLOGUE

★ ★ ★

"Why do you want to leave Iraq?"

The frightened family of six stared at us quizzically.

"Don't you already know what happened to us?" asked Danial, the father. "We thought that was why you're here."

He was right. That *was* why we were there. Over the course of the past week, my husband, Joseph, and I had interviewed more than four hundred Christians who had been driven from their homes by Islamic extremists and were now anxiously seeking asylum outside Iraq.

While many Muslims were also suffering, Christians were far more vulnerable. When ISIS or other Islamic insurgents took over a city, the Christians were ordered to leave their homes or convert. Many fled—but then had nowhere to go. They knew that Christians who sought refuge at UN camps were often intimidated, attacked, or persecuted in other ways.

"We want to know what happened to *your* family specifically," I told Danial. "If we are going to find a safe country willing to take you in, we must know the details of your stories so we can explain why these governments should help."

What I didn't tell him was that Joseph and I were also vetting those we interviewed. Our job was to ensure that there weren't any elements of ISIS or other extremist groups in the mix—anyone who could pose a threat, now or in the future, to countries willing to provide them refuge. As former CIA counterterrorism and counterintelligence specialists, we had the perfect backgrounds for such an undertaking.

By this point in the week, after meeting with hundreds of people, Joseph and I were beyond exhausted. We had to turn off our feelings in order to get through the interviews, which were filled with one dramatic story after another. We didn't have the physical or emotional bandwidth to process the depth of the tragedy these people, and hundreds of thousands like them, had endured. There was a job to do, and we had to get through it, tired or not.

That is what I told myself, anyway. At times, it was impossible not to respond to the utter desperation evident in so many faces. Not long before my interview with Danial, I'd sat across from a young husband and his wife. We had barely begun the interview process when their little boy began squirming on his mother's lap. Soon he was not only struggling to get down, but he became quite vocal, breaking the conversation with the chatty disruptions of a bored toddler. Both parents snapped at him, desperately trying to rein him in.

As I read the panic in his mother's eyes, I realized how terrified they were that their son might be jeopardizing the interview. I got out of my chair, knelt down in front of the mother, took the little boy's hand in mine, and asked, "*Kifak habibi? Ismak eh? Kam omrak?*" ("How are you, my love? What's your name? How old are you?")

Both parents told me his name was George, and his mother helped hold up three of his fingers to indicate his age. While I focused on the boy, squeezing his adorably chubby cheeks, faint smiles appeared on the family's anxious faces. I grabbed a plastic toy car from the table behind me and handed it to George.

As I noticed his parents visibly relax, I was struck again by the unfairness of the situation. This little boy was one of millions of Iraqis displaced by war. In a way, he was fortunate—he had lost only his home; his immediate family was still intact. Now his father and mother were desperately trying to get them out. They had no idea who we were or exactly what we were doing—only that we were working to find a safe haven in another country for one hundred or more Iraqis.

After concluding our interview with George's parents, we'd conducted several others without incident. The interview with Danial and his family proceeded like those before it until the family's eighteen-year-old daughter, Miriam, asked, "Can I please add my fiancé, Hamad, to the file? He is a convert from Islam to Christianity, and we are in danger if we stay here in Iraq."

"Where is Hamad now?" Joseph asked.

"He lives with his family here in Erbil," she explained.

That's odd, I thought. Most Muslim families are not at *all* accepting when one of their members rejects Islam.

"They are not happy about his conversion," she continued. "But he's not in trouble with them so much as ISIS."

"Why is that?" Joseph asked.

"Hamad's mother used to be a Christian. She converted to Islam when she married a Muslim man many years ago. When ISIS took over Mosul where they resided, ISIS was looking for people to shake down for money. Even though she was a Muslim convert, ISIS heard that she was formerly a Christian who still had Christian family members, so they kidnapped her and demanded a ransom. Hamad was frantic to free his mother, so he sold one of his kidneys. He sent the money he received to the kidnappers, and they released her."

What? I leaned forward in my chair. "Wait a minute. Your fiancé sold his *kidney* to pay a ransom for his mother?"

"Yes."

Joseph and I exchanged furtive glances. There was something very fishy about this story, and the more questions we asked, the stranger it got.

I suddenly had a flashback to my CIA days, in which we'd heard some really tall tales in the debriefing room. Experience had shown that the more far-fetched the story, the more likely it was to be a fabrication. But every now and then, a source would tell us something outrageous that we didn't initially believe but that would turn out to be shockingly true. Which one was this?

We needed to determine whether Hamad had *really* converted to Christianity. Was he a brave man willing to risk death for his newfound faith, was he just a liar seeking a way out of Iraq, or was he an Islamic extremist parading as a Christian convert to gain entry into another country?

What had begun like dozens of other interviews that week had taken an ominous turn. If we incorrectly sized up this man's intentions, we might be sentencing him to death at the hands of ISIS—but if he were somehow allied with them, we might be jeopardizing the lives of countless innocent people.

My stomach tightened as I looked back at Miriam's face, willing her to reveal something more about this man. She remained inscrutable, her eyes downcast, her hands folded demurely in her lap.

"Miriam," Joseph said. She glanced at him shyly. "We will need to speak with Hamad. Please ask him to come by this evening." She gave a quick nod.

Hours later, Joseph and I were back at the trailer that served as our office, waiting for the couple to arrive. My mind raced as I tried to put the pieces together.

The sound of heavy footsteps on the trailer steps, followed by the squeak of the door, made me look up. Miriam walked in first, trailed by a passive-faced young man.

On the surface, Hamad seemed just like any of the hundreds of other men we had interviewed—quiet, and with a vacant expression that resulted from utter defeat, from not being able to provide for or protect their families.

But Hamad was single. He didn't have a family to protect or provide for. The vacancy in his eyes was not one of embarrassment or failure; it was . . . *something else.*

Something was off about this guy *and* his story. I wasn't sure what it was, but I had every confidence that Joseph and I would get to the bottom of it. After all, this is why we had come to Iraq. This is what we had been trained for. We knew what converts looked and acted like, and we knew what terrorists looked and acted like. If this guy *was* bad news, we'd figure it out soon enough.

As Hamad sank down into the chair across from us, a rush of adrenaline coursed through my veins. *This guy doesn't know who he is up against.* Joseph and I stole a quick glance at each other. Neither of us showed the slightest trace of emotion, but the feeling was palpable.

We've got this.

CHAPTER 1

THE SPY NEXT DOOR

I never dreamed of becoming a spy. My dreams were for a much more pedestrian future: a comfortable home in the suburbs, a good, solid career, a couple of kids, and a white picket fence.

In fact, if you had told me twenty years ago that my calling would involve traveling to war zones or dealing with insurgents, I would have thought you were crazy. I wasn't exposed to such things growing up.

My dad, a traveling life insurance salesman, was on the road a lot, and my mom stayed home with me and my little sister, Julie. When I was six, my family followed my maternal grandparents from rural Pennsylvania to Mount Plymouth, Florida, a little town in the center of the state. We lived in "the sticks," which meant we were surrounded by cow pastures, orange groves, pine forests, and swampland. Sturdy oak trees dripping with Spanish moss and a tiny lake full of lily pads and reeds—not to mention herons, turtles, frogs, alligators, and water moccasins—added to the wild beauty of that rural setting.

Though I never strayed far from home as a child, I occasionally got glimpses of the wider world. Our neighbor Gladys paid Julie and me to water her plants each summer while she was on vacation. I would skip over to the house and water the dozens of houseplants. Before returning home, I'd sit on the floor in front of Gladys's bookcase and spend hours pulling issues of *National Geographic* off the shelf and carefully paging through their colorful, glossy spreads. I was transfixed. The cultures were so intriguing to me, and their strangeness made me ache for the rest of the experience: the sights, sounds, and smells that would accompany such forays into the unknown.

Occasionally missionaries would visit our little country church to talk about their work in other cultures. Julie and I still remember a few words in Portuguese thanks to the visiting missionaries who taught us a gospel song in that language. Being able to "learn" a foreign language left a lasting impression on me.

Still, the fact remained: My family was simple and didn't discuss politics, debate international affairs, or opine on world events. We were blissfully ignorant of military conflicts and foreign coups d'état. The only inkling I had that a crazy world existed out there was back in the eighties when I started seeing television broadcasts about hijackings of passenger airplanes.

I remember asking my mom, "Do you think it's possible *we* could ever get hijacked?"

"Oh, honey," she said, "you have nothing to worry about. It's only flights in the Middle East that get hijacked, and you'll never go there."

For sure, I thought, *I'll never go there.* (Spoiler alert: Never say never.)

Those who grew up with me and knew me as a sweet, southern girl are probably still shocked that I would even apply to the CIA. After all, how could the little ballerina voted homecoming queen—the girl who openly and frequently talked about her faith—get involved in clandestine activities that required such manipulation and deceit?

Michele Rigby, international spy.

It was—to say the least—a wild contradiction.

But as it turns out, that is *exactly* what the CIA was looking for.

Like most people, my only context for the CIA and its work was what I knew from TV and movies, so I had no idea what was real and what was fiction. All I knew was that it seemed like a place where only the world's most sophisticated and smartest human beings applied—not normal people like me.

Regardless, when the career center at Georgetown University announced that CIA representatives were coming to discuss job opportunities at the secretive organization, my curiosity got the better of me—even though I *knew* I wasn't the type of person they were looking for. So . . . like a meek little nun, I entered the library with my head bowed low and quickly took a seat in the back corner of the room.

After all, I reasoned, *it can't hurt just to listen, right? What do I have to lose?*

I was finishing up my final year of graduate school at the Center for Contemporary Arab Studies, and as much as I would love to say I had a clear career path in mind, the truth is, I had no idea what I wanted to do. And don't let the Arab studies focus fool you. My interest in the Middle East was more personal than professional.

In addition to being a floundering grad student, I was a newlywed.

I had met my husband, Joseph, during my senior year of high school. As a cheerleader, I often held get-togethers at my house after football games, and one night, one of my classmates brought along a young man from Egypt whom his church had been helping. His name was Joseph Assad, and he was unlike anyone I had ever met before.

We all sat with rapt attention as he told us what it was like to grow up in a part of Egypt that had given birth to a virulent form of Islamic extremism. He described the experience of being threatened by classmates whose parents were members of secret terrorist cells in the city and of being deliberately blocked from entering the university (or any college) in Egypt because he was Christian.

Though it's embarrassing to admit, prior to meeting Joseph,

I didn't even know that Egypt was a country. To me, it was just an ancient civilization, a historic land that I saw on the History Channel and read about in the Bible. Nor did I know that there were Christians in the Middle East, or that they had been so brutally persecuted for centuries.

Joseph's story amazed me. Having lived a remarkably sheltered life, I was astonished to meet someone who, at the age of nineteen, already knew what it meant to stand strong in the face of such intense intimidation. This wasn't just being picked on by the mean girls at lunch. This was life and death, and I was utterly and completely stricken. As I sat listening to Joseph share his testimony, I thought, *I want to marry someone just like that.*

Five years later, I did.

Joseph opened my eyes to a world I never knew existed. Shortly after we met, we traveled to Egypt as part of a mission team sponsored by Campus Ministries at Palm Beach Atlantic University. Despite all the drama in the region, my parents agreed to let me go. They trusted God, and they knew that he would take care of me. Looking back, it was incredibly brave to let their eldest daughter travel to the far side of the world, where the only thing dicier than being a woman was being a Christian. But they had the courage and the spiritual discernment to let go.

I, on the other hand, was the picture of naiveté. With no idea of the challenges before me, I jumped into this new adventure with the enthusiasm that only the young and inexperienced can muster. No one warned me of the intense heat, the swarming flies, the blood-hungry mosquitoes, or how hard it is to communicate with people who speak a different language. Almost immediately, the romantic notions I had created in my mind of how amazing this trip would be were replaced by the harsh reality of puking my guts out and nearly passing out from the heat and stress of physical labor.

During that trip, I saw things that I'd never seen before: gun-wielding soldiers on every other street corner, women shrouded in *hijabs* and suffocating black *abayas*, villagers washing their pots and pans in the Nile, donkey carts hauling their wares to market, and mud-brick homes situated along dusty, pockmarked roads.

We were enveloped by a world starkly different from our own. Had we known what we were getting into, some of us probably would not have signed up for the trip. Thank God I set off unaware, or I would never have received the blessings of being a member of that team. Not only did I learn a lot about myself and my faith, the trip made me realize how little I knew and how much there was to discover in this great big, beautiful world.

The following fall, I enrolled at Palm Beach Atlantic, where Joseph was beginning his sophomore year. Eventually I chose to major in political science. That gave me the opportunity, three years later, to return to Egypt as part of a study abroad program. In addition to studying politics, culture, religion, history, and the Arabic language, I had the chance to climb Mount Sinai, go scuba diving in the Red Sea, explore the great pyramids of Giza, meander through the busy stalls of the historic Khan al-Khalili market, watch the whirling dervishes in Old Cairo, tour the world's oldest Christian monasteries, and even star in an Egyptian television advertisement for Eva skin care products. (I was "discovered" by a television producer in an ice cream shop.)

We also spent three weeks in Israel and Palestine studying one of the hottest and most contested topics of the early nineties. The Oslo Accords had just been signed, and intense negotiations were continuing in an effort to keep both sides engaged and the process moving forward in a constructive manner. We met with political leaders, community organizers, and educators on every side of the issue. The briefings we received were sobering and insightful, taking on even more meaning as we made our way across Israel and the West Bank. The issues weren't theoretical but flashed regularly in front of our eyes. We could see the problems, and we could feel the tension as we explored the contentious Temple Mount and the Jewish, Arab, and Armenian Quarters of Jerusalem's Old City.

We also sailed across the Sea of Galilee, peered over the mountains of the Golan Heights into Lebanon and Syria, and followed the footsteps of Jesus in Bethlehem, Galilee, and Jerusalem. It was the education of a lifetime.

There is no question that traveling to the Middle East irrevocably changed the course of my life. The differences between my value system and the worldviews of the various Egyptians, Palestinians, and Israelis I interacted with made me hungry to understand them. What influenced their thinking, and what factors shaped their outlooks on life? I wanted to unlock the mysteries of human behavior and understand other people's frames of reference.

The summer after I graduated from Palm Beach Atlantic, we married and moved to Washington, DC, where Joseph began working as a Middle East research director at a think tank focused on human rights and democracy. At the same time, he worked on acquiring a master's degree at George Mason University in conflict analysis and resolution. Joseph's experience testifying before the US Congress and the United Nations Human Rights Commission in Geneva and focus on conflict and diplomacy in the graduate program prompted him to consider a career working for the government. To this end, he took the foreign service exam that is required to become a diplomat at the State Department. While awaiting the results of the exam, he began applying for similar jobs that could take advantage of his unique background, experience, and education.

Three months after moving to Washington, DC, I obtained a job working as an administrative assistant in the government relations department of a humanitarian organization before enrolling in Georgetown's Arab studies program. Naturally, my family and friends wanted to understand my plans for the future. "What will you do with an Arab studies degree?" they asked.

My answer didn't exactly induce confidence. "I'm not sure."

I knew that the degree was a stepping-stone to a variety of careers in journalism or with a think tank, the government, or an international organization. But what *I* would do with it? I had no idea. I just felt this insanely strong pull to study the Middle East. Travels to the region had whetted my appetite, and I had a burning desire to dig deeper, to learn more.

And so I did what I had always done: I heeded the urge deep within my soul, the feeling that I just had to take a particular course of action. I had made a decision very early on in my life that I would follow God's lead no matter where it took me. That visceral sense of direction had never led me astray, so I listened to it. Two years later, that same urging led me to the back of a crowded library to listen to a CIA representative describe a career path I would never have imagined for myself.

I don't remember much about what the recruiter said that day, but I definitely did not leave that room thinking I was the type of person the CIA was looking for.

Later that afternoon, while inserting my résumé in various recruitment files, I saw a box in the career center with a sign on it that read, "CIA: Place Résumés Here." Hundreds of hopeful applicants had flooded the box with their résumés. I threw mine on top. I don't know why I did that, other than the fact that I desperately needed a job. I was applying for any and all job opportunities.

A couple of weeks later I received a telephone call from a woman saying she was a hiring coordinator at the CIA. The agency had reviewed my résumé and liked what they saw. Now they were inviting me to a personal interview.

I was floored. *Out of all of those résumés, they picked mine? How is that possible?* I spent days preparing for that interview, but what I could not prepare for was the strange sensation of driving up to the gates of the massive, intimidating compound located in Langley, Virginia.

I swerved off Route 123 toward the main entrance and carefully followed the signs that separated the visitor line from the employee entrance. With great caution, I pulled up next to the guard gate to check in as I had been instructed. As I handed over my identification to the security officers, my heart felt as if it were beating out of my chest. I thought of Charlie, standing at the iron gates of the great chocolate factory preparing to enter the impenetrable fortress. Like him, I had gotten the Golden Ticket, and I was gaining admission to a place that I had only seen in the movies. The security officers were curt, further adding to the distinct sensation that I was utterly out of place, infringing on a top-secret facility that I really shouldn't have access to.

Despite my nervousness, the interview inside the great building went extremely well. The woman who interviewed me was intelligent and friendly. Soon thereafter, I received a conditional offer of employment to become a leadership analyst at the CIA.

The position is described online in this way:

> Leadership analysts . . . are responsible for providing U.S. policymakers and other relevant decision makers with assessments and analyses of foreign leaders and legislators/representatives, as well as other key members in the science and technology, social, cultural, economic, and military fields. . . . Leadership analysis is best defined as studying all facets of leaders, including their psychological components. This field of study, which is often seen as an offshoot of political psychology, utilizes the tools of psychology by exploiting the psychological traits of the individual in questions [sic]. Leadership analysts use this study of the psyche to analyze the leader's character traits within the context of society and culture.[1]

How they looked at my résumé and decided I was the perfect fit for this job, I have no idea. But then, who was I to question the CIA?

The offer was contingent on my ability to pass the polygraph test, medical examinations, psychological examinations, and a background investigation, all of which I was somehow able to schedule and complete while finishing up my degree.

In May 2000, I graduated from Georgetown with a master's degree from the Center for Contemporary Arab Studies. This had not come easily. The Arab studies program did not confer the degree until students passed the dreaded Arabic proficiency test, which included a written and verbal examination. But all the effort (including the Arabic-induced headaches) was worth it because I was going to work for the CIA!

Or so I thought. A week before my start date, I received an odd letter in the mail. It was from the agency, but it wasn't thick like all the other correspondence I'd received from them. The envelope contained one sheet of paper, a short message on CIA letterhead that said, "You no longer meet the requirements for this position at the CIA." The job offer had been rescinded. Bam. No explanation. Just like that. Gone.

My head was swimming. *What did I do wrong? Why do I no longer meet their requirements? What requirements are they referring to? What does this mean? What could I possibly have done to have jeopardized this job?*

After all the time and effort I'd spent to get a degree from Georgetown and secure the job, all I was left holding was a cold, impersonal rejection letter. I was devastated.

Maybe they are right, I thought. *Maybe I'm not a fit for the CIA after all, because I sure didn't see* this *coming.*

The next day, even though I was still in shock, I started my job search from scratch. I applied to every foreign affairs, think tank, advocacy, and intelligence-related job in the Washington, DC, area. Rejection after rejection piled into my in-box. Everyone seemed to have plenty of experts on the Middle East. The organizations and agencies that did have openings wanted people with years of experience. It's the conundrum every new graduate faces: How are you supposed to get experience if nobody is willing to give you a chance?

I would never want to repeat this period of my life. I was flooded with depression and insecurity. My chances of getting a job seemed just as impossible now as they had five years ago when I showed up in DC with a basic college degree. Despite my having obtained a graduate degree from a top school, nothing seemed to have changed. I was back to looking for temp jobs, competing against people who'd never been to college. I was placed in support roles under the direction of other recent graduates who had slid into these amazing positions. What did all these new graduates have that I did not? Why could they get jobs and I couldn't?

Every prayer I lifted up to God seemed to hang in the air, unheard or unanswered. In the silence I prayed, "God, where are you?" and "God, please show me where to go."

No answer.

The lack of direction made me feel empty, scared, and unsure of myself, wondering whether God had even heard me or was withholding something fabulous from me. Little did I know that he was moving the chess pieces where they needed to be, setting the stage for my future.

CHAPTER 2

THE RIGHT STUFF

Several months later, Joseph and I met a friend, Justin, for dinner. He was anxious to tell us that he had applied for a position in the CIA. He was at the very beginning of the process but was giddy with excitement because the agency had responded to the résumé he had submitted, and he had already been through one round of interviews. The wound I had received from the agency was still raw, so it was hard for me even to *hear* those three letters, never mind give support to a friend who desperately wanted to work there.

Not only that, but I had finally gotten a job with the Academy for Educational Development, a nonprofit organization focused on education, health, and economic development in countries all over the world. My job as a program associate was to design and execute a marketing plan for a national fellowship program.

I loved my new colleagues, and I thought the organization's mission was honorable. But it hadn't taken me long to realize that I was not a good fit for the position. For one thing, I didn't know much about marketing. Still, at this point in my career, I was simply grateful to have some positive forward momentum and the chance to catch my breath after losing the analyst position.

To his credit, Justin knew what I had been through and was

sensitive to my predicament. More important, he had something interesting to share. He hadn't applied to be an analyst, the position I'd been hired for; he had applied to be an operations officer.

What I didn't realize was that the CIA was split into multiple segments, known as directorates, each with a unique mission. The CIA consisted of the following:

- The Directorate of Operations (which would be called the National Clandestine Service from 2005 to 2015, when it would be renamed the Directorate of Operations)
- The Directorate of Intelligence (which would be renamed the Directorate of Analysis in 2015)
- The Directorate of Science and Technology
- The Directorate of Support

The Directorate of Operations collected and evaluated intelligence; the Directorate of Intelligence analyzed the information, placing it into context for policymakers and other intelligence consumers; the Directorate of Science and Technology ensured intelligence collectors had the technical tools they needed to do their jobs; and the Directorate of Support ensured the CIA had the necessary staff to execute the full range of intelligence activities.

Now it is likely that I heard this description of the CIA during the information session I attended at Georgetown, but having no context for the kind of people who get hired by the CIA, I didn't think much about its makeup or organization. So when I threw my résumé into the CIA box and was later contacted by recruiters regarding the analyst position, that's the road I went down. I had no idea there were other options.

"The place to be," said Justin, "is the Directorate of Operations." The men and women in this directorate identified, developed, recruited, and handled sources to acquire secret information of interest to US policy makers.

Granted, this seemed even more of a long shot—at least where I was concerned. While Justin and Joseph could easily see themselves in the middle of all the action, I could not even begin to envision myself in such a role.

After listening to Justin, Joseph decided to apply. He thought that I should too, but I declined. I had no choice. In the rejection letter I'd received, I had been told that I could reapply to other jobs at the CIA, but I had to wait an entire year before doing so. Six months had already gone by, but I wasn't in any rush to start that whole ugly process all over again. I was more than happy to wait and watch, to see how far Joseph and Justin would move through the convoluted employment process first.

Joseph submitted his résumé and almost immediately heard back from recruiters. He received a phone call in which they asked basic biographical questions and queried why he was interested in working for the CIA. They must have liked his responses because shortly thereafter, he received a letter in the mail inviting him to an informational session to learn more about the Directorate of Operations.

The event took place at a facility in the northern Virginia area with a group of about sixty candidates. One speaker described what it was like to be an undercover officer and work abroad. Another described the three main career thrusts: operations officer (OO), collection management officer (CMO), and staff operations officer (SOO). All of these types of officers are involved in the collection and dissemination of human intelligence—some more directly than others.

Recruiters asked the candidates to carefully consider which of the positions they preferred since they'd need to choose one before leaving the meeting. It seemed a little nuts to ask applicants to make this decision so early in the hiring cycle, before anyone had a clear understanding of which position was a good match. But again, who was I to question the CIA?

They also explained that the hiring process was long and intrusive because the CIA needs to be sure that they hire people with backgrounds, experience, and personalities best suited to the job. They are looking for a strange combination of qualities: They want people who are honest, but can lie. They want people who have not broken the law, but who are willing to do so (by carrying out intelligence acts abroad, we are breaking the laws of the foreign country). They want people who are authentic and forthright, but who have the capacity to manipulate. They want people who can work well in a team, but who can execute operations by themselves (most operations are solo). They want people who will plan and fully coordinate their operations in advance, but who are able to make changes on the fly, according to circumstances.

To summarize, the CIA is looking for walking contradictions.

The hiring and vetting process is also intensive because recruiters are seeking complicated human beings who can be trusted with some of the nation's most sensitive tasks. Furthermore, being an intelligence officer is not something a person does for only eight hours a day. Working undercover, leading a secret life, and lying to most people about what one really does is a full-time job. Intelligence is an all-encompassing profession that requires sacrifice in the service of a greater cause. This is not something you waltz into halfheartedly.

Officers don't just *live their cover*; they must be able to *defend* it. Their lives, work, and well-being depend on their ability to do this convincingly, so they must be able to handle the pressure that this entails. *Defending their cover* refers to their ability to answer questions about themselves and their jobs without inviting additional scrutiny or leading people to doubt their identity or intentions. Such questions come from a variety of people, all the way from unwitting family, friends, and casual observers to potentially hostile groups such as foreign governments, security services, police, undercover officers, or enemy groups.

To respond successfully to inquiries about their identities, jobs, activities, associations, or travel, officers have to be able to react quickly, to think on their feet. They must be clever and creative. They cannot give any indications that they are disquieted by questions. And above all, they must respond with confidence and grace. Maintaining calm under the most trying circumstances is something every officer must be able to do, over and over again. Preparation and consistency are key, but there will always be situations they never see coming and must respond to anyway.

CIA agents have to learn to appear normal and maintain the facade that "nothing's going on here," even when they are doing something that would appear fishy to bystanders. When I'd become an agent myself, I once had to play the part of a source who may have been compromised by a terrorist group during a training exercise conducted for another government entity.

The students in the training exercise were instructed to maintain constant surveillance on me to flush out the truth. They put me through a multihour exercise, making me walk for miles through all kinds of locations to determine whether I was dragging bad guys to the meeting site. Then to ensure I wasn't wired, the students gave me directions over my cell phone to lift my shirt and show my belly while turning around in a circle. They were presumably hiding out in a parking garage fifty yards in front of me, using binoculars to see whether I was wired or being followed. Now this command would have been fine had there been no casual observers around, but I was walking through a park, with many people behind me on the trail. *How do I do this without looking like a total nut or raising the suspicions of these bystanders?* I wondered.

I quickly raised my shirt to show my stomach, while dancing around in a crazy circle and howling, "Ahhhh! Bee! Get out, get out!" Nobody blinked.

That was an instance of thinking fast during a fleeting operational scenario. Keeping a clear head when dealing with unexpected incidents is a critical aspect of the job.

Maintaining their cover is a burden officers bear throughout their career in the Directorate of Operations. But it doesn't stop when they leave the CIA: They must protect their cover even after retiring from the agency. Dropping cover requires special permission, so officers who leave the CIA are legally obliged to protect that cover, to maintain the stories they have told, until given special dispensation to say otherwise.

In addition to the pressures of maintaining their cover, candidates must be aware that intelligence is a risky job. In many places in the world, recruiting and handling spies is a dangerous business. Not everyone can handle the pressure of carrying out illegal acts under the noses of foreign security services that are actively looking to identify (and ultimately detain) spies and thwart CIA operations.

Intelligence officers know what the worst-case scenarios are and are taught how to minimize the risk. Though they don't fixate on all that can go wrong, if they're discovered abroad in hostile territory, their activities or associations could land them in prison or get them killed. In the best-case scenario, they would be detained, interrogated, and then expelled from the country. Such incidents rarely occur thanks to the painstaking planning that goes into every operation, big and small. But candidates must be cognizant that this isn't a game. The threats are real, and the missions can be perilous.

Vetting practices are stringently applied throughout the employment process to ensure that enemies of the United States do not penetrate the ranks of intelligence officers. Joseph later told me that at his initial meeting one of the recruiters, who had spent most of his career in the Middle East, joked to the group, "For all we know, there could be an al-Qa'ida member sitting here amongst us."

Being the only person of Middle Eastern descent in the room, Joseph felt a little awkward. He hoped nobody was looking at him and wondering whether he was a terrorist or counterintelligence threat.

At the end of the meeting, applicants filled out a form confirming their continued interest in being considered for the CIA. Each candidate was asked to choose one of the three positions they had heard about in the session. Joseph checked a box, handed in the form, and then came home and told me all about it. He was so excited.

As for me, I was still conflicted. The CIA made perfect sense for someone like Joseph. He was smart, confident, and a world traveler, and he had already proven his courage in the face of intense opposition. While I had my degree and a handful of mission trips under my belt, I thought that I was less of an action person and more of a people person. All the spies I had seen on TV or in the movies were hard-nosed, operational types. I was more relational, more sensitive. I just wasn't sure I was wired for a position like this.

A few weeks later, Joseph was invited for three days of interviews and processing. That is where he met a recruiter named Jill. Jill spent hours getting to know Joseph, asking him questions like "Why do you want to work for the CIA?"

Personally, I think candidates' answers to this question go a long way in showing recruiters applicants' understanding of the job, as well as their motivations for wanting to join. For instance, a candidate who answers, "Because I'm really good with a weapon" doesn't have a realistic understanding of the CIA's mission and activities. The job is not a law enforcement position.

Joseph's response was quite different: "Because I was born in the Middle East and spent most of my formative years there, I understand the threat of Islamic extremism to the world. I suffered as a young Christian at the hands of extremists in my hometown. Given this background, I feel I have a deep understanding of both Islam and extremism, and believe that I can make a contribution to America's security. As a new immigrant, I value the freedom that this country stands for. Many Americans take these freedoms for granted. I don't. I would be honored to defend those freedoms because I know what it is not to have them. Furthermore, I speak Arabic, and I look Middle Eastern . . . I can blend in."

At some point during the interview, Joseph mentioned that he had a spouse who knew the Middle East well and had a graduate degree in Arab studies. This *really* got Jill's attention. After asking some questions about me and my background, she told Joseph that I would *also* be a good candidate for the NCS. She suggested that Joseph share this information with me and that if I was interested, I should apply—immediately.

When Joseph told me how interested Jill was in me, I was dubious. After all, the agency had already turned me down once, and I had no idea why. Still, Joseph's chances were looking extremely good, and I had to admit, it *would* be kind of cool to work side by side. So I threw caution to the wind and reapplied. What could it hurt to try? The worst thing they could say was no.

As soon as I submitted my résumé, Joseph alerted Jill. A couple of weeks later, my phone rang. It was a recruiter for the Directorate of Operations who wanted to ask me a few questions. I couldn't believe my ears. *I thought I had to wait a year. What exactly did Joseph say about me to that woman?*

The recruiter was surprisingly friendly and easy to talk to. She asked me a variety of questions to test my knowledge of international affairs. To my amazement, I passed the interview and was invited to a small gathering at a public location to learn more about the agency's recruitment process, much like the one Joseph had attended a month or two before.

The recruiters explained that they were searching for men and women with a deep curiosity about the world. They wanted people who were well-traveled, adventurous, and familiar with other languages, and who had studied abroad. Even more specifically, they wanted emotionally intelligent individuals with solid people skills who could read others well and key into their personalities, moods, motivations, and feelings.

I almost fell out of my chair. I had never heard such a strange job description. It was as if they were describing me to a T. I wanted to jump up and down like a rambunctious little kid with my hand in the air yelling, "Me! Me! Me! That's me!"

I have always had an uncanny ability to figure people out. It is not enough to know *what* someone does; I have to understand *why* he or she does it. I am driven to identify people's values, ascertain their strengths and weaknesses, and ultimately interpret why they behave the way they do. People are complicated creatures, and I am motivated to figure them out because it helps me to make sense out of life. It brings order out of the chaos.

In addition, I was born with a strong empathetic nature. Back when I was in the third grade, a new boy named Joey joined our class midway through the year. I assumed from Joey's high-water pants and straggly hair that he was probably from a poor background. His clothes were dirty, and he smelled as though he didn't bathe regularly. He was shy and withdrawn, with eyes full of sadness. Joey clearly needed a playmate, but I was a girl, and this was third grade. Someone might have accused us of "liking" each other, and that would have been unacceptably embarrassing!

None of the kids wanted to hang out with Joey, so I went to one of my male friends and implored him to intervene.

"Ben, you know the new boy, Joey, right? Will you play with him during recess? I think he needs a friend. I would do it, but I'm a girl."

That afternoon, Ben reluctantly brought Joey into the play group, and it was the first time I saw Joey having a good time at school. I felt such a sense of relief to know that Joey wasn't sitting in the corner nursing a broken heart.

This same concern for others' well-being and emotions surfaced regularly at home, too. Whenever my parents argued, I would compile a list of things that each of them could do to meet the other's expectations. I desperately wanted them to get along, to feel better. When I presented the list to my parents, they were shocked that a ten-year old would be trying to help them work out their issues. But I did. It was just my nature.

I also became quite adept at reading body language. For example, when my mother came home from work, I knew whether she'd had a good day or a bad day within seconds of her parking her car and walking in the door: The way she carried her bags, the way she breathed, and the speed with which she greeted us told me a lot. I adored my mom and was every bit as familiar with her behavior and emotions as she was with mine.

I never imagined that this proficiency in reading and understanding others would be the foundation for a career in intelligence. The traits I always considered weaknesses were actually perceived as strengths—by the CIA of all places!

Throughout the briefing, the recruiters kept throwing out the words *espionage* and *manipulation* while monitoring the crowd for telltale signs of anxiety. They announced—in no uncertain terms—that this was not a game. This was real life. We would be hired to manipulate others in order to obtain critical intelligence.

One recruiter fixed us with a somber stare as he explained, "Intelligence officers recruit spies to commit espionage against their country or turn against the other members of their insurgent group. If this is unpalatable to you, if it goes against your values or morals or just doesn't fit your personality, then please *self-select* out of the process."

Several people stood and left the room right then, never to return.

Strangely, I did not find the recruiter's explanation off-putting. Words like *espionage* have such negative connotations, but I saw them as being acceptable if applied in a particular way. For me, the ends justify the means *if* what is being done is in the best interests of those involved in the transaction.

In other words, my motivations are key. I would never be comfortable trying to persuade someone to act in a certain way if I was doing so with malicious intentions. If, however, I can find a way to appeal to someone in an honest and forthright manner (arguably one of the most effective methods of selling anything), then I don't see my values as being incompatible with the requirements of the job.

In my mind, manipulation meant that I would be using my powers of persuasion to shape another person's ideas or behavior. I would be working to get something I needed from him or her, which would require a strategy and the intention to achieve a certain set of objectives.

A variety of professions require such skills to do the job well. This is what salespeople, marketers, real estate agents, business associates, and diplomats do. The significant difference is that the stakes in the CIA are higher and far more serious than sales bonuses or the bottom line. The couple walks off the car lot without buying a Toyota from you, negotiations break down and the business deal fizzles, the potential client does not choose your company. Such situations pale in comparison to the life-and-death scenarios that play out in the world of counterterrorism and counterintelligence.

The other critical piece to point out is that the recruiters were not suggesting that we should be Manipulators (with a capital *M*), only that we should have the emotional maturity to compartmentalize how and when we "turned it on."

CIA officers need to be wise to the world and knowledgeable of the risk. Intelligence officers need to know how to play the game. But it should not be a self-serving exercise, nor is it about officers hiding their hand or employing their people powers in the worst possible ways. Unlike in the movies, the CIA doesn't resort to blackmail. The agency doesn't twist people's arms, issue threats, or seek to intimidate anyone in order to obtain their cooperation. That kind of manipulation is out of the question. Ours is a much more subtle game.

As the recruiters continued to talk, I conceptualized the mission and could clearly see myself being a part of it. I was all too aware of the experience of the canaries in the coal mine—the Christians of the Middle East, who had already suffered persecution at the hands of the Muslim Brotherhood, Egyptian Islamic Jihad, and al-Qa'ida. Having become intimately familiar with the nature of those attacks and the ideology behind them, I knew what was coming to the West.

The threat emanating from terrorists in the Near East region was significant; they had already transferred their attention from local targets such as military, police, and security services to US interests at home and abroad. Al-Qa'ida had shown its global ambitions as an international terrorist organization by attacking the US embassies in Nairobi and Dar es Salaam in 1998, and the USS *Cole* in Yemen in 2000. We were definitely on the terrorists' radar.

Instead of being frightening, the idea of being part of the counter-terrorism mission excited me. I have always been fiercely patriotic. And I am extremely loyal. It was clear that this would be no easy battle. Indeed, if words like *manipulation* scared the people in that room, then counterterrorism was far beyond the borders of what they could handle.

Many things intimidate me, but I had no problem with any of the explanations the recruiters provided. Instead of being put off by descriptions of what CIA intelligence officers are expected to do for their country, I got more and more antsy with excitement and found it difficult to stay in my seat. The recruiters' straight talk did not give me pause. I was all in, if they would take me—*if* being the key word.

Three weeks after that informational meeting, I received an unscheduled phone call from a different recruiter. Unfortunately, the second phone interview did not go as well as the first. The interviewer asked which part of the world I knew the most about. Without hesitation, I proudly answered, "The Middle East!"

"Great," she said. "I'm going to ask you about Latin America." (*Uh-oh.*) I hardly knew a thing about my southern neighbors. I had tried to learn by reading newspaper articles on Central and South America, but I quickly found myself bored and reverted back to pieces on Africa and the Middle East.

The interviewer asked me the name of the person who had just been elected the president of a country in Latin America. She reminded me that it had been a landmark election. I was so embarrassed—I had no idea. I stalled. I hemmed and hawed, hoping the elusive answer would just magically pop into my head. After giving what turned out to be the wrong response, I apologized to the recruiter and said, "I don't want you to think I'm not educated about world events. I just don't focus very much on Latin America."

My performance was a total fail. I deeply regretted being so unprepared for those questions and began to beat myself up. *It wasn't even a difficult one! I should have read more newspaper articles! I should have devoured the* Economist *cover to cover! I shouldn't have skipped the Latin America section!* But there was nothing I could do about it now. I'd had my chance, and I blew it.

Despite thinking that my candidacy had come to an abrupt end, a month later I received another phone call from the CIA. The purpose for this phone call shocked me—I had made it to the next level and was being asked to come in for extensive personal interviews, as well as three days of physical exams and psychological testing. I was floored. *How did I make it through the sifting process when I flubbed the last phone call so badly?* Well, I wasn't about to ask. I just accepted the offer and scheduled the upcoming interview.

A couple of weeks later, I went to a satellite CIA facility for an interview that lasted several hours. The sheer length of our conversation gave the recruitment officer plenty of time to get to know me. I discovered that it's hard to hide our deficiencies or strange personality quirks from potential employers when we're questioned long enough.

Although I was nervous, I felt comfortable speaking to the officer. In fact, I prefer interviews to written application forms, as I believe they give me the best chance to express myself and to connect with potential employers. I felt confident about the expertise I had gained through all my travels and degrees, and I felt passionate about working for the US government. Like most people, I'm far more interesting in real life than I am on paper, and I wanted to show the interviewer who I really was.

Everything was going smoothly until the woman explained that we were going to do some role-playing to see how well I could think on my feet. Knowing my specialization was the Middle East, she asked me to pick a country in that region. From out of nowhere, and for some unknown reason, I chose a place I had never been to and knew the least about in the Middle East.

"Saudi Arabia," I blurted out. *What? What did I just say? Where did that come from?*

Naturally, out of all the countries in the world, it turns out my role-player just happened to be an expert on Saudi Arabia's history and culture. I knew several other countries in that region like the back of my hand, but no, I chose the not-so-magical kingdom. Internally, I was kicking myself, desperately hoping that I would not reveal how little I knew about Saudi Arabia. I wondered if I was about to replay the experience of the phone interview in which my lack of knowledge of Latin America became glaringly obvious.

Somehow, by the grace of God, the role-playing session proceeded without a hitch. I was able to react quickly, think on my feet, and handle myself with confidence and tact. Instead of being a liability, the role-play was the seal of a great interview. I left the room feeling that the interviewer had really gotten to know me as a person and had dug down to the core of who I was. I had presented myself well. As a result, the interviewer knew about my life, personality, motivation, expertise, and preferences in intimate detail, and she could make an informed decision as to whether or not I was suitable for the clandestine service. I surely had no idea, but I was hoping that she did.

After completing several days of personality inventories and psychological testing, I was seated in front of a psychologist, who opened the conversation in a very unorthodox manner. Mind you, at the time, I considered the CIA to be an all-knowing, omnipotent giant, so I was utterly intimidated. The doctor informed me, "Michele, based on the way you answered the questions on the psych exam, we have determined that either you're lying or you are a psychopath."

Huh? I swallowed hard. *Oh, Lord, how do I respond to that? What should I say?* Neither option he'd given me was palatable or true.

"Um, sir, I was definitely *not* lying," I countered. "I just found some of the questions hard to answer because they were unclear; I would answer them differently depending on the situation or circumstances."

He stared at me for what seemed like an eternity. My heart was racing, and my palms were sweating. The interview never really recovered. It was a bust. I don't remember anything else we discussed; all I remember is that I couldn't wait to get out of that chair. I practically flew out of the psychologist's office as soon as he released me. This time I was certain that he was drawing a big X on my recruitment file, and I was about to be kicked out the door. Even now, I don't know if he was having an off day or if there was some method to his madness. But for whatever reason, months later, I found out I was still in the running.

The next step was a polygraph test. I need to clarify something. To say that a polygraph is *not* a *big* deal is a *big* fat lie—unless you *are* a psychopath, which, clearly, I am not. The examiners tell you not to be nervous while they hook your body up to a strange-looking device with all manner of wires, finger clips, and sensors that measure your heart rate and respiration. You are told to clear your head and relax, but as the examiner asks whether you have ever lied or cheated, a movie reel of material flows through your mind—every sin you have committed in your whole life. The polygrapher reminds you that you need to clear your head and *just* answer the question, but all you can think of is *I'm a sinful person. I've made plenty of mistakes in my life. What else am I forgetting to confess?*

It is at this point that all serious Catholics, evangelical Christians, Mormons, and other conservative people of faith completely fail the exam because we know—based on decades' worth of preaching—that if we have even considered a sin in our hearts and minds, it's as if we've *committed* the actual sin. We feel so guilty for our transgressions that the polygraph goes haywire, making it look as if we just tortured and killed someone in the waiting room before waltzing in for the exam. For people like us, the polygraph is akin to hell. There is no way around it. Ironically, the polygraph is a torture device that is most effective with people who have a conscience. The rest seem to get through it without a hitch.

And yet somehow, I came out on the other end. It took me numerous sessions, but at some point the polygrapher declared that I had sufficiently passed the test. Despite a less-than-stellar phone interview, struggles getting through the polygraph, and a miserable meeting with the psychologist, I was offered a position in the CIA's Directorate of Operations. It had *finally* happened. Despite the suspicion I had lugged around for years that I was less intelligent than everybody else in DC, I was exactly the way I was supposed to be! It seemed I had finally found my niche.

Even more exciting, while I was going through all that processing, Joseph received word that he had been accepted into the Directorate of Operations and had already begun his secret agent training. Unfortunately, because I started the process later than he did, we wouldn't be in the same training group. But we had both made it through the hiring gauntlet! Joseph and Michele Assad— secret agents in training.

Years later I learned that the rejection I had received regarding the analyst position was a meaningless form letter. I hadn't done anything to jeopardize my employment. The Directorate of Intelligence had simply overhired for the positions they needed to fill, assuming that some of the candidates would not make it through the background checks, polygraph, drug testing, or other aspects of the employment processing. Because my background investigation took longer than other people in line for the job, they slid into the available positions first, and I was relegated to the cutting room floor. It was maddening to realize that I had allowed myself to be weighed down by the scarlet letter of shame and rejection, only to find out that there was never anything wrong with me.

But here's the interesting part. Had things gone smoothly, had I actually started work as an analyst, I would not have fulfilled my calling to serve in the Directorate of Operations—a much better fit for my gifts and personality. The CIA does not want its employees to shift from one directorate to another, so once you're in one, that's where you stay. I could not have started out in the Directorate of Intelligence and then later moved over to become a clandestine agent. While a few people have managed to make the great leap, it is extremely difficult to do and requires the intervention of senior officers. It takes years to accomplish *after* you make your mark as an analyst. It is easier to come in from the cold than to transition from one directorate to another.

Had I started work as an analyst, my life would have been very different. I wouldn't have spent much of the next ten years of my life overseas. I wouldn't have served on the front lines of the war on terror. I wouldn't have been involved in intelligence collection efforts and operations that saved so many lives. I wouldn't have become a counterterrorism or counterintelligence specialist. I wouldn't have discovered the fullness of my gifts. I didn't know all that, but God did. He had a much better plan for me.

This turned out to be one of the biggest lessons of my life: When we are seeking God and trying to align ourselves with his will, we will occasionally miss the boat. We are human beings. We do this. But God doesn't give us only one chance to get it right. He will do whatever is necessary to get us back on track. I now realize that God threw me off course to get me back on course. The whiplash I experienced from this course correction was painful and shocking. But it taught me to trust the Force greater than I.

CHAPTER 3

DON'T JUDGE A SPY
BY HER COVER

Joseph was midway through his training when I began mine. I was sworn in as a member of Class 10 just four months after the September 11 tragedy. Joseph was one class ahead of me. He had already completed the first half of training and, along with the rest of his class, had transitioned over to "The Farm," a CIA covert training facility, for the second half of the program.

While he was able to give me a vague overview of the training process, the CIA doesn't allow trainees to share specifics with the next class. Most of the training exercises were designed to trip us up and expose potential weaknesses in our character and abilities. Therefore, it was vital that we all came in blind. Even though I had made the cut, I was still feeling a little insecure and wished that I could know the outcome ahead of time—would I be able to get through this, to pass the training and come out on the other end?

After a few weeks of administrative processing, my group left headquarters for a secret satellite facility to begin training. Classroom instruction and discussion were followed by role-playing exercises out on the streets with a cadre of experienced intelligence agents as we learned the ins and outs of planning and executing intelligence operations. Most notably, we started learning about cover—how to be one thing while pretending to be another.

The television show *Alias* was on at that time, and I thought that Sydney Bristow was the coolest character ever. Sometimes, to overcome the intense stress, I would pretend that I was training to be Sydney (of course, without the cool blue wig and hand-to-hand combat). I know—real professional. What can I say . . . sometimes you play mind games to get yourself over the hump, and this is just one of the things that worked for me.

My training partner was a young man named Adam, a former police officer from Boston. The two of us had very similar personalities. In fact, when everyone in the class took the Myers-Briggs personality type inventory, Adam and I were an exact match. Adam was so much like me it was ridiculous. He was like a male version of myself, which I found strangely comforting as we embarked on this crazy journey to become intelligence officers.

Our first training instructor was a guy named Jim. He was a living legend at the CIA—the kind of spy who lived and breathed operations and set the standard for all the young officers who came after him. By the time I started the training program in 2002, Jim was well past his glory days and two decades into retirement. Regardless, he was full of life and brimming with energy. He talked with great fondness of his time in the field and was eager to tell stories of his early years in the CIA. I couldn't believe my good fortune at getting placed in his charge for the first half of training, when mentorship from your instructor is key to learning the ropes.

While our class was much larger, mentorship sessions took place daily in a small and much more intimate group setting, which included one instructor and two students. After shaking our hands, Jim sat down to introduce himself to me and Adam. "Welcome to the CIA," he said. "I'm here to help you get through training. Please feel free to ask me questions and let me know if you need additional explanations on the topics you will be introduced to in this course." I nodded and smiled, hoping he'd notice that I was tracking with him.

But within a few minutes, I noticed something odd. Instead of looking at both of us, Jim faced Adam the entire time. He talked to him in the tiny student office as if I wasn't even in the room, pausing every so often to spit the red juices of his chewing tobacco into a Styrofoam cup. I tried to quietly scoot my chair closer to Adam's so I'd be in Jim's line of sight. His eyes remained locked on Adam.

"One of my jobs," Jim said, "is to help you visualize how the classroom instruction fits into real-life operations." He told us that he'd spent most of his time in the field and was even mentioned in Ronald Kessler's bestselling book *Inside the CIA*.

Adam and I stared in awe at the legend, saying over and over, "Wow, that's so cool, sir."

After Jim left the room, Adam turned to me and said, "Well, that was weird. Did he even look at you?"

"You noticed that?" I asked.

"Of course I did. How could I *not* notice?"

This was where Jim's age, and the fact that he was from a completely different era, became evident. As training progressed, Jim seemed shocked when I'd do well in the exercises and get positive feedback from the instructors. He didn't know what to do with the fact that I was succeeding. I assume that in his mind, I should have been in a secretarial or support role, not collecting intelligence in the messy and dangerous world that he had dealt with in his prime. So he kept ignoring me.

I decided not to take it personally.

Fine, I thought. *Underestimate me. But in the process, I will learn everything I can from you—even if all of your wisdom is directed at Adam over on the opposite side of the room.*

Still, it's hard to prevent judgment like that from seeping into your subconscious. After all, the training program was designed to be extremely challenging in order to weed out anyone who wasn't suited for the demanding life of an undercover intelligence officer. And the truth was, I had no idea if I was capable. It wasn't like I had role models I could look up to and compare myself with. All I had seen up to that point was an instructor cadre that was mostly older, white, male retirees. The only female instructors in this part of the training program taught the report-writing modules. I had no idea if I fit the 007 mold. Was I capable of recruiting and running sources or managing counterterrorism operations? Was I supposed to be there or not?

Then about a month into training, Adam walked into our shared office with his head hanging low and closed the door. I could feel something was wrong.

He said, "Michele, we need to talk."

I took a deep breath and braced myself. He sat down next to me and got right to the point. "I'm quitting the program. I don't think I'm cut out for this. I've talked extensively with my wife, and we are not prepared to live this kind of life: working undercover, having to move every couple of years, and managing all the stress that entails. We just don't want to do it. I've thought long and hard about this decision, and I wanted to tell you what I was feeling, so you know why I've made the decision to drop out."

My heart sank. I was crushed. I thought so highly of Adam, but I also knew he was making the right choice. Being a spy is not a part-time job, and it requires the sacrifice not only of the intelligence officer but of his or her entire family. The pressures of living undercover are shared with one's spouse, so if he or she doesn't feel comfortable with it, then there's no use forging ahead. It is not a lifestyle for everyone.

Of course, when Jim learned the news later that morning, he was shocked. He had assumed that Adam was more suited to the clandestine service than I was. He tried desperately to change Adam's mind. But my partner was clear on what he wanted out of life—and the CIA was not it. And with that realization, Adam left the program.

He cleared out his desk and was gone the next day. Now Jim was stuck with me.

The training sessions got really weird after that. Because nobody else was in the room, Jim actually had to talk to me, so I took the opportunity to work on him. I wanted to change his mind about me, and now that I had him all to myself, I thought I might have a shot at it.

I decided to tell him funny stories about the time I spent in Egypt to show him that I was not some sheltered young lady. I told him how I'd encountered a dishonest camel guide in Cairo. After I'd paid twenty-five Egyptian pounds and enjoyed a beautiful loop around the Giza Plateau, the young man said to me, "If you want to get down, you're going to have to pay an extra fifty pounds."

I crossed my arms, sat up straight in the leather saddle, and said, "That's fine. I've got all day."

His face contorted, wondering if I'd understood him correctly.

He explained again, "You pay fifty pounds, and I let you down."

I put my hands on my hips and said, "Well, good. I don't want to get down."

He was shocked. He'd never had that response before. He'd extorted money from hundreds of tourists with that line, but now he couldn't get me off that camel quickly enough.

I also told Jim about the time in Palestine when my friend Tony and I were in the Muslim Quarter looking at trinkets in a tourist shop. For some reason Tony was trying to find a key chain with Arafat's likeness as a gift for one of his professors. The shopkeeper was making small talk with us when he asked, "Do you like Arafat?" Because we had not yet grasped the complexity of a question like this with all its potential trip wires, we naively responded, "Sure!"

He asked, "Why do you like Arafat?"

"Well, um, because he decided to make peace?"

It turns out that this was *not* the right answer. The man turned ten shades of red, and his eyes grew wide as he glared at us with disgust. Spittle flew out of his mouth as he started screaming, "You like Arafat? You like Arafat?"

Before we could amend our statement or say anything more, the man screamed, "Arafat is a traitor! He shook hands with the enemy! He thinks to make peace with the enemy? How dare he! Arafat should be killed like a cow! Do you know how we kill cows?"

Bewildered, we slowly shook our heads no, while carefully inching backward toward the exit. Then in a thick and angry voice, the shopkeeper said, "I will tell you how we kill cows: We chop them up into little pieces!" As he said this, he used his hands to demonstrate what it looks like to dismember something by karate chopping it into small chunks.

Smiling uncomfortably, Tony and I quickly turned around and flew out the door. I glanced back over my shoulder to see the shopkeeper standing there—his face aglow with anger, his eyes full of rage—as we scrambled down the ancient cobblestone street.

By sharing these stories with Jim, I was seeking to communicate something more profound than a few humorous anecdotes: *Don't mistake my smile for weakness or my sunny disposition for naiveté. I may not know exactly what I'm getting into here at the CIA, but I'm tougher than I look. I'm ready to see what I'm capable of.*

I wasn't just a tourist with a couple of trips under my belt; I had wandered far off the beaten path into Upper Egypt, Alexandria, and the Sinai desert, immersing myself in the cultures. I was careful to mention that I had also traveled to Kuwait, Morocco, and Israel. Although I looked young, I was no pushover.

The stories helped soften Jim up a bit, but I could tell he wasn't convinced. I still had to prove I was operationally minded and capable of serving as a covert intelligence officer. He needed to see that I could take the heat, so he turned it up . . . way up.

One morning, I received a folder from Jim that provided instructions for the day's scenario. Each student was to drive to a local restaurant to meet with an instructor posing as a nuclear scientist. The brief described the source as a person who worked for the type of country that we would characterize as a pariah state. My classmates and I had never worked against *hard targets*, people from countries or cultures that were difficult to recruit from either because we had minimal access to them or because their ideology was so hardwired that there was little chance they'd agree to work with the CIA. Because we'd be dealing with a hard target, we assumed the exercise would be more challenging than any we had already faced. Our job was to develop rapport with the subject, while working to authenticate his identity and assess his value.

All the students were given the same scenario, although the instructors would play their parts differently, depending on their personalities and the students' performances. We went into that training scenario expecting to meet a walk-in who had risked his life to make contact with the world's preeminent intelligence-gathering agency.

As I drove to the meeting location, I was trying to focus on what I needed to achieve. Up until this point, all restaurant meetings had been straightforward, so I told myself there was no reason to worry about this scenario. The mechanics of the meeting were the same, although the story and inherent challenges of meeting with a hard target were unique.

It will be fine, I assured myself. *Just get inside the restaurant, order a nice salad, and engage the instructor like you always do.*

I cleared the first hurdle by arriving at the restaurant within the prescribed five-minute window. I carefully parked the car, exited the vehicle, and slung my purse over my shoulder. As I started walking through the white gravel parking lot toward the restaurant, I noticed a gentleman in his midfifties pacing back and forth on the walkway next to the entrance. He looked fidgety. I realized that this was probably the instructor posing as "Malek," so I walked over to him and delivered the oral paroles I had carefully memorized. (*Oral paroles* are code words we exchange to ensure we're talking to the instructor and not the mechanic from down the street on his lunch break.)

The gentleman responded with the appropriate code words, but then the scenario took an unexpected and unwelcome turn. I was presented with a very difficult "target" who didn't want to meet with me because I was a woman. He had me jump through many challenging hoops that seemed to test my resolve and ability to deal with difficult personalities.

One of the drawbacks of my being open, smiley, and easy to engage is that these qualities often confuse people and lead them to inaccurate conclusions about my personality and capabilities. Those who deal with me for only a short time may hastily assume that I am one-dimensional, not serious, lacking in intelligence, or naive.

My instructor needed to test my determination and grit, as well as my ability to remain focused even when I faced unexpected obstacles. I needed to demonstrate that I could be firm when necessary. The role player quickly found out that, despite my friendly demeanor, I was willing to be assertive.

It reminded me of an encounter I'd had in Cairo. I had purchased a bottle of water from a street vendor, and he was counting the change back to me in Arabic while he laid the bills in my hand. Having just learned Arabic numbers, I knew that he had skipped one. Momentarily forgetting to be polite, I jumped in and said, "No, you forgot *ashara* [ten]!"

As soon as I said it, I was horrified. In American culture, calling someone out in this manner is not the most polite way to address a vendor's "oversight," but instead of being offended, the old man chuckled and joyfully handed the missing bill back to me. He wasn't embarrassed at all. He was beaming and patting me on the back, as if to congratulate me on properly standing up for myself.

While this may seem like an insignificant experience, it offered me one of the greatest lessons of my life: No one will respect you if you don't stand up for your own interests. People do not walk on eggshells in the Middle East; they pursue their interests without apology and resolve their differences by hashing them out loudly, in front of others, not by hiding the issue or delicately dancing around it.

With lessons like this under my belt, I began to amend the way I interacted with the world. I started to understand how critical it was to take a harsher tone or act more aggressively when my well-being or security was at stake, practices that seemed to go against the Southern culture in which I was so firmly anchored.

Eventually Malek and I did get to the meat of the exercise, but that seemed to be secondary to testing my knowledge and resolve. I think the instructor had been told to increase the stress level as much as possible to see if he could dominate and throw me off balance. It didn't work; I did not cave. I remained focused and intent on achieving my objectives.

The next day, Jim said, "I heard you did pretty well yesterday."

Wait, did Jim just give me a compliment?

Jim was slowly realizing that I was not just meeting but exceeding the standards the instructors had laid out for this and other exercises. I might not just be good enough to scrape through my training; I might even be sufficiently talented and determined to do the hard work of a CIA agent.

CHAPTER 4

A MODEL SPY

Even though Jim was slowly starting to come around, the cold, hard truth is that—even today—certain jobs in the agency are considered a better fit for men. When a job involves dealing with rather unsavory individuals (like terrorists) or revolves around cutthroat business dealings, the gender bias leans even more dramatically in a man's favor. People assume that a strong male presence is more effective in certain scenarios. I suppose that's true if you are battling it out in an ultimate fighting competition, but it's not often that intelligence agents are expected to enter the ring and face off against Hulk Hogan or The Rock.

I can't blame other people for operating under old assumptions about gender. I myself assumed that men were better at serving in the core collector roles (the people who recruit and handle spies) since most of the agency's sources are men and many come from incredibly paternalistic cultures.

It's a fairly logical view unless you understand the psychology of espionage. The key is to be able to correctly read your opponent. Espionage is all about psychology, and when you master the ability to read others while thinly disguising your own hand, you can turn your "gender liability" into an advantage.

In the CIA, smart women tap into the misplaced assumptions of the adversary by using the element of surprise. It's almost like playing poker. When a criminal, terrorist, or potential business partner does not expect a woman to be his equal, you—the woman—hold all the cards. When you finally reveal your hand, his jaw drops in disbelief. A woman can change the terms of the engagement. She can use all her attributes, intelligence, and empathy to win the game before anyone realizes that she's even playing.

Unfortunately, I didn't realize this when I began my career with the CIA. I wish someone had told me back then about Virginia Hall—one of the first female spies ever to work for the US Office of Strategic Services (OSS), the precursor to the CIA. She is perhaps the best example I've found of a woman allowing people to underestimate her—and then using it to her advantage.

Virginia had wanted to be a diplomat for as long as she could remember. She loved to travel, and she had a faculty for languages and an adventurous spirit. Her dream was to work her way up in the Foreign Service to eventually direct a US mission abroad. As lofty as these aspirations are now, back in the 1920s they were downright unrealistic. In the early twentieth century, there was no such thing as a female ambassador. But Virginia was intent on pursuing this goal, and like a good diplomat in training, she mapped out a course of action and began taking steps toward its realization.

Twice, she took—and failed—the Foreign Service exam. Undeterred, she decided to travel abroad to gain some practical experience, working first at the US embassy in Warsaw, Poland, and later at the US consulate in Turkey. While there, she suffered a horrific accident. An avid outdoorswoman, Virginia loved hiking, hunting, and horseback riding. One day while hunting with friends, Virginia was climbing over a fence when her shotgun accidently discharged. She looked down to see her left foot hanging in shreds. By the time she made it to the hospital, gangrene had set in, and her leg had to be amputated below the knee. Soon thereafter she was fitted with a wooden leg. The restoration of her mobility, even through a clumsy "peg leg," must have been a relief for such an active woman. But I'm sure it wasn't considered very womanly, at a time when a woman's appearance was of utmost importance.

Still, Virginia was not the kind of person who would let a gunshot wound and amputation get in the way of her dreams. As soon as she was well enough, she went to work as a clerk at the US consulate in Venice, Italy. While there, she submitted her application for a Foreign Service position, but she was rejected on the grounds that she wasn't "able-bodied."

Virginia tried valiantly to resuscitate her dream, launching numerous appeals to senior State Department officers, but to no avail. Dejected and demoralized, Virginia realized she wasn't going to get anywhere with the State Department. Despite her best efforts, she was unable to break into a bureaucracy that didn't welcome females (let alone female amputees) into its ranks.

Unsure of what to do next, Virginia decided to spend the summer of 1939 in France. Unbeknownst to her, the decision to go to Paris placed her in position to respond to a crisis that would soon envelop a significant portion of the world.

On September 1, 1939, after a long and unsettled summer in Europe, Hitler invaded Poland. Britain and France responded to Hitler's aggression by declaring war on Germany, and World War II was officially under way.

Wanting to be useful to the war effort, Virginia enlisted in the French ambulance corps to help evacuate casualties from the front lines. She drove the ambulance, negotiated dangerous terrain, and contended daily with the drama of war—all with a wooden leg!

Virginia continued her service in the ambulance corps until France surrendered to Nazi Germany the following year. This meant that Virginia was now trapped in hostile territory. She knew she had to escape, and a month later, she successfully crossed into neutral Spain before making her way to England.

After arriving at the US embassy in London and providing an incredibly insightful debrief on the conditions in France, Virginia took a job at the US Defense Attaché's Office. But it took only a few months for Virginia to realize that the embassy's desk job wasn't doing it for her. That wasn't where she needed to be.

Here's where the story gets *really* interesting. At some point during her time in London, the British noticed Virginia's potential and pitched her to work for the newly established British Special Operations Executive (SOE). Launched by Winston Churchill, the new agency's objective was to link up with resistance movements and empower them to defeat the German occupiers. Churchill's marching orders to the new group were simple and straightforward; they were to "set Europe ablaze!"

This was the opportunity Virginia had waited for without even knowing what it was. The offer appealed to Virginia because she deeply believed she was supposed to be on the front lines, not the sidelines, of the conflict. Virginia accepted the recruitment proposal right away. She completed the SOE's new covert training program and in April 1941 became a special agent. The woman who could not get hired by the State Department to represent the United States in diplomatic functions or to mingle at social soirees suddenly found herself preparing for deployment to Vichy, France, where she would bear the code name "Germaine" while assuming the persona of Brigitte LeContre, a French-American reporter for the *New York Post*.

Virginia immediately distinguished herself as a resourceful agent who could accomplish what most others could not. She spent the next fifteen months working in Lyon organizing, funding, supplying, and arming the French Resistance. She rescued downed Allied airmen, making sure they made it safely back to England. She oversaw SOE parachute drops designed to supply Resistance fighters. She organized sabotage attacks against German supply lines. She engineered POW escapes from German and Vichy French prisons and camps. She even served as a liaison for other SOE agents operating in southern France.[1]

Virginia was so effective in her missions that she flew to the top of the Gestapo's most wanted list, even though they didn't know exactly who she was. Operationally astute and brilliant with disguises, Virginia was able to hide her true identity from her enemies; they didn't even know that she was an American. But that didn't stop them from circulating posters offering a reward for her capture, describing her as the "woman with a limp. . . . She is the most dangerous of all Allied spies. We must find and destroy her."[2]

Only the most clever, courageous, and fortunate agents stayed alive and remained effective in spite of the Germans' penetration of the Resistance. Only a few agents escaped the clutches of the Nazis once their cells were compromised and their identities, locations, and activities were discovered. It was so dangerous to operate behind enemy lines that the life expectancy of an Allied radio operator (one of Virginia's many roles) in 1943 was just six weeks.[3]

In late 1942, with the Gestapo hot on her heels, Virginia slipped away from the ever-tightening dragnet by using one of the most risky avenues of escape—she hiked across the snow-covered Pyrenees Mountains into Spain, in the middle of winter (despite being labeled unfit for service because she wasn't "able-bodied"—*take that, State Department!*). Throughout the war, Virginia remained one of the Nazis' most elusive targets, frustrating any and all attempts to find and finish her.

Following her Houdini-like escape from the claws of her adversaries in France, Virginia was recruited by the OSS, and in 1944, she reportedly parachuted back into France with her prosthesis in her knapsack. Disguised as an old farmhand, she trained Resistance battalions, organized sabotage operations, supplied intelligence on the German army, performed the critical duties of a radio operator, worked as a courier, located drop zones for Resistance forces, and helped prepare the ground for D-day.

After the war, Virginia transitioned from the OSS to the newly created CIA and remained there until her mandatory retirement in 1966.

Virginia embodied everything I wanted to be. She was adventurous, gutsy, courageous, headstrong, and incredibly intelligent. She wasn't easily dissuaded from accomplishing her tasks, and she used everything at her disposal to engineer success. She pushed every boundary presented to her, willing and able to drive right to the edge without letting fear get the best of her. She instinctively knew how to transform her disadvantages into advantages; her obvious limp, for example, became an opportunity to disguise herself as an old woman or a beggar. Incorrect assumptions about her physical limitations allowed her to skirt surveillance by employing methodologies her enemies did not expect. In this way, Virginia never drew their attention and instead used her disability to blend right into the landscape.

Virginia wasn't good enough for the State Department, but she was good enough to take on the Gestapo. She wasn't good enough to sit behind a desk reading and writing cables, but she was good enough to execute hundreds of military and intelligence operations against the Nazis.

The training exercise with Jim and Malek was designed to expose my weakness as a woman operating in the high-stakes field of international espionage. But what they hadn't counted on was the experience I had gleaned studying and working abroad in the Middle East. When they looked at me, they no doubt saw a petite, timid little girl who would crumble under the pressure.

Of course, plenty of men had underestimated Virginia Hall, too.

CHAPTER 5

KEEP CALM—AND CARRY A WORKING COMPASS

During that year of training, we learned all aspects of HUMINT (Human Intelligence) operations, including how to spot, assess, develop, and recruit an agent; debrief an agent; vet information; identify counterintelligence threats; spot surveillance; carry out covert communications; execute high-threat meetings; protect sources; conduct dead drops; and write intelligence reports.

There were so many aspects of training that I often referred to it as "boot camp for intelligence officers." Students were constantly observed and their performances rated by instructors. And the instruction didn't end once we began working in the field. Before deployment to dangerous postings, CIA officers had to be recertified, not only on the Glock and M4, but in the Overseas Personality Security Course. Since our work was a matter of life and death, the staff had to be certain that we had the ability to clandestinely run an operation and keep ourselves, as well as our assets and information, safe. I did great at the psychological stuff. And I turned out to be quite astute at the shooting and high-performance driving segments. However, my performances in two of the other paramilitary exercises were not my finest moments—especially the ambush and land navigation.

Even though the ambush exercise only mimicked an attack, I hated the idea of being in such a vulnerable position. Along with the other students, on the day of this exercise I slid the protective face mask over my eyes, pulled the protective vest over my long-sleeved shirt, tucked my pants into my combat boots, pushed the gun into the holster on my hip, grabbed the semiautomatic weapon loaded with paint-filled Simunition cartridges, and climbed into a station wagon with other trainees. We watched as another car full of trainees pulled out and headed into the forest. For some reason, my pulse started racing. I tried to calm myself down. After all, this wasn't real: fake terrorists, fake ammunition, fake ambush . . . no worries, right?

Knowing that I would have to scramble out of the car, I wanted to test my door to make sure it opened easily. The lock released, but when I tried to press down on the handle, it wouldn't budge. The door was jammed shut. *Thank goodness I had the foresight to try the door.* My eyes scanned the vehicle, frantically searching for the next best exit.

The other trainee in the backseat was a gentleman who was significantly overweight (we'll call him Larry). I felt bad for Larry. He probably hated this part of the training too. But my sympathy quickly dissolved into a selfish concern that he probably wouldn't be able to move very quickly once the terrorist attack unfolded. If I was to avoid getting shot, exiting his side of the vehicle was probably not my best bet. I'd be better off scrambling over the seats to escape through one of the front doors.

Our instructors stood outside the vehicle. Once they confirmed that we had our seat belts on and were sufficiently geared up, they told the student in the driver's seat to follow the little dirt road into the woods. The only other instructions he was given were to drive about twenty-five miles per hour and to just "keep going." They didn't say how far to drive, but I guess that was the point. We weren't supposed to know where the ambush would occur (hence the term *ambush*).

The driver put the car into gear, and we slowly rolled into the eerie calm of the thick forest. As the station wagon rumbled down the dirt path, we eagerly scanned the horizon, searching for the attackers. A couple of students cracked jokes to break the tension, but I could not relax. I was breathing hard into my face mask, causing a cloud of warm breath to accumulate on the plastic screen. Yes, I'll admit it: I was terrified. This training exercise was the antithesis of fun for me. But as much as I despised it, I knew I desperately needed it. After all, I would be deploying to locations where the possibility of an ambush was not out of the question.

Without warning, a loud explosion pierced the silence, followed by a quick succession of deep thuds as the car was pelted with rounds. The driver yelled, "Contact left!" signifying the direction from which the attack had been initiated. Suddenly the car's engine died. We were unable to get off the "X" in the relative safety of the vehicle— the preferred course of action if you were to experience this in real life. Then four masked men emerged from the woods, aiming their AK-47s and firing at my side of the car. Someone yelled, "Get out! Get out! Get out!" and the trainees started scrambling out of the right side of the vehicle.

As I suspected, Larry was having a difficult time responding to the stress. He was fumbling with his door and couldn't seem to get it open. *I had a feeling this would happen!* As expected, I would need to climb into the front seats in order to get out of the vehicle. Because I was saddled with so much gear, scrambling over the center console was as tricky as I thought it would be. I was not exactly agile, but this option was still quicker than waiting for Larry to move. As I scaled the seats and fell into the front, he was still trying to get his door open.

I didn't know where the attackers were at that moment, but I desperately hoped they hadn't made their way to the right side of the vehicle and weren't lying in wait for me to exit. Unfortunately, I couldn't waste a moment to look. I had one focus—get out of the car. When I finally crawled out of the front passenger seat, Larry fell sideways out of the vehicle and into the mud. In his panic, he had forgotten to unbuckle his seat belt and was still very much attached to the car. Worse yet, he couldn't figure out how to extract himself from the awkward mess. As he tried to get up, he let out a yelp. *I wonder if he hurt himself.*

At this point, the attackers were crossing in front of the vehicle, so I decided it was time to get out of Dodge. I took off running and headed for the tree line just yards away. Meanwhile, Larry lay wounded in the mud (he had twisted his ankle) and was soon getting "shot up" before the instructors realized that he was, indeed, injured. Meanwhile, I followed the rest of the students into the woods, running like hunted prey.

I crashed through the undergrowth, quickly catching up to the others. We were desperate to get out of range of the attackers. Even though they could not see us anymore, they were still able to shoot. The exploding rounds kept whizzing by and striking us on the backs of our legs, rear ends, thighs, shoulders, and arms. As a round hit the back of my leg, I gasped at the stabbing pain and ran even faster. The volley of paint-filled bullets continued, following our group deeper into the forest.

Without warning, the officer in front of me tripped on a tree root and fell hard into the mucky swamp. It was too late for me to change direction, so I tripped over his feet and slammed down on top of him, hitting my head hard. Then the guy behind me, who had been right on my heels, came crashing down on top of us, splaying arms and legs all over. There we were, a writhing pile of America's best and brightest, covered in paint splatter, mud, sweat, and dirt. Navy SEALs had nothing on us.

We left training that day battered and bruised. But as painful as the simulation was (to both my body and my ego), it taught me the importance of pushing past fear and discomfort. That's what the instructors were trying to condition us to do—to conquer our tendency to freeze during critical moments. They wanted to be sure we had the capacity to act when action was most needed.

According to behavioral scientists, the human tendency to freeze in the context of a threat may be a native biological response to extreme stress. Though it is quite typical to freeze when you are being attacked, paralysis is your enemy. However, if you think through and even practice your options ahead of time, you are less likely to freeze. That's why it's important for soldiers, police, firefighters, and anyone else who must operate within the context of rapid responses and life-or-death situations to be trained with drills that are as realistic as possible. The idea is to develop muscle memory for things like aiming and pulling a trigger while under extreme stress or using one's vehicle to get off the "X" and away from danger, if necessary.

Given enough training, certain skills and behaviors become so automatic, they become almost impossible to turn off.

Case in point: Several weeks into my training, I had driven from my townhouse in Alexandria, Virginia, to Washington, DC, during a rare break to join some friends for Sunday brunch. As I came around a bend in the road, a car about fifty yards in front of me (going the opposite direction) slowed down to about ten miles per hour as it passed a water treatment facility. As it did, I saw a dark-haired male in the passenger seat surreptitiously lift a camera and snap a few pictures. The car then sped away as the camera disappeared from view. The way the man lifted the camera and took pictures without looking into the viewfinder or focusing the lens seemed terribly sneaky. Since water treatment facilities aren't normal tourist destinations or typical subject matter for photographers, I immediately became concerned.

Terrorists case potential targets in order to identify vulnerabilities, and they design attack plans using photographs, videos, and sketches. They have to obtain these materials without anyone knowing what they're doing, so they try to look inconspicuous and fly under the radar of the casual observer. It's the same strategy robbers use to case a bank or convenience store prior to hitting it.

This was a particularly sensitive period in our nation's history, just six months after 9/11. We were fully engaged in the Third World War (i.e., the war against terror) and painfully aware that al-Qa'ida was preparing for additional attacks against the homeland as well as US interests abroad. There had been a spike in surveillance activities against US infrastructure, including bridges, fuel depots, oil refineries, military facilities, national landmarks, financial institutions, and government buildings.

That was it for me. I flew like a race car driver to the next light so I could do a U-turn and pursue the suspicious vehicle. There was no question: I had to get his license plate number, vehicle description, and as many details as I could about the driver and his passenger. I swerved in and out of traffic for several miles before I was close enough to obtain the identifying information.

Luckily, I had a notepad and pen in my purse, which I had been using in my own surveillance runs. I captured the data and submitted it to the FBI's tip line as a suspicious activity report. I never heard back. To this day, I have no idea who the two dark-haired men were or what they were doing in the blue rental car, but their behavior didn't seem normal or natural to me.

Likewise, a few weeks later I was at a toy store in the mall, shopping with my six-year-old niece, when I noticed a male, who looked about forty, crouched down by the Barbie dolls. His hair was greasy and unkempt, his shirt half tucked in, his appearance disheveled. Something about this guy made the hair on the back of my neck stand up. He wasn't the kind of person who normally perused the doll section. From the moment I had turned into that aisle and laid eyes on him, I couldn't help but focus on the strange man. *Is he shopping alone?* I wondered. *If not, where is his daughter or the small child he is with?*

Each time shoppers walked by, the man furtively glanced their way. His placement (in the toy store by himself) and behavior (the furtive glances at other shoppers) had clued me in to the possibility that something was amiss. Having just finished surveillance training, my senses were primed to notice anything unusual and to identify anything out of place, so I focused on his demeanor as my family and I shuffled by.

As I keyed in on his face, I saw his expression completely change and his eyes bug out of his head when my niece walked by. The look on his face was evil and wildly inappropriate in ways that I won't even try to articulate. It sent chills down my spine. I wanted to effect a citizen's arrest in the toy store immediately. But since I couldn't prove the guy was the monster that every cell in my body sensed, I simply ushered my niece—and the rest of the family—out of that aisle and exited the store. Looking back, I wish I had alerted store management to the potential problem, but I did not yet have confidence in my intuition and assessments.

The point is, my training was changing my perception of the world. I was picking up on details I might have normally missed. By honoring my God-given intuition instead of questioning it, demeaning it, or squashing those flashes of insight, I was seeing a different dimension altogether. The more training I received and the more frequently I applied the concepts I'd learned, the more sensitive I became. I was becoming more attuned to my environment—I was becoming a spy.

One of the last paramilitary training exercises we did tested our land-based navigational skills. Naturally, on the day we were to be tested, a freak snowstorm dumped two feet of snow in the region. Being a Florida native, I had seen this much snow only twice in my life, so I was completely out of my element. While I would have preferred to retreat inside and sit by a cozy fire sipping a hot cup of coffee, I was going to have to spend all day outside in the frigid cold, navigating a large forest and zigzagging my way from waypoint to waypoint.

There were already plenty of existing challenges in the terrain without the snow, but Mother Nature had found a way to make the task even harder. I figured the course would take about twice as long to complete because we'd have to trudge through a mixture of snow and piles of decaying leaves shed from the thousands of deciduous trees that fall.

Dressed in multiple layers that included cold-weather fatigues and combat boots, each student set out on a unique course. Initial waypoints had been issued that morning as we stood at the starting line surveying the picture-perfect snowdrifts. We were given a full day to finish the exercise, which required us to navigate in and around dense forests, rambling streams, large hills, dense thickets, and nasty thornbushes (my absolute favorite). The area was chock full of lakes and swampland that needed to be avoided, although the snow made these hazards harder to identify before we stepped into them.

After a week's worth of navigation training, I was still nervous, but I also realized how far I had come. I felt confident I could complete the course even though I was cold and uncomfortable in the snow. With a backpack containing a map stuffed into a waterproof pouch, coordinates for each waypoint, a compass, a pencil, a whistle, an MRE (meal ready to eat), and water, I set out from the starting line. I kept sinking in snow that went past my knees and, in some areas, up to my thighs. A mere forty-five minutes later I reached my first waypoint. I was feeling really good about myself, thinking, *Yay! I can do this!* After pausing for a moment, I took a drink of water and read the second set of coordinates that had been placed on top of the red barrel marking the first waypoint. After checking my compass, I got my bearings and set out for the second waypoint.

Approximately two-thirds of the way into the second leg, as I was traversing a severe dip in the terrain and crossing a narrow valley that cut between two steep hills, I suddenly stepped into a stream that I could not see beneath a thin layer of ice and snow. I quickly pulled my foot out of the freezing water, but despite my military-style combat boots, my foot was soaked. Even worse than the cold water stinging my frozen toes, I could *not* figure out how to get past the creek. With all that snow, it was hard to determine an appropriate crossing point. So . . . I moved farther upstream to a place where the creek was not as wide and crossed it, carefully maneuvering on slippery stones and decaying tree trunks lying in the muck.

I had safely crossed the stream, but I had also made a mistake. By wandering off course to find a crossing point, I had lost my bearings. Every time I tried to set a course, I found myself facing a different direction. *Which way is north?* I wondered. *Is the compass broken? Am I misreading it?* My pulse picked up, and I started to get nervous. But I fought back the fear of helplessness, knowing that I had to be calm in order to get myself back on track. *It's no big deal,* I reassured myself. *You just need to focus.* In the midst of the mental chaos, I almost forgot that my foot was quickly freezing into a block of ice.

After carefully considering the land features around me in relation to the detailed physical map we had been given, I tried once again to establish the direction I should be heading in. Pushing the frustration out of my head, I tried to be decisive and set off toward a series of steep, undulating hills. After twenty minutes of plodding through difficult terrain, I clambered up the last hill hoping to see the red barrel marking the next waypoint. But there was nothing— just empty forest. I wandered around the area for another twenty minutes desperately looking for that barrel, but I could not find it.

I prayed and prayed. Then I panicked. I couldn't imagine backtracking all the way to the stream. It had taken so much energy to get to where I was now standing. *Even if I return to the babbling brook, how will I change course?* I had been so confused. I don't know what I was doing wrong, but I could not get a good read from that compass. I wished I had someone to consult, but it was just me, myself, and I in the vast, swampy forest. The snow made it eerily quiet, which further isolated and deflated me. I had no idea what to do.

That was the moment when I considered the very last resort—throwing my hands up in the air in defeat and blowing the whistle. We'd been told to use the whistle if we were lost or hurt. It might take a while for the instructors to hear it through the thick forest, but someone would eventually find me.

Failing the land navigation exercise did not mean I would fail the entire program. The paramilitary courses were supplemental and had no bearing on our graduation from the clandestine training program. Still, not making it through land navigation training would be embarrassing, and giving up after only *one* barrel would make me look like a fool.

I reluctantly put the whistle up to my mouth and sat motionless for a few seconds, trying to get the courage to blow it. Turns out, I couldn't bear to go down in defeat so early in the exercise. Even though I was thoroughly lost, I didn't want to embarrass myself by showing the instructors I couldn't make it to the second waypoint.

Out of sheer desperation, I set a course in a random direction and started walking, all the while thinking of that television show *I Shouldn't Be Alive*. All these silly people kept wandering farther and farther off-course. The more they walked, the more lost they became. Next thing you know, they were hanging on to the edge of a cliff freezing to death. (Okay, so maybe I wasn't *that* desperate, but I *was* lost—and thoroughly confused.)

With images of death running through my mind, I was stunned when, ten steps later, I pushed through the forest wall and tripped onto asphalt. Just like that. I felt like I had just emerged from the crowded darkness of the wardrobe into beautiful, magical Narnia. All that drama, and I had been only steps from a well-trodden road.

Seconds earlier, I had almost given up. But now I knew exactly where I was. I finally had a sense of direction. It took only about ten more minutes to reenter the forest and find the second barrel. Thanks to my training, I had successfully fought off the panic trying to push its way into my mind and kept moving. In the end, that's what saved me and enabled me to complete the exercise—the simple strategy of putting one foot in front of the other.

Now that I'd mastered the fine art of walking, my training was finally complete.

I was ready to take on the world.

CHAPTER 6

INTO THE DESERT

In December 2002, after a year's worth of blood, sweat, and tears, I successfully passed the CIA's clandestine training program. By February 2003, I also completed the optional paramilitary training program. That was it. I was done. I was officially a member of the Directorate of Operations, ready to get to work as a CIA intelligence officer.

Joseph, having started his training before me, had just completed his first six-month assignment, while I finished up the last half of my training. While most of my colleagues were scheduled to spend a year or two at headquarters preparing for their overseas tours, I was slated to go to the field right away. As it happens, there was an immediate need for two agents in ████████. Fortunately for the CIA, Joseph and I were both familiar with the Middle East, we both spoke Arabic, we were both cleared for duty, *and*, unlike most of the other agents, we were willing to go just about anywhere.

We were scheduled to deploy in April. As a result, the month of March was a mad rush to prepare for the big move. We set to work immediately, sifting through all of our belongings. Whatever hadn't been sold or given away was packed up by a moving service a week before we were scheduled to fly out of Washington Dulles International Airport.

The packers emptied the house of all its contents over the course of two days. It happened so quickly I barely had time to process the magnitude of this international move. By 4 p.m. on the second day, the packing was almost complete, and Joseph and I stood in the front yard of our townhouse in Alexandria, Virginia, watching as the last few items were stuffed inside the moving trucks. We signed the paperwork, and then—quite unceremoniously—the two trucks slowly pulled away from the curb.

As I watched the moving trucks make their way down the street, it suddenly hit me: *This is it! There is no turning back now.* We were completely committed. Those trucks were hauling away the remnants of our old civilian lives. We now stood on the precipice of a lifestyle and career that we could barely conceive—a new country, new culture, new jobs, new boss, new colleagues, new house . . . one of the few constants in our lives would be each other.

My eyes welled up with tears, a rare emotional moment when I acknowledged the enormity of this sudden change. I swallowed hard and asked Joseph, "Is that it?" Joseph put his arm around me as the tears rolled down my cheeks.

"I know." He tried in vain to comfort me. "I know. It's hard, but we're going to be okay. We'll be fine."

I had to let go—let go of my earthly possessions, my family, my friends. I was releasing everything I knew for everything I did not. I had to trust God. I had to move forward, as intimidating and scary as it was. I had to keep it together.

That night we checked into a local hotel, where we'd remain until we got the final go-ahead to board our flight out of Washington Dulles. That was the beginning of our nomadic existence, which would continue for the next fourteen years.

Of course, there was more to our transition than a simple change of address. Going undercover is a strange and complicated process that essentially involves . . . well, frankly, disappearing.

We were allowed to tell immediate family members our true affiliation, but only if we felt certain that they could bear the burden of knowing and protecting this secret information. In other words, if your mom was a talker who would be so terribly proud that she'd want to shout from the rooftops that you were working as a covert counterterrorism specialist overseas in ████████, then you probably shouldn't tell her. Or if Dad was a worrier and knowing this information would mean he'd spend the next two decades glued to the television, certain that you were going to show up on the evening news (and not in a good way), then maybe you shouldn't tell him.

As for me, most of my immediate family knew. They were very proud, but they were also concerned for our safety, as our expertise in the Middle East meant we were likely to be sent from one war zone to another. They did their best to hide their concerns from us, but I know it wasn't easy for them. Naturally, they became avid consumers of news coming from the region, and they prayed . . . often. And, of course, they sent us care packages and stepped in to bear the burden of taking care of our mail and helping to manage our personal affairs while we were away. My sister, Julie, had a real estate power of attorney, which enabled her to buy and manage a rental property (on our behalf) while we were abroad. My dad had a general power of attorney for all other matters. And before we left the United States for our first tour, we presented both of them with a notebook containing important personal data: bank account numbers, safe deposit box keys, and a copy of our wills (which I'm sure comforted them immensely). And in case of emergency, the CIA had their contact information and knew whom to inform if anything happened to us.

Hours before we left our hotel in Tysons Corner, Virginia, we called several members of our family to let them know we were about to depart. I told my dad, Art, and stepmom, Crystal, "I love you both so much. Thanks for being there with us every step of the way. We really appreciate it."

My dad's voice sounded a bit tentative. I could tell he wanted to be positive and was doing his best to hide his concerns. "Of course we're sad you're leaving, but you know we'll be praying for you every day," he said. "We know you probably won't be able to get in touch right away, but let us know, as soon as you can, that you made it." As usual, he was supportive. If my parents had any doubts, they didn't say anything. Whatever concerns they had, they must have laid them at the feet of God.

Julie had offered to send treats from home, including anything we had forgotten or couldn't find at our new posting. "I can't wait to hear what you think of ████████. I know it's scary, but you'll do great. You'll rise to the challenge as you always do. Write us when you can. We will be anxiously awaiting your updates."

"Thanks, honey. I'll call or write as soon as I'm able. I don't know how well the telephone system or Internet works on that end, but we'll find out soon enough."

"Please be careful, Shell."

"Of course I will. I love you, Sissie."

Hanging up was difficult. I didn't want the conversations to end. I swallowed hard and tried not to cry. I had no idea when I'd see my family again or how often we'd get to talk. Minutes later, Joseph and I loaded our bags into the taxi and headed to the airport.

After a very long flight, I looked out the plane's window as we descended toward boulders, rocky outcrops, and huge craters. The dusty brown landscape below us seemed devoid of life, and it felt as if we were infringing on a private space, like astronauts flying in to set up shop on the dark side of the moon. The tiny dots of civilization nestled in the majestically folded mountains were the only evidence that we were still tethered to planet Earth.

As the plane made its final approach to the small international airport, the feeling creeping up on me was not what I expected. Instead of the normal excitement I felt when traveling to new places, I felt a deep and foreboding sense of isolation. Joseph and I stared out the windows of the airplane at our new surroundings, then looked at each other with pensive and slightly worried expressions.

Feeling a mounting sense of anxiety, I questioned the wisdom of agreeing to serve in this place for our first tour. Putting words to the jumbled thoughts in our cloudy minds, I asked rhetorically, "What have we done?"

Neither one of us could answer. All we could do was survey the ground and wonder what we had embarked upon.

Extensive jet lag and exhaustion from thirty-three hours of travel and transit were doing us no favors. It made the first glimpses of our new home feel quite jarring. The country was nearly in its natural state . . . a wild, unbridled beauty. The lack of development contrasted starkly with all that we were familiar with: the sprawling metropolis of Cairo, the bustling Marrakech souk, or the nouveau riche skylines of the Gulf Arab states. We'd been all over the Middle East, but despite our familiarity with the region, we were unprepared to live so far off the grid. The reclusive nature of our new environment—simple, small villages separated by deep gullies and miles of dirt roads, with limited infrastructure—engendered doubt about my ability to adjust to this new place. Despite extensive travel in the area, I simply had no frame of reference for what I was about to experience.

I couldn't blame anyone but myself. When Joseph and his buddies had been discussing potential first tours and saying how cool this country must be, I'd responded, "Well, why don't we go there?"

He looked at me like I was crazy and asked, "You'd be willing to serve in ███████?"

"Why not?" I said.

There were two slots available in the CIA station for people with our skill sets, so it sounded like a good idea. For headquarters it was a coup since few officers were willing to go to ▮▮▮▮▮. Plus, they got two Arabists for the price of one.

The other distinct advantage to serving here was that the deployment was to occur a month or two after my graduation from training. This was something every officer desired, but was rarely able to arrange. But staff in ▮▮▮▮ were desperate to fill the two slots and asked headquarters to send us out as quickly as possible. That's why when we arrived at the tiny airport with one barely functioning luggage carousel, we were shocked that no one was waiting to receive us, as is customary in the clandestine service. Joseph used his new cell phone to get in touch with our point of contact. This person, in turn, made some calls and found out that we had somehow been forgotten. Someone at the office eventually secured a driver to retrieve us from the airport.

We had learned weeks before that our residence was not yet ready for occupancy, so the driver took us to the one hotel in the capital city that had sufficient security to house Americans and other Westerners. This temporary arrangement was not ideal or even close to it. Living out of a hotel for a month or two—even in the United States—would be hard. But doing so in this part of the world? Very challenging. Adding to the difficulty of moving six suitcases and four carry-ons into one small room was the fact that the hotel turned out to be a relic of another era. It was dark, decrepit, and in a state of disrepair.

After we crammed ourselves into the dusty room, our contact told us not to go anywhere. Al-Qa'ida had just threatened to attack US and other foreign interests in the capital, so the embassy had warned American citizens to avoid going into the city or moving around too much. As I recall, we arrived on a Thursday morning, and at that time, weekends in that country were Thursdays and Fridays. We were instructed to keep a low profile and stay in the hotel all weekend. After giving us this unfortunate news, our contact provided us with the emergency telephone number for the marine guard force at the US embassy, and then left.

Talk about feeling trapped and deflated. There was no television and spotty (if any) Internet, and the food was barely edible. I consider myself fairly adaptable, but this new situation strained my usually optimistic self.

Given the lack of options and the need to fight a serious dose of jet lag, we decided to do the very thing we had been warned against: explore the old city. We were bored beyond tears and wanted to get a sense of the place that would serve as our home for the next two years. It was, after all, one of the oldest continuously inhabited cities in the world, a cultural and architectural icon that we had read about and were dying to see firsthand. So I put on my most conservative clothes, and we took a taxi from the hotel to the entrance of the old city.

Stepping out of the car was like stepping out of a time machine. It wasn't long before everyone within eyeshot was unapologetically staring at me, like I was Marty McFly in *Back to the Future* emerging from a DeLorean in 1955. Having been the target of much staring in the Middle East, I was used to being the center of attention. But for some reason, I felt more out of place than ever. I dropped my eyes to the ground, trying to avoid eye contact with the men, as they would literally turn their heads to watch the alien woman walk by.

As we navigated through winding dirt streets and moved deeper into the souk, or marketplace, I started to notice spray-painted graffiti (in Arabic) that read, "Death to America. Death to Israel. May God curse the Jews." The message had been applied to doors, walls, and storefronts.

Realizing the level of hostility that the people in this area might harbor toward Americans, Joseph whispered to me, "No English." I complied. He then spoke to me in heavily accented Lebanese Arabic, most of which I didn't understand. But I pretended like I was completely engaged in the conversation. In order to hide my American-accented Arabic, I limited my responses to *na'am* ("yes") and occasional head nods, pretending I was a native speaker of the language.

The obvious point of this exercise was to hide the fact that *we* were the potential targets of those signs. Joseph could get away with this easily. The locals would never take him for an American with his dark hair and olive-colored skin. They would assume he was from a neighboring (and friendly) country. For me, the ruse was more difficult due to my very Western appearance, but the goal was to pass for a light-skinned Lebanese national.

We continued "chatting" quietly in Arabic, cutting short our dalliance in the historic district, leaving behind mosques, *hammams* (bathhouses), and homes dating back to the eleventh century. We made our way out of the souk's maze to a paved road where we could hail a taxi.

We returned to the dank and musty hotel with its numerous layers of security. Most Western government officials and business-people used this property, so there was a dedicated security staff to check the undersides and trunks of vehicles for explosives, which included the use of a swab to check for TNT, TATP, and other chemicals used by bomb makers.

Although the whole weekend was a wash, we had high hopes for our first day at work. Even if living conditions were difficult and the threat situation was heightened, at least we could find purpose and meaning in the workplace.

A fellow officer picked us up at the hotel to take us to the compound for our first day of work. After flashing our new passports and making our way through the multiple layers of security, we finally entered the facility. It was secure, but the space was small and cramped.

Joseph and I made the rounds, meeting our new colleagues before being led into the boss's office. Instead of getting up to welcome us as we walked through the door, he remained seated at his desk. He ignored us, tapping away at the keys on his computer for what felt like an eternity.

Without looking up, he said, "Have a seat."

We sat down, feeling awkward and uncomfortable, wondering how long this was going to go on. Being a student of human behavior, I realized that he was trying to send us a message. And it was something to the effect of "I hope you feel as unimportant and inconsequential as I think you are."

When he finally looked up, he had a harsh look in his eyes that made my heart drop. With a complete lack of warmth and an anger that seethed right below the surface, he welcomed us to ▆▆▆▆ by saying, "I inherited a broken station. I am trying to put it back together again. It has not been easy, but I'm determined to get things up and running. I expect you to do your jobs and not give me a hard time. Do not mess this up. Do you understand?"

Completely freaked out, we nodded and managed to mutter, "Yes, sir."

Thoughts were swirling inside my head. *What is wrong with him? Why is he angry at us? What in the world have we just walked into?*

Then our new boss summarily dismissed us, saying, "You can go now."

He didn't speak to us for the next three months. The leadership—or lack thereof—was astounding. And it wasn't like I never saw him. We'd pass each other in the hallway, though he would not acknowledge me. I decided to be the bigger person, so every single time I squeezed by, I would address him directly, saying, "Good morning, sir," with all the positivity and respect I could muster. And I kept doing it, even though he pretended like he didn't hear me and acted as if I didn't exist.

In fact, sometimes, I felt as though I literally *didn't* exist at the CIA. No matter how qualified I was, it became clear early on that there would always be one thing working against me—I was a woman.

Joseph seemed to earn people's respect immediately. They just automatically assumed he knew what he was doing. But when it came to me, there was always a certain air of skepticism—almost as though they questioned why I would even *want* to do this job.

After my first several weeks in the field as a collection management officer (CMO), I asked my boss, "Will I ever get to handle or recruit any sources?"

"Why would you want to do that?" he asked incredulously.

I paused for a moment. *Is he kidding? Is he really asking me this question?* I gulped hard and then explained, "Because that's what the agency just spent the entire last year training me to do."

"Well, we don't need you to do that. It's better if you stay in the office and do the work here."

Seriously?

When I asked someone in HR about this misunderstanding, I was told, "Women seem to work better in the role of collection management officers versus operations officers, who are mostly out on the street recruiting and handling sources. Your husband should take that job, and you should be a CMO. Women don't know how to deal with Arabs."

Again I thought, *Seriously?*

I was crushed. All the officers in my class had been told by trainers that, like operations officers, CMOs would recruit and handle sources (though we'd also have other work), but apparently the field managers never got that memo.

The reality was that HR officers and field staff funneled women into one role and men into another with complete disregard to experience, cultural understanding, and linguistic skills.

Once I realized this, I was completely deflated. Maybe I *was* better behind a desk than in front of a source. After all, they would know, right?

Meanwhile, any chance of improving the status quo was undermined by a couple of female officers who were still mired in the mentality of high school gossips. They created an atmosphere of backbiting and distrust, spoiling any remaining opportunities for a collegial workplace.

It was incredibly frustrating. *God has brought us so far*, I thought, *and this is where we landed?* It made no sense. How could a workplace be so cold and unsupportive? How was this situation acceptable in light of the fact that we had given up everything to come here? We'd sold our car and our home in Alexandria, packed up everything we owned, uprooted our lives, and moved halfway around the world to a place nobody wanted to live or work. We were willing to sacrifice a great deal in the service of our country, but this . . . this is not what we anticipated. This was not the reception we'd expected to receive from our colleagues.

Despite the hostile work environment, I remained committed to my job. I made a lot of mistakes, but I kept bungling along, trying to figure out what I was supposed to be doing. I really needed guidance on how to make the transition from training scenarios to the real world, but from the looks of it, I was going to have to slog through and figure it out on my own.

It took a good six to eight months, but I finally started to catch on, and after seeing our work firsthand, the boss *eventually* warmed up to Joseph and me. We actually became friends.

Unfortunately, it didn't last long. When our first boss finished his tour, he was replaced by Bad Boss 2. This gentleman didn't get the job because he was a good leader or was particularly knowledgeable. Rather, he'd just hung around long enough and knew the right people. He couldn't run an operation to save his life and was keenly aware of this fact, so he masked his insecurities by hiding from everyone. Holed up in his office, he emerged only to berate someone or to use the bathroom. I think he was terrified we would see through his facade, which we did. What made it worse was that he was spiteful and vindictive toward his officers. I didn't know whether to dislike him or feel really sorry for him. In the end, I think I did both.

While I don't enjoy delving into details regarding the negative aspects of my agency experience, I think it's important to understand that although the job was supremely cool, it wasn't all smiley faces and unicorns. I had more than my fair share of bad managers and uncomfortable situations at the agency, but through them all, I learned so much—primarily to put my head down and just do the work. It takes time, but eventually people will recognize your substance and your spirit and respect that.

In the meantime, I trusted that God had a plan—he always does. It might not be clear as day, but it's always there, preparing us for what's to come. Case in point: Though this obviously wasn't intentional, Jim's early reluctance to engage with me during my training helped prepare me for the cold shoulders I got from Bosses 1 and 2. Had Jim been warm and welcoming, the reception we received in ███████ would have been even more jarring. And compared to what lay ahead, navigating office politics was like a walk in the park.

CHAPTER 7

MR. & MRS. SMITH

As far as the CIA was concerned, having a husband-and-wife team at their disposal was quite the coup. Not only were we willing and able to go places most other agents weren't, but because we were married, we were something of a "buy one, get one free," if you will. Even though we both received salaries and danger pay, we required only one set of housing-related expenses, which included rent, furniture, utilities, water delivery, appliances, a twenty-four-hour guard force, etc. Simply put, we were a bargain.

Of course there were advantages for us as well. For one, we provided each other with invaluable emotional support. Who are we kidding—ours was a weird job, and not one that a lot of people could relate to. Being able to share that experience with your spouse—to have someone who understands everything you're going through because he or she is going through it right alongside you—is priceless.

And unlike many agents, we always had someone to lean on when times got tough and the pressure of living in war zones and other dangerous places started to get the best of us. We were able to spend birthdays, holidays, and weekends together—even if some of those were spent in the office. And we always had the comfort of knowing that wherever we went, there was an extra set of hypercommitted eyes watching our backs and scouting for danger on our behalf.

Most important, we carried the burden of living undercover together—equally. This is hard to do when one spouse isn't a CIA officer because he or she is always on the outside, doing everything possible to be supportive, but never fully understanding the burdens of this crazy life.

Still, when we were working with sources, we never let on that Joseph and I were anything more than colleagues. After all, why give the enemy a potential advantage? To this end, we tried hard not to let our nonverbal behavior give away our real-life status. Of course, the effort to keep this personal information under wraps made for some interesting and humorous situations, despite our best efforts.

Once, for example, we were debriefing a midlevel Sunni insurgent who was very close to insurgent leadership. Joseph had talked him into cooperating with the US government and—quite miraculously—agreeing to stop carrying out attacks on Coalition Forces. At one point, Joseph invited me to debrief Khalid directly to acquire information in one of my areas of expertise.

Khalid was an egocentric, street-smart Iraqi with a dangerous ideology: By his own admission, he was a Salafist, meaning that he belonged to an ultraconservative form of Islam that gets much of its support from Saudi Arabia. Some Salafists are jihadists, and Khalid was in that category. He espoused offensive jihad (i.e., proactive violence) against those deemed to be enemies of Islam.

Not just any case officer could handle a source like Khalid. It had to be someone who knew how to interact with a tough jihadist and ultimately talk in a way that would resonate with him. This was not difficult for Joseph. His high school was full of kids whose parents were members of the Egyptian Islamic Jihad. And a few of those students became founding members of al-Qa'ida. Joseph saw them in action every day and was familiar with their mentality and behavior. Given these unique experiences living (and defending himself) in the lions' den, Joseph could walk the walk and talk the talk when needed.

Knowing Khalid's assumptions and hang-ups enabled Joseph to reframe the debate. He explained that the United States was not the enemy. Instead of achieving their objective of expelling Coalition Forces from Iraq, the insurgents were achieving the opposite: More and more troops were being sent in to restabilize the mess we had made when we removed Saddam Hussein from power and dissolved the military and police forces.

Meanwhile, al-Qa'ida was growing like a cancer, taking control of large swaths of Sunni territory. Tribal leaders and insurgent groups needed to focus on wider issues of governance and control versus worrying about Coalition Forces. The quicker the insurgents backed down, the quicker the Coalition could withdraw its troops and leave the country.

Khalid was a smart guy. As soon as the situation was presented to him in this manner, from a more strategic perspective, he got it. And he was surprisingly able to influence the positions of other insurgents and help them understand this new equation. The time Joseph spent with Khalid was very valuable. He proved to be an exceptional source, getting the insurgents to cool down as well as to act as a bulwark against al-Qa'ida.

In order to make Khalid more open to engagement, Joseph never told him he was a Christian. Khalid assumed Joseph was a Muslim, and Joseph did not disabuse him of this. To support this facade, Joseph had to take on a different persona, which involved a different name (Jamal), a slight vocabulary change, and attention to his behavior. For example, there are certain phrases that Muslims will use and Christians will avoid, such as *bismillah* ("in the name of God"). Some Muslims use this phrase when they are about to begin a new task, such as eating, driving, or even searching the Internet. Joseph also had to be aware of simple behaviors like knowing who should stand to the right or the left when entering or exiting a room together. These were nuances that Joseph had to follow to keep up the ruse.

The other tradition quite pertinent to this story is that most Salafist men don't wear gold rings. They follow *fatwas* (Islamic judgments) based on the *hadith* that say it is permissible for a man to wear a ring as adornment, but it must be silver. Women may wear gold rings and other gold jewelry, but it is generally understood in conservative circles that men should not. (Hadith are historical collections of the sayings and actions of Muhammad that Muslims use to further illuminate the teachings of the Qur'an.) Aware of this stricture, Joseph removed his gold wedding band prior to meetings with Khalid.

As a Salafist, Khalid supported a strict interpretation of Shari'a law that segregates men and women and teaches that a woman's place is in the home. Therefore, I was not sure how amenable he was to being debriefed by me, a foreign (and non-Muslim) woman of childbearing age. When interacting with men like this, I've encountered a variety of responses. On one end of the spectrum is total avoidance; some men eschew eye contact or touch of any kind, including a handshake. The next option is polite engagement. And on the other end of the spectrum are those excited to interact with a woman, who use every opportunity to touch or get close to me.

From the moment I walked in the door, Khalid was extremely friendly. Joseph introduced me as "Sarah," a colleague specializing in counterterrorism issues. I had not yet spoken any Arabic, so Khalid assumed that I didn't know any. He looked over at "Jamal" and committed one of the Middle East's most unforgivable sins. Having no idea he was commenting on Jamal's wife, Khalid said, "You didn't tell me you were bringing someone like her to the meeting! Wallahi ['I swear to God'], if you had brought ten women that looked like her, you would have won the war. We would have all surrendered."

Having a difficult time with the Iraqi dialect, I couldn't catch exactly what he was saying, but I did realize one thing: it was highly inappropriate, and there was a sexual vibe to it. Joseph tried to laugh at Khalid's joke but was obviously extremely uncomfortable. He had to play along, but having an insurgent hit on his wife, especially in a place where making inappropriate comments about someone's spouse could get you killed, was a strange experience. Khalid was trying to be lighthearted and witty (many Arabs love joking around), but he was unknowingly pushing all the wrong buttons. If he'd had any idea what he was doing, he would have been mortified.

Embarrassed by Khalid's lack of decorum, I walked over to the corner of the room to get a bottle of water out of the mini refrigerator. As I bent down to retrieve the water, Joseph came up beside me and whispered, "Take your ring off."

The distinctive gold wedding ring, which I normally took off before meetings, was shining brightly in the fluorescent lights. I glanced over and realized that Joseph was wearing his matching band (the two rings were identical). He'd forgotten to take his off too. After slipping the band off my finger, I stood up and shoved it into the front pocket of my pants, hoping that Khalid wasn't watching me. With his back to Khalid, Joseph slid the ring off his finger, holding it in his hand to conceal it from Khalid's view.

We walked back to the center of the room and sat down around the glass coffee table. We made some small talk before Joseph launched into business. (Joseph acted as the translator for this meeting, enabling Khalid and me to communicate, and carefully hiding the fact that I had some knowledge of Arabic.) He explained that I was there to ask Khalid some important questions and requested that Khalid give me his utmost attention. As I started to explain my purpose for coming to the meeting, Joseph somehow lost his grip on the gold band, and it fell out of his hand. Instead of merely landing on the table, it slowly and majestically bounced—in slow motion . . . *ding! ding! ding!*—across the glass table until it landed right smack in front of Khalid. *Smooth.*

Joseph quickly reached over and scooped it up, hoping Khalid hadn't had time to process what had just happened. Trying to deflect attention away from the bouncing gold ring, I launched into my portion of the debrief. Khalid looked slightly puzzled, but apparently wanting to keep up with the conversation, he moved on.

In times like this, Joseph and I looked less like Mr. and Mrs. Smith and a lot more like Inspector Clouseau. It would have been a difficult life if we had done it alone. But working together made all the difference.

On one rare occasion, we even found ourselves working against another husband-and-wife team—and the outcome was not at all what we anticipated.

Thanks to Hollywood, most people have a very glamorous impression of the CIA. But the cold hard truth is, officers spend a lot more time prepping for meetings and writing up results than actually executing an operation. This is the side of intelligence work the public doesn't see but that requires a great deal of effort.

The other time-consuming activity is developing targets—people officers pursue a friendship with, in the hope that they will eventually decide to work with the CIA. In intelligence parlance, this is called a recruitment. But getting someone to the point where they are willing to risk their lives to do this is no easy task. Joseph and I had to systematically build a solid foundation of friendship and trust, the hallmarks of every successful recruitment. If we were developing a nice person, then this could be a real treat. But many of the targets we were trying to recruit were not the most upstanding human beings.

That was the case with Sayf. He worked for a government whose relationship with the United States was highly antagonistic. His government had sponsored numerous terrorist attacks against US targets, so our countries weren't exactly friends. Sayf was definitely of interest to the CIA.

As it happens, Sayf was newly married to a wonderful young lady named Amina. As was the custom in this country, the marriage had been arranged by their respective parents. But despite it having been arranged, Sayf and his bride seemed to be very much in love, and within months of saying "I do," Amina became pregnant. By the time we met the young couple during our second tour, they had a one-year-old son.

Joseph began a friendship with Sayf, and we started seeing the couple quite often for coffee and tea or dinner. They were extremely generous when hosting us at their villa, often placing ten different delectable dishes in front of us for a meal, which I'm certain must have taken all day for Amina to prepare.

One weekend, in order to return the favor, I spent all day cooking a meal for them. I was quite nervous because it is a challenge to figure out how to satisfy the tastes and cultural expectations of people from different backgrounds. Many people in the Arab world have a limited palate; they are used to certain types of dishes and rarely branch out. It's the opposite of the United States, where we're all about trying new foods and discovering new cuisines. My problem was that I didn't know how to prepare the dishes this couple was used to. The meals I was used to making were completely foreign to them.

I have served many diplomats and international guests through-out my career, and I've been shocked by how often my guests have given me feedback on what would have made the meal more palat-able. "A little more lemon" (in the dish that took two hours to pre-pare) or "If you had put less sugar in the [homemade triple-layer] cake, it would be much better."

It's strange. I can't imagine ever correcting a host or hostess who's spent all day preparing a meal—no matter what it tastes like. But in the Middle East, these kinds of critiques are normal. (And for the record, I'm a pretty good cook!)

Despite my nervousness, the meal went well. I served my mother-in-law's famous creamy chicken curry, which is actually a southern Indian dish that we have adapted to suit our own tastes—for us, the more fla-vor and fire, the better! In addition, I prepared roasted red pepper and chickpea salad, lamb *kofta* with garlicky yogurt dip, Turkish *pide* (simi-lar to small pizzas), and homemade brownies with chocolate chunks.

Even if my offerings weren't like their traditional dishes, they didn't criticize my efforts. Furthermore, I was just happy they ate. There have been numerous occasions when I've spent all day preparing dinner for guests, only to have them tell me they weren't hungry and then refuse to touch a morsel.

After we finished eating, we moved to the living room to have coffee, tea, dessert, and mixed nuts. Joseph had told me in advance that he was going to take Sayf out for a walk around the grounds of our apartment building in order to try to coax some intelligence out of him. I was excited that we might be at the point in the relationship where Sayf was willing to share sensitive insights about the authoritarian regime he worked for. If he did indeed share information or express discontent with his regime's policies, it would represent a breakthrough in the relationship.

At the appointed time, Joseph and Sayf stood up and informed us that they were going for a short walk. Amina and I replied, "Okay, have fun!"

At this point, the situation got somewhat harder for me because I didn't have anyone to translate for me and Amina. She was from a well-known but very sheltered tribe in her country, and her dialect was so unique—I'd never heard anything like it before. It was completely different from the Modern Standard Arabic (MSA) that I'd studied at Georgetown or the Egyptian dialect I'd learned in Cairo. Amina's vocabulary and accent were so distinctive that her Arabic sounded like a different language altogether.

Because of this, talking to her was tortuous. It required the engagement of every brain cell for me to comprehend what she was saying. After about twenty minutes, I had expended my full complement of Arabic. But as hard as it was, I kept telling myself that it was worth the effort if Joseph was making progress downstairs with Sayf.

Twenty more minutes crept by . . . minute after painful minute. I was desperately hoping that Joseph and Sayf's walk would end soon, that they would come through the door and save me from myself. As

I thought about how pathetic my Arabic was, Amina started discussing family issues. She said she thought American culture was not very honorable because there was so much divorce. She said something about Americans having loose morals and rampant sexuality. Furthermore, she asked me, "Why don't Americans value their families like Arabs do?"

Now these are complicated topics in any language, but trying to respond to these value judgments in Arabic . . . I get a headache just thinking about the linguistic gymnastics I employed trying to respond to her questions in a meaningful way. I was completely inept and incapable of explaining the intricacies of my people and my culture to Amina.

I kept looking at my watch, thinking hours had elapsed, but alas, it had been only five minutes since my last desperate glance at the timepiece. Talk. About. Awkward. Amina and I had exhausted our ability to communicate, and we were creeping up on an hour since Joseph and Sayf had left the apartment. I thought to myself, *He'd better be getting some great intel!*

For someone who likes to make conversation and enjoys connecting one-on-one, it was the height of discomfort to sit there and merely stare at Amina. I tried playing with the baby, but he was tired. I showed Amina some of my photographs, we looked at picture books, and then we tried to teach each other a couple of useful words in our respective languages. And then we ran out of things to do. Amina yawned. I yawned. The baby yawned. We were exhausted. It had been two hours since the men had taken leave of us.

I twiddled my fingers. Amina played with her head covering. The baby yawned again. After an interminable wait of about two and a half hours, Joseph and Sayf returned. I could not have been more relieved to see two people walk through the front door.

Because everyone was so clearly tired at that point, the family thanked us for the meal and immediately went home. Once they had gone and we had put on sound masking (to hide the conversation from any potential hidden audio devices), I asked Joseph what I had been dying to know all night: "So how'd it go? What did you get? What happened?"

His one-word reply was strange. "Nothing."

"What?"

"Nothing."

"How's that possible? You were gone for two and a half hours!"

"You're not going to believe this," he said, "but we didn't talk about anything. We didn't even take a walk. We got into his car, and he drove to a local bar to meet his girlfriend. I had to sit there, twiddling my thumbs, while he kissed and groped her. It was ridiculous."

Quite shocked, I said, "What? Are you kidding me? He used his time with you as an excuse to go see his girlfriend . . . at a bar?"

"Yep."

"While I babysat his wife?"

"Yep!"

I could not believe what I was hearing. "So Sayf was smooching his local girlfriend while his wife was sitting on my couch, telling me how immoral American culture is?"

"Yes indeed!"

Smoke was coming out of my ears. "This is so wrong in so many ways!" I said.

And that, my friends, is the joy of being an intelligence officer. Sometimes things go really well, and sometimes they are simply terrible. Sometimes they are exciting, and sometimes you're so bored you just want to poke your eyes out. And sometimes you have to babysit someone's wife so he can execute his own covert activities.

Either way, it's all that much more enjoyable when you have someone to share it with.

CHAPTER 8

GET OFF THE "X"

About a year after we arrived at our first post, I headed out one morning to make the twenty-minute drive to the CIA compound. Joseph was traveling, so I was by myself and more nervous than usual. It took about twenty minutes to get from our house at the southern edge of the city to the CIA compound. My colleagues and I had to be especially careful when navigating the streets of this unforgiving place because as American citizens and US government officials, we represented the perfect targets for al-Qa'ida, whose presence was well established throughout the city.

Because of the training we had received, we knew that we were most vulnerable in our vehicles while coming and going from our residences, and while entering and exiting the work compound. These were the easiest places for attackers to lie in wait, to *set up* on us.

I was keenly aware that American diplomat Laurence Foley had been assassinated at his residence in Amman, just seven months before we began our deployment in a country with elements far more hostile than those in Jordan. The gunmen shot Foley just as he was about to get into his car and drive to work. The two killers—a Jordanian citizen and a Libyan citizen—carried out the operation at the behest of future al-Qa'ida in Iraq leader Abu Musab al-Zarqawi.

I had no intention of becoming another fatality—if I could help it. I carefully exited the walls of our compound and scanned the empty lots around me, looking for anything or anyone that seemed to be out of place. Nothing appeared strange or amiss, and I left home without incident. As I drove out of the residential neighborhood and onto the main street, I checked my rearview mirror often to ensure no one was following me.

About halfway to work, I came to a stop at a red light. I patiently watched as a couple of pedestrians crossed the street in front of me. One of the men, who was walking very slowly, glanced up at the vehicle and saw me through the windshield. I was sitting by myself in the driver's seat of a large SUV. As the man's eyes honed in on me, they flashed the look that I know well after living in some of the most conservative cultures in the world. It was the look of a hungry dog that had just seen his first meal in days. It was a look of perversion, depravity, and darkness that was so revolting it made my skin crawl. You would have thought I was completely unclothed in the driver's seat. For the record, I was wearing a long-sleeved shirt, so all he could see was my face and neck, but apparently that was just too much for him (or whatever spiritual darkness was in him).

He stopped crossing the street and planted his feet squarely in front of the vehicle. To my horror, he started gesturing with his hands, acting out an incredibly inappropriate sexual act. I was startled. I could not believe what I was seeing. I had traveled quite a bit, but I had never encountered anything like this before. *How can he possibly think it is all right to do this in public? This kind of behavior isn't okay in any country, in any culture. Blakhh.*

I figured the man would get it out of his system and move along, but he just stood there in his white *dishdasha* (long, flowing robe), *kaffiyeh* (head wrap), and Western-style sports jacket with the tag still sewn onto the sleeve. He continued making the obscene gesture for what seemed like an eternity. Soon other men on the sidewalk started noticing, and I felt my face flush. I was mortified. The light eventually turned green, but I couldn't go anywhere with this man standing directly in front of the vehicle.

Getting more and more annoyed, I gestured toward the sidewalk and yelled, "Get out of here, you jerk!" I kept waving my arms, shouting at him to move in both English and Arabic. He couldn't hear me through the glass, but I kept shouting nonetheless. Meanwhile, a small crowd of men started taking interest in the spectacle and began moving toward the car to get a better look at me. They didn't appear to be disturbed by the man, but they were supremely interested in *me*. They just *had* to see what was behind the glass, eliciting such a reaction. Ever since I'd joined the CIA, it seemed like I was either ignored because I was a woman or the center of attention. I just couldn't catch a break.

After living in ███████ more than a year, I knew how quickly men swarm a vehicle in the wake of a car crash. It was the strangest sight. Hundreds of men would surround the vehicle, pushing their faces up against the glass and trying to look at the people inside—particularly if there were women. (No, they really *don't* have enough to do.) They would stand there, noses scrunched up to the window, just staring. The chance to see a woman, up close and personal, was an opportunity they could not pass up. And that day at the intersection, I was the only female for miles.

In ███████, women aren't permitted outside the home, with the exception of trips to the vegetable market, the grocery store, or the homes of family and friends. Local women are *munaqabeen*, which means that they are completely shrouded in flowing black cloth. No part of their bodies can be seen, with the exception of their hands. ███████ is such a conservative country that if an advertisement on the street bears a woman's face, it isn't long before someone defaces the sign, blotting out the perverse image. Outside of their mothers, sisters, daughters, or wives (yes, plural), men don't really know what other women look like.

My stomach clenched as I shifted from being shocked and appalled by the man's behavior to realizing that he was placing me in danger by causing a scene and refusing to move out of the way. ████████ is one of the carjacking and kidnapping capitals of the world. In fact, one of my predecessors at work had been carjacked right there in the city. She related the story to me like it was no big deal, because those were the good old days when the kidnappers would treat you like an honored guest. They would often use Western hostages as leverage to negotiate with the government for some essential service they needed in their village, like a school or medical clinic.

More recently, however, kidnappings had turned into a deadly sport that usually ended in the deaths of the victims as a result of botched government intervention or al-Qa'ida's involvement.

Kidnappings weren't necessarily planned in advance. Rather, foreigners were often a target of opportunity. Tribal men would take foreigners captive and sell them to al-Qa'ida for desperately needed cash. And one thing I knew as a counterterrorism officer—those kidnappings never ended well.

With all of this racing through my mind, I knew I couldn't let fear take over and cause me to freeze. I couldn't just hunker down and hope the situation didn't deteriorate further. Without thought, my security training kicked in, and I felt the sudden urge to "get off the 'X.'"

In CIA lingo, the "X" refers to the site of an attack. This is the location in which the attackers have the greatest advantage because they control the environment. Attackers increase their chances of success by stopping, surrounding, or disabling your vehicle, making it difficult for you to get away. From a target's perspective, the "X" is the position of greatest vulnerability, where you have the least amount of control over the outcome of a situation. Therefore, we are taught to do whatever we can to get off the "X" and away from that location.

At that intersection, I was sitting squarely on the "X." The crowd of men approaching the vehicle was growing by the minute, and if there happened to be any extremists amongst them and they discovered I was alone . . . well, I didn't want to wait to find out what might happen. Unfortunately, I was sandwiched between the instigator and a beat-up sedan idling a couple of inches behind me.

Like a zombie movie unfolding in slow motion, local men, bearing various types of weapons—mostly ceremonial knives—were advancing from every direction. They were emerging from storefronts and sidewalk perches along the road to get as close to my car as possible. Within the span of two minutes, the group of bystanders had expanded and was now a crowd of twenty or thirty leering men. Very shortly my SUV would be surrounded and I would be unable to move.

My mind raced. *What do I do? How do I get out of this?*

In a moment of sheer desperation, I took my foot off the brake. The SUV lurched forward, and the front bumper hit the man with a soft thud. I wish you could have seen his face—his expression was one of pure shock. Never in a million years did he think I would be bold enough to hit him with my vehicle. But he quickly recovered and defiantly regained his stance in front the SUV, even more determined to stand his ground.

At this point, even more men were succumbing to curiosity— they just *had* to know what inside the SUV was causing such a scene. Out of the corners of my eyes, I could see the zombie men closing in. They were crossing the street and walking up the sidewalk toward my SUV, and as they walked, I could see the glint of their knives affixed to the wide belts slung across their skinny waists. My panic grew. My thoughts were jumbled and desperate. I would be surrounded in seconds. I had to get out of there.

I took my foot off the brake and tapped the gas pedal. I hit the man harder, and he fell back several steps onto the pavement. I yelled, "That's right, you creep—get out of the way or I will run you over!" I held his gaze, wild-eyed, while revving the engine like the crazy woman I had just become. *Vrooom! Vroom!* His eyes widened. He threw his hands up and began to slowly back away from the car. The crowd of men temporarily froze and stared in shock, wondering what I would do next.

The second the pervert stepped out of the road, I gunned the gas and shot through the intersection. My heart was pounding, and I was shaking violently. I raced through the city toward the office, refusing to stop for any more stop signs or traffic lights. When I finally made it to the relative safety of the CIA compound, adrenaline was surging through my body. It took hours for me to calm down.

That day was a stark reminder of how quickly things can spiral out of control when you live in a place like ▮▮▮▮▮▮. Who knows what would have happened if I had just sat there in shock, waiting and wondering to see what was going to unfold. The longer I had stayed on the "X," the less control I would have had over the situation, and the more likely it was that I would have been at the mercy of people who did not have my best interests in mind.

There are many stories of people—both diplomats and civilians—who became paralyzed by fear and ended up victims of brutal terrorist attacks. Incidentally, that's why the fight-or-flight response is now called the fight, flight, or freeze response. Because sometimes when the odds are overwhelming and we don't know what to do, we neither fight nor flee. More often than not, people die by simply *not doing anything*. That's what the instructors were trying to condition us for in the simulated ambush—to conquer the tendency to freeze. They wanted to be sure we had the capacity to react, to move.

That training came in handy more than once, including on a trip Joseph and I made to Egypt over a holiday weekend. Joseph was traveling elsewhere at the time, so I went ahead of him, landing in Cairo a day before he was scheduled to arrive. The next afternoon, three family members and I drove to the airport to pick him up.

Egypt's airport infrastructure is notoriously unhelpful. At that time, there were no flight status monitors. Neither was there a central terminal or information desk from which to obtain data on departing or arriving flights. Family and friends just sat and waited for their loved ones to emerge from the customs area.

We had been there about half an hour before I realized that Joseph's flight had landed. I knew that an acquaintance of ours was on the same flight, and I saw him exit the sliding glass doors of the international arrivals hall. I assumed Joseph would either be right behind him or exit momentarily.

Instead, another hour went by.

And another thirty minutes.

At the two-hour mark, I started to panic. It appeared that all of the passengers from Joseph's flight had moved through customs because travelers from other destinations were now exiting the arrivals hall. I knew, beyond a shadow of a doubt, that he had boarded the aircraft and that the aircraft had made it to Cairo.

We waited another tense hour as I paced the floor. As the minutes ticked by, I started considering the worst-case scenario: What if authorities thought Joseph still did human rights work and were intent on making him "disappear"? They have been known to do this to people involved with humanitarian organizations. Joseph had worked for the democracy and human rights think tank more than five years prior, but government officials might not be aware that he no longer worked there. Years ago we'd found out that Joseph's human rights work had landed him on Egypt's black list—alongside Islamic terrorists and violent criminals. We had broken our own rule by letting Joseph travel into Egypt by himself, something we avoided since we didn't trust the authorities. The Mubarak regime had a record of detaining and torturing those on its black list, and this wasn't a chance I wanted to take—that Joseph could end up receiving the same treatment as terrorists because of his Christian background and human rights work.

Three hours had passed since I saw our acquaintance emerge from customs. It shouldn't take this long for Joseph to come out. I was wondering what—if anything—I should do.

As my stress climbed to a ridiculous level, I knew I couldn't sit there any longer. It was time to get off the "X." I had to act. It was possible Joseph was being held somewhere inside the airport, and if so, I needed to get to him quickly. My best bet would be to make it clear that I knew he had arrived and was in the airport.

I decided to confront the security officer manning the exit door. His job was to ensure nobody illegally entered the secure part of the airport. I grabbed my passport, put it in my right hand, and walked up to him. Speaking only English (because in that culture, English speakers are respected), I informed him, "I am an American official. My husband is also an American official. He is inside that hall. Your people are holding him. I am going to give you ten minutes. I better see my husband in ten minutes, or I will walk in that hall and find him myself."

He was shocked. He said, "Ma'am, you can't do that. You can't go in there."

"I know, but if you don't produce him for me in ten minutes, I will walk in there—legal or not. Do you understand?"

He just stood there, so I continued, "You'd better hurry up; the clock is ticking. You have ten minutes."

He got on his walkie-talkie and spoke to someone. He looked uncomfortable. He started pacing in a tight little circle in front of the arrivals hall exit doors. I stood a few feet away, tapping my foot and checking my watch every few minutes, desperately hoping that the officer would see me and know that I was serious.

Five minutes went by, and I approached the officer again. "You have five minutes. If he doesn't walk out this door in five minutes, then I'm going inside. This is your warning."

He protested, "Ma'am, you can't do that! This is the secure part of the airport. You can't go in there. You'll get arrested!"

"I know, and I'm prepared for that. Just so you are aware: You'll need to call the US embassy and tell them that you just arrested one of their citizens. Do you have that number? Because you're going to need it."

What am I doing? I could hardly believe myself. The boldness I felt, the determination that I had to act, was bursting at the seams. I'd do anything to be sure that Joseph was all right, even if it meant causing an international incident.

I turned around and walked back to my family, whose mouths were agape. They'd never seen me act like this, so they were in shock. I said, "Okay, guys. I'm about to walk into the arrivals hall. If I don't come back out again, call the US embassy and tell them I've been detained and that Joseph is in there too."

Not knowing what else to say, they whispered, "Okay."

My hands were shaking. I took a deep breath, checked my watch (it had been thirteen minutes), and walked toward the officer, carefully holding my American passport in the air. I quietly prayed, "Please, God, help me!"

The officer watched me approach. I could see the fear in his face, wondering what I'd do. I announced in very clear English, "I am an American citizen. My husband is an American citizen. You are holding my husband inside. I am going to find him."

With this, I approached the glass doors, which slid right open, allowing me to proceed into the customs area. The officer ran after me, yelling, "Stop! Stop!"

I started walking very fast. I wasn't sure where I was going, but I wanted to look like I knew. So I walked with purpose while scanning the horizon, trying to plot my next move. About three different officers saw me breaking the security barrier and started converging on the crazy American lady. I started yelling, "Where is my husband? Where is my husband?"

At that moment, I caught a glimpse of Joseph at the other end of the hangar-like customs area, briskly walking toward me. *Thank you, Jesus!* A man came running over and shoved a passport into Joseph's hand. A few steps later, Joseph and I met and stole a quick hug. He said, "What are you doing in here?"

"I was trying to find you!"

As it turns out, Joseph had not been formally detained, only told to sit on a bench and wait. He was never given a reason why he was being held and unable to proceed through passport control and customs. He was simply told, "One minute," which irritatingly turned into more than three hours.

Concerned, he told one of the officers, "If you don't release me soon, I will walk out of the arrivals hall without my passport. I will notify the US embassy that you were harassing an American official, and I don't think you want that to happen." He had no idea that I was making similar threats, informing officers I was about to break through security to find my spouse.

Strangely enough, this special attention came to an end once they learned that Joseph was no longer involved in human rights work. Though they were a little late to the game, they finally figured out that Joseph was working for the US government. He never received that kind of treatment again.

Given my boldness in these two situations, it might surprise you to learn that my natural inclination is to remain on the "X." I like routine, and I highly value stability. At my core, I am very much a homebody. I am not a fly-by-night kind of person. When change is presented to me, I tend to face it with much trepidation. I get nervous about what to expect and whether I will succeed in the new endeavor, and I often get wrapped up in the "what-ifs." I have to concentrate on moving myself forward because the process of opening up to new possibilities is unnerving. Venturing outside my comfort zone goes against the grain of who I am and stokes my deepest insecurities.

Was it hard to be a CIA officer with all of the challenges and change that entailed? Yes. Scary? Of course. But if I was going to fulfill my life mission, I had to conquer my instinctual tendency to freeze in place. Fear would get me nowhere. Faith, however, would take me to places I never imagined.

CHAPTER 9

CAUGHT BETWEEN IRAQ AND A HARD PLACE

One of the biggest challenges of counterterrorism work is that you are constantly relocating. Just when you've finally adapted to your new surroundings, the agency moves you to another country and you have to start all over again—new city, new culture, new supervisors, new colleagues. Sometimes they take into account your preferences for where you'd like to serve, but most often field requirements trump personal desires.

Case in point: I had no intention of serving in Iraq. I thought I had done my duty by serving in ███████, the other place no one wanted to go. Several colleagues tried to reassure me by saying, "Don't worry, you've already done your time; there is no way they would put you on the short list for Iraq." But by the fall of 2005, the situation in Iraq was deteriorating, and one by one people were getting yanked from their other tours and being sent to one of the most unpopular wars in modern history.

Anxiety continued to build as Iraq went down in flames, fanned by our unrealistic democratic experiment, the intervention of outside forces (i.e., Iran), and sectarian fault lines that widened by the day. Statistics certainly didn't help US government recruitment efforts:

In 2005, there were nearly eleven thousand roadside bombs in Iraq.[1] Deaths on every side of the equation—military and civilian—were spiraling out of control, suggesting that 2006 would be the worst year yet.

That's why I had been relieved in early 2005 to find out our next post would *not* be Iraq, but a place that many senior officers fought hard to get. Several jokingly said that they'd be willing to give up their firstborn if it meant they could get posted to this particular location. Joseph and I just got lucky. So after taking five weeks of leave back in the United States, we deployed to our new home country, excited to see what this tour had in store.

The first couple of months were uncomfortable since our apartment wasn't ready and we had to live in temporary quarters, but once we finally got placed in a beautiful new building on the outskirts of town, we were happy as clams. It was a modern, airy apartment with a beautiful balcony overlooking a verdant green valley. A month later, we received our household goods and were finally able to get settled.

███████ was wonderful—so much so that I was in culture shock. For the first time in almost two years, I could actually walk the streets without worrying about getting kidnapped. I could wear normal clothes and nobody would look at me funny. In fact, nobody stared at me at all! The food was healthful and delicious, which was in severe contrast to the food at the last post, which made us sick for almost two straight years. It was no longer necessary to soak my fruits and vegetables in bleach to make them safe to eat, and I could dine freely in restaurants and not have to worry about running home with a bout of diarrhea.

Then about a month later, I got a weird text from Stacey, a close friend of mine who was serving at headquarters.

Hey M! I heard you're going to Iraq!

I quickly wrote back.

No, honey, we're out here in ████████. Just started. Been here about five months. I just unpacked all my stuff.

There was a bit of a pause. Then she responded.

Well, I'm pretty sure you're being redirected to Iraq. I was in a long discussion about it this morning with HR folks who were trying to hunt down some Arabists who could help out with The Surge.

My heart dropped through the floor. I could not believe what I was reading. I reread the texts again to be sure I hadn't misunderstood my girlfriend. I asked her one more time,

Are you sure it was me they were talking about, not someone else? Maybe someone with a similar name?

Once more she said,

No, it was you and Joseph. 100%. They were trying to figure out where you were and they knew we were close friends . . . so they included me in the discussion.

My head started spinning. I wondered how in the world they could let me and Joseph deploy to a new country, just to pick us right back up and throw us into a war zone. It was crazy. It made no sense. Furthermore, the war was raging in Iraq. I honestly could not think of a worse place to be.

Instead of completely freaking out, I decided to pray about it. I prayed, and I prayed. I begged God not to let them send us to Iraq. Then I let my family in on the horrible secret and asked them to pray. They got right down on their knees, petitioning God not to send their daughter, sister, niece, or cousin to Iraq.

But no matter how hard we prayed or how fervent our protestations to headquarters, it was all for naught. We soon received the communication that nobody wanted to get, advising us to begin the paperwork for our return to Washington, DC, followed by immediate deployment to Iraq.

I was devastated. There was a lump in my throat that would not go away. I could hardly think straight as I repacked my household effects and prepared to fly back to DC. To further add to the stress, I had to retake the weapons course before I could launch to Baghdad. The agency required qualification on the Glock semiautomatic pistol and M4 rifle every two years, so I was overdue for the training—especially if I was to be deployed to the war zone.

To make matters worse and to add to my emotional distress, three days before I was scheduled to leave ████████, I woke up in the middle of the night with hives on my arms and stomach. I wasn't sure what I was having an allergic reaction to, but it didn't worry me too much. Eventually the discomfort passed, allowing me to go back to sleep, and the next day, there was no sign of hives or any indication of what had made them occur.

The next evening, I woke up again after sleeping for a couple of hours, and the hives were back. But this time, they were larger and had spread to other areas of my body. I was baffled, unsure what was causing this nightly flare-up. I took some allergy pills and tried my best to go back to sleep, which I eventually did. I woke up the next morning a bit worried about the hives, but they soon disappeared. Before long, I was attending to the hundred things I needed to accomplish on my last day in this beautiful country.

After Joseph and I completed all of our administrative requirements, we returned to the apartment, where only our luggage was now waiting. We went to sleep (not so soundly), thinking about our return to the United States and impending tour in Baghdad. Hours later, I awoke to the awful sensation that my body was on fire. The hives, which kept disappearing during the day and returning each night, had come back with a vengeance. Worse, they were growing in circumference, morphing into giant patches of swollen, burning skin. Instead of having a hundred hives on my tummy, I now had three large hives wrapped around my midsection. It was the same with both arms and legs. A few enormous hives appeared to be swallowing up my entire body.

Just when I thought it couldn't get any worse, I realized that I was having trouble breathing. Joseph called the doctor. He told Joseph I was going into anaphylactic shock and to get me to the hospital immediately. It seemed I was having a severe allergic reaction to the antibiotics I had been on for a rare bout of food poisoning, and it was critical that I get to the hospital before my airwaves constricted any further. I had never experienced anaphylactic shock before, and I was terribly scared, wondering whether we'd make it to the hospital in time.

Over the next few hours in the hospital, I shook uncontrollably as epinephrine and a large dose of Benadryl coursed through my system. The doctor said that he could not in good conscience let me fly back to the United States later that day, but I was adamant. I was on a very tight schedule that included a day at headquarters to sign papers and then a week's worth of weapons training before we boarded the flight that would take us to the war zone. There was no time to waste. I had to get on that flight or it would throw everything off.

Thinking back now, I have no idea why I cared. Why did I push so hard, begging the doctor to let me travel the next day? Why didn't I just accept that the situation was out of my hands, and have headquarters reschedule weapons training for the following week? Why not take some time in the United States to relax, heal, and prepare for the assignment? But I pushed hard, and the doctor reluctantly let me board the plane and leave ████████ that afternoon.

The first flight was uneventful. The second flight from Europe to DC was fine until I awoke from a nap to a stinging sensation on my stomach. I went into the bathroom, lifted my shirt, and looked in the mirror. I could not believe my eyes. Those darn hives were back, and they were spreading . . . again. Fear flooded my mind. Was I headed toward anaphylactic shock for a second time—*midair*?

I returned to my seat and gave the awful news to Joseph. I decided not to do anything for about an hour, hoping the hives would just go away. When I couldn't ignore the burning any longer, I thought it wise to tell the crew that I might be on the threshold of a medical emergency.

The flight attendants were very responsive. They reacted quickly, learning all they could about my situation and then advising the captain. The captain arranged for priority landing at Washington Dulles Airport, and we were moved into first class so we could be the first off the plane. Thankfully, we touched down before I got worse.

As the plane taxied down the runway, we could see the ambulance right there on the tarmac, next to our gate, ready to whisk me away to the hospital. I was extremely embarrassed to be the object of all this activity. The other passengers waited patiently while representatives from the Department of Homeland Security boarded the plane, stamping our passports and arranging our quick transition off the aircraft and into the ambulance.

After spending the next few hours in Reston Hospital Center recovering thanks to the massive dose of Benadryl they administered via IV, I was discharged just before sunrise. We checked into our hotel, got a few hours of sleep, and then headed into headquarters. I was not keen on being there—it's never fun schlepping around the building trying to complete all of your administrative requirements in one day, but papers had to be signed and we had to check in with numerous offices to prepare for the looming permanent change of station.

Our first stop was the human resources department to meet with Flo, who had been processing our file and helping us prepare for Iraq. She had never been particularly friendly, but we had no choice but to deal with her. She was in charge of the transition and would tell us what we needed to do on the only day we had at headquarters.

When the receptionist called Flo and told her we were there to see her, Flo surprised both the receptionist and us by saying that she was too busy to meet. I found that odd since she knew we were coming and we had only one day to accomplish all our tasks. Therefore, I decided to walk over to her desk and personally see what was going on.

Flo's back was to us, so she didn't realize that we were standing behind her.

"The Assads are here to see you," the receptionist announced.

With an irritated inflection in her voice, Flo responded, "Well, I do *not* have time for the Assads. They'll have to come back later. I had a terrible commute this morning. I have had a very bad day."

Normally I am amicable and calm. I despise confrontation, preferring to be a peacemaker. It takes a great deal to push me over the edge, but Flo had officially flipped the switch.

"*You've* had a bad day?" I barked.

Suddenly everyone in the human resources department froze—even Flo, who refused to turn around and face me, which only added to the level of anger now surging through my bloodstream. I repeated myself, even louder this time.

"*Really*, Flo? *You've* had a bad day?"

Once again, I was met with silence and her unwillingness to turn around and face me like a respectable human being. You could feel the tension building in the room. Unable to contain myself any longer, I said, "Flo, let me tell you what a bad day is: It's being sent, against your will, to a raging war zone where hundreds of people are dying every day. It's getting pulled out of a great tour after a few short months and being told that you are going to Iraq—*after* serving two years in another war zone. It's having an allergic reaction and going into anaphylactic shock the night before getting on a plane to come home. It's rushing to the emergency room and trying to get there before you stop breathing. It's getting sick again on the airplane three hours before landing in DC.

"Just hours ago, I was in the emergency room receiving an IV in an attempt to stave off another episode of anaphylactic shock. And the day after tomorrow I begin a week of weapons training before I can board the flight straight to the gates of hell! I would happily trade a bad day with you, Flo!"

You could have heard a pin drop. There wasn't one person in the room not leaning forward in their chair to hear the unusually direct confrontation. As I turned around to walk away, I advised one of Flo's colleagues sitting nearby, "You're going to have to find someone else to process this file, because Flo's having a bad day." No one argued.

Every night of weapons training that next week, I woke up multiple times in the middle of the night covered in welts. I went through multiple packs of Benadryl and slathered hydrocortisone cream all over my body before climbing back into the bottom bunk and trying to sleep through the night with dozens of strangers in the communal quarters. My sleep that week was plagued by jet lag and fiery welts. This was not the ideal physical condition to be in for Glock requalification, but I was determined to get through it.

Each exercise required us to draw our concealed weapons and shoot quickly and accurately before returning the weapons to the holsters hidden beneath our vests. We shot at targets from various distances, incorporating reloads and malfunctions into the scenarios. We shot from behind cover, completed target differentiation exercises, and moved carefully through shoot houses while encountering and responding to "hostile fire." Each student expended thousands and thousands of rounds that week. The continuous shooting and magazine reloads shredded my hands and fingers. Wrapping them up in medical tape each day helped me get through the week.

The hardest part for me was the first day. My hands shook uncontrollably, and it took a couple of hours to work the nervousness out of my system and feel comfortable in the arena. Strangely enough, I've never been scared of guns, and I wasn't scared of the Glock itself, but I had a hard time transitioning to the multidecibel commotion of fifteen students shooting at the same time. Earplugs and headphones were helpful, but the noise level was still unsettling for me. Once I got used to the racket, I felt much more calm and in control.

Despite all of the unusual challenges that week, I made it through. On the final qualification test, I shot 30/30 and was added to the list of people able to serve in war zones. (A minimum of 26/30 shots was required to pass the timed test.) I suppose I could have derailed the deployment to Iraq by "failing" the test, but I've always been fiercely competitive, and I don't like to fail. Still, it was hard to reconcile the notion that I was capable of holding my own in a deadly, highly combustive environment with the reality that I was, in fact, headed for a deadly, highly combustive environment. There was no avoiding it. And now, no delaying it. Ready or not, Joseph and I were headed for Iraq.

CHAPTER 10

WELCOME TO HELL ON EARTH

As the government plane approached Baghdad International Airport, the pilots executed an unconventional descent. They carefully maneuvered over the designated airspace and then descended to earth in a tight corkscrew pattern. Coming in for a normal landing would have subjected us to the very real possibility of getting shot down by anti-aircraft missiles. Flight attendants had us close the window shades and turn off all electronic equipment inside the cabin so we would "come in black." They didn't want the insurgents to be able to see the plane and shoot us down from the edges of the airport.

In addition to Joseph and me, a couple of other passengers were embarking on a one-year tour of duty, but the majority were being deployed on a short-term, temporary basis. Regardless of who we were or what we were doing there, this peculiar descent further reinforced the notion that we were about to experience something beyond the bounds of our experience or comfort zones. We had left the security of home for a place in which corkscrew countermeasures were necessary to avoid getting shot out of the sky. We suspected that it was going to be a tough year, and I can confirm that Iraq did not disappoint.

Joseph and I were relieved when the plane touched down in the wee hours of the morning. We were white-knuckled through the entire descent, holding each other's hands, praying that nothing would go wrong. After we had deplaned, administrative officers gave us a security brief and took photos for our new badges. After the "Welcome to Baghdad" speech, we were each issued a helmet, a Glock, an M4, a holster, two magazines, a secure radio, and a Kevlar vest. Then we patiently waited for our turn to board the helicopter that would shuttle us from the airport to the CIA compound in the Green Zone. This was much safer than traversing the infamous "Route Irish," aka IED Alley, which was riddled with explosive devices freshly buried in the road every day. There were several helicopter runs each night ferrying officers back and forth. The helicopters flew low and fast, skimming over the tops of the buildings, making it harder for insurgents to see them coming.

However, there was a time crunch: If we weren't able to make it over to the compound before sunrise, we would be stuck at the airport until the following evening, when the city would be under curfew again and we could operate more securely under the cover of darkness.

Because our plane had arrived much later than expected, only half of the group was able to make it over to the CIA compound before the sun began to rise. The rest of us had to wait until the following evening.

Getting stuck at the airport felt like being in purgatory. Joseph and I had made it all the way to Iraq but had not yet arrived at our final destination. There was nothing to do but wait and ponder what was to come. The gaudy interior of the airport further added to the sensation of being in a time warp. The VVIP buildings designed for Saddam Hussein were dripping with 1970s decor: golden fixtures, marble, mirrors, and self-glorifying murals of Saddam. They reflected the trappings of a bygone era and the cult of personality that had been strategically erected around him. There wasn't much to do as we waited for darkness to fall again. We stretched out mealtimes, read books, and lounged around on the overstuffed couches.

When it was finally time to go, we gathered the bags and equipment and headed to the staging area. As I waited to board the helicopter, I suddenly felt like I was entering the Twilight Zone. I kept thinking, *How in the world did I get here?* I had never imagined myself working in a war zone, so I was feeling the shock and awe of being dropped into an alternate reality—and not one of my choosing.

After approaching the helicopter in a single-file line, we carefully climbed the tiny stairs, trying to balance all of our belongings as the rotors cut through the hot desert air, kicking up every piece of dust on the ground. We sat down inside, crowded together like sardines. The gunners put on their night-vision goggles and assumed their positions at the doors, which were open to the night sky. I could see the pilots checking their colorful screens and preparing to lift off. These were not things I knew. They were not things I'd mentally prepared for. *What am I doing in such a place?*

I probably should have been nervous about the ride to the compound, but the truth is, I loved every minute of it. I was thankful to be sitting close to the gunner so I could see Baghdad out the door below. Seeing the city from above, in the middle of the night, almost made me forget the battlefield it had become. Because the city was under curfew at that hour, it seemed peaceful. It was a momentary reprieve from the hell that was Iraq.

I had tried everything to avoid this place, so my goal was modest: Just get through it. I could not comprehend why my life had taken such a sudden and difficult turn. *Why, Lord, why? Why didn't you protect me from this terrible place?*

Even though God had not prevented us from going to Iraq, I still had every confidence that he would keep Joseph and me safe while we were there. After all, he had seen us safely through our first and second tours. Joseph and I had both been through enough to realize that every now and then, God was going to throw us into something that seemed way over our heads—usually to prepare us for even greater challenges down the line. And there was no question about it. This time, we were in *way* over our heads.

The sirens were typically the first indication that our enemies had launched rockets or mortars at the Green Zone, which housed several Iraqi ministries and Coalition Forces compounds. The sound of the sirens—*Wonk! Wonk! Wonk!*—was followed by a strangely detached voice that rang out over the loudspeakers, warning, "Incoming. Incoming. Incoming."

The rocket identification system gave us up to five seconds to get to cover. If we weren't already in a hardened facility, we could access bunkers strategically placed throughout the compound. They were close enough that we could usually reach one before rockets started hitting the ground.

As long as we were in the work villa, we were mostly safe. The villa used to belong to one of Saddam Hussein's sons. It was considered a hardened facility, which meant that the building could withstand a direct hit from rockets or mortars. (However, the office I worked in was lined with windows, so we had to sprint out each time the alarm went off.)

At least half of the CIA staff, including Joseph and me, slept in small trailers spread around the compound. Unlike the villa, these trailers were extremely vulnerable to indirect fire attacks. Referred to as pods, they were so thin they shook violently when helicopters passed overhead, as they did every fifteen minutes or so due to our proximity to a helicopter landing zone. If the sirens went off in the middle of the night, as they often did, it was best to ride out the attack in a nearby bunker. Luckily the entrance to the bunker was right outside the front door of our pod, making it easy to access, which we did hundreds of times during that tour.

The attacks had been traced to a group of Shi'a insurgents. When they began firing at the International Zone (IZ), aka the Green Zone, they didn't know what they were doing. Therefore, the majority of rockets were imprecise and, fortunately, hit insignificant targets or landed in agricultural areas. It was the equivalent of shooting from the hip instead of strategically aiming the weapon. But at some point in the early fall of 2006, everything changed.

I suspect that Iranian trainers were brought in to teach the insurgents how to better calibrate their launches. The drastic difference in results suggested that the insurgents had been schooled in how to set proper coordinates and calculate trajectories. Furthermore, they may have had "spotters" in the Green Zone, Iraqis who worked with Coalition Forces in a variety of roles and so had access to our compounds. These Iraqis were either sympathetic to the enemy or members of the insurgent group, but either way, they helped the shooters tweak their aim and improve the efficacy of indirect-fire operations. The imprecise rockets and mortars morphed into terrifying little projectiles that could reach their intended targets with increasing and disturbing accuracy.

Once the Shi'a insurgents could breach the heavily fortified Green Zone, the balance of power shifted. They could hone in on Saddam's former palaces and presidential compounds expropriated by Coalition Forces leadership, diplomats, intelligence agencies, security companies, and Iraqi government ministries. Our little security bubble had been penetrated. We transitioned from feeling fairly secure to being sitting ducks. Our tours of duty would never be the same.

In the beginning, we were embarrassed to show too much concern. I casually sauntered toward the bunkers, hiding the fact that I was terrified inside. One does not want to look uncool in the war zone, you know. Only a couple of rockets landed every few days, meaning I could still pretend that a war wasn't raging outside the Green Zone.

But within a few weeks, the terrorists had gotten the hang of it and were volleying multiple rockets at a time, several times a day, into the formerly cozy IZ. The insurgents used portable platforms to carry out a shoot-and-scoot strategy that enabled them to hide from

Coalition Forces. Because the insurgents could launch from a different location each time, they got away before we could pinpoint their position and shoot back. The insurgents took to this newfound game of cat and mouse with gusto, volleying numerous mortars at a time before disappearing into the crowded streets of Sadr City, a Shi'a enclave in northeastern Baghdad.

Once we started getting hammered regularly, I morphed from "cool" into "crazy," running like a bat out of Hades to get inside the bunkers. Cool didn't matter anymore; safety was my only concern. By then, I had made a decision to do everything possible to avoid becoming a victim—*if* it was within my power to do so. I mentally prepared myself by knowing where all of the bunkers were and calculating where I was in relation to them every time I stepped out of the work villa. The split second the alarm went off, my whole body was primed to respond. As these bunker runs became a mainstay of our existence, all the cells in my body were ready to act the moment the system was triggered. Living in a constant state of readiness to run was a special kind of stress that took a toll on us physically and emotionally.

One of my military colleagues told me that if I heard the toylike din of the rockets spinning through the air, it wasn't a bad thing. That meant the rockets were set on a course farther afield. I'd heard that strange buzzing noise over my head a few times as the rockets sped toward their final destination. But as that officer told me, "It's the ones you don't hear that you have to worry about." Unfortunately, we didn't usually hear the rockets until they hit the ground and exploded into a thousand pieces. The ear-popping detonations were followed by shock waves that rippled out from the point of impact. They felt like earthquakes rumbling beneath our feet.

As we sat in the bunkers breathlessly waiting for the shelling to stop, the smell of burning refuse would begin to waft through the air. After the indirect fire subsided, we called our respective phone trees and checked in using call signs to identify ourselves. Security officers couldn't announce the "all clear" until every officer and employee had checked in. This could take anywhere from five minutes to half an hour depending on how quickly we responded and the amount of damage that needed to be surveyed. Security officers had to comb the compound to ensure there were no injuries to take care of or unexploded ordnance to manage.

Getting caught outside when the rockets rained down was even more uncomfortable once the temperatures started to soar. On a particularly bad day, I had already vaulted into the bunkers three separate times. As I was on my way to the chow hall (which was not a hardened facility), the alarm went off yet one more time. I jumped into the nearest bunker, which was now at capacity holding ten of my colleagues and ten Iraqi workers.

It was terribly hot. The thermometer had swung all the way to the extreme end of the reading, indicating that it was well over 120 degrees. The twenty-year-old Iraqi worker standing in front of me was sweating profusely. Beads of sweat ran down his arms, slipping off the tips of his fingers like an icicle melting in the hot sun: drip . . . drip . . . drip. I don't know how he did it; I don't know how *anyone* worked outside in that heat. The sun was so intense that when the gold cross I wore around my neck swung away from me and then fell back on my chest, it singed my skin. *Was the cradle of civilization always this hot, or did people adjust as the temperatures slowly rose?* I marveled.

As we patiently waited for the all-clear signal, the smell of sweat, body odor, and burning rubber hung in the fiery air. As awful as I felt, I knew that the workers in the bunker felt far worse. It was an unforgiving war in an unforgiving land.

In addition to dealing with rockets and mortars, almost every morning between six and eight we woke up to a massive car bomb detonating on the streets of Baghdad. These bombs were timed to occur during rush hour in order to inflict the greatest number of casualties. The enormous explosions were followed by a *whoosh* as shock waves emanated from the epicenter of the attack, violently shaking everything in their path, including the walls of our thin-skinned pods.

The morning routine was always the same: a car bomb went off, and my stomach churned as I realized two things: (1) dozens of innocent people had just died, and (2) I was still stuck in Iraq. It was a Groundhog Day existence, a bad dream that I desperately wanted to wake up from but never did. There was no respite from the tension, no place to go to unwind. It was an unrelenting cycle of stress and anxiety.

In spite of all the chaos, there was much work to be done.

CHAPTER 11

FACE-TO-FACE
WITH THE ENEMY

Several months into our Iraqi tour, there was a terrorist attack on an NGO (nongovernmental organization) convoy near Yarmouk, Baghdad, that resulted in the death of a US citizen. We decided to try to collect intelligence on the terrorist operation. I asked officers to query their sources about the event to see what we could unearth regarding the identities of those responsible for this brutal attack.

Even though Yarmouk wasn't far from the Green Zone, it had become an incredibly dangerous neighborhood. Ethnic cleansing in Yarmouk had hit a fever pitch, as it had in the rest of Baghdad. The Sunni residents who were the majority sect there had pushed out most—if not all—of their Shi'a neighbors. The fear of "the other" and the interminable violence against the opposite sect had turned Yarmouk, and indeed much of Iraq, into killing fields. Sunnis were killing Shi'a and Shi'a were killing Sunnis.

But that wasn't the only problem. There was intracommunal violence and power plays in which Shi'a killed Shi'a and Sunnis killed Sunnis for control of neighborhoods, government positions, and leadership of insurgent groups. Any Iraqis who wandered into the wrong part of town and were not the "right" sect, religion, or group faced the very strong possibility they'd never come back out. The bodies of those who found themselves in the wrong place at the wrong time would often be discovered hanging from light poles or left on the side of the road to be eaten by wild dogs. Bodies were piling up in the streets. Relatives were scared to collect the corpses, as some were wired with IEDs that would explode if they were moved.

In the midst of this chaos, an American NGO official planned to visit Yarmouk to carry out a prodemocracy training project at the headquarters of a prominent Sunni political party. To facilitate this meeting, the young woman had been assigned a personal security detail (PSD) that included three vehicles: one to handle the principal, one to take up the lead, and a third to follow the others. Each vehicle would have at least two security contractors to support the move between the NGO compound and the party headquarters.

The security retinue successfully delivered the official to the meeting location and remained there throughout the one-and-a-half-hour visit. At the conclusion of the meeting, party officials reportedly asked the American trainer if she would like additional security for the move out of the neighborhood. According to those same officials, she declined this offer.

What she might not have realized was that her convoy had to drive through an area referred to by locals as the "Triangle of Death." The party headquarters was located at the northwest corner of that triangle, and the visitors would have to travel south and then east to get out of the neighborhood. They had to traverse one of the most dangerous corridors in Yarmouk, largely under the control of local PSDs attached to prominent local families and informal neighborhood watch groups. Because there was no law and order, these groups functioned less like security groups and more like urban street gangs. The young men dressed in knockoff Adidas tracksuits and *shibshib* (sandals) were simply thugs. They terrorized the neighborhoods they pretended to protect. They knew little of religion or ideology.

I don't know the motives for what happened or how far in advance the operation was planned . . . but what unfolded next was a complete nightmare. The first car in the security retinue pulled out from the heavily fortified compound and headed down the street. Its progress was halted by a car that appeared to be stalled in the middle of the road. The second vehicle with the principal inside pulled up behind the lead car. It took a few seconds for the drivers to realize that this wasn't a broken-down vehicle but an ambush.

Without warning, shooting commenced. All kinds of weaponry were used in the assault: handguns, AK-47s, and an RPG (rocket-propelled grenade) launcher. The rear vehicle, which had been delayed leaving the compound, couldn't see what was happening through the smoke. It slammed into the middle vehicle, coming to an abrupt standstill.

The three cars sat limp in the road with their tires blown out. The terrorists approached the convoy and tried to open the doors of the middle vehicle, presumably to take the principal hostage, but they could not get the car doors open. Frustrated, they threw a grenade under the car. A few seconds later it exploded, turning a bad situation into an impossible one. In the midst of the chaos, a couple of guards from the other vehicles were miraculously able to extract themselves and crawl away. However, the young principal and her driver could not get out and perished inside the burning vehicle.

The ground was littered with spent shell casings, indicating the overwhelming barrage of force the attackers used. A plume of black smoke rose from the burning wreckage of twisted steel, fractured glass, and melted plastic. It smoldered for two days.

Because my primary responsibility in Baghdad was to manage the collection and dissemination of terrorism intelligence and the Sunni insurgency, I was best placed to figure out which sources might have access to the information we were seeking. Getting anyone to talk in this neighborhood would be a challenge. Those who weren't affiliated with an insurgent group feared the insurgents and looked upon Americans as unwelcome occupiers and/or enemies.

Nevertheless, we wanted to make the effort, to do what we could to identify the men who had ordered the attack, as well as those who had perpetrated it. After studying the case, I came up with a list of questions case officers could use with their sources to obtain insights on the attack. What was the purpose of the ambush? What, if anything, did the terrorists hope to achieve?

To begin, I ran traces to see whether any of our sources had ever provided reporting on Yarmouk. Then I looked at a map and tried to gauge which of our sources lived or worked near Yarmouk and might have heard about the attack through friends, families, or insurgent contacts. Based on the results of those inquiries, I made a list of sources who might be able to give us some insights into those involved in the attack. Then I drew up a long list of questions that I hoped to have answered.

One thing intelligence teaches you is that you don't know what a source is capable of unless you really get to know him and continually explore "areas of opportunity" together. For instance, you could find that one of your sources has a brother who lives in Yarmouk and, even though he hasn't reported on that area before, might be able to glean some information when visiting family. Therefore, simply reviewing notes in a source's file is of limited use. To really know whether your source has or could gain access to the information of interest, you must have a discussion with him.

Even when a source doesn't seem to have natural access, if he is sufficiently motivated and resourceful, he can surprise you with the details he can obtain using basic elicitation skills. Even hearsay or thirdhand information can be useful in generating leads or helping to focus future collection efforts.

When I approached the case officers and told them about the high-priority collection requirement, many invited me to directly debrief their sources in their next meetings. Those interviews were a welcome break from the sedentary existence of a CMO, the position that I held in Baghdad. My responsibility was to manage the acquisition and dissemination of intelligence collected in and around Baghdad. Each CMO had a particular focus, and I was responsible for the terrorism and Sunni insurgent accounts. I partnered with the operations officers (the case handlers) to manage their terrorism reporters. We worked hard to determine access, design debriefing questions, assess responses, and verify the intelligence before we disseminated it to the intelligence community.

In order to do this, CMOs are tied to their computers, processing intelligence reports, reading cables, interpreting SIGINT reports (signals intelligence gleaned from electronic communications and weapons systems), fielding questions from military colleagues, and coordinating on analytic assessments. We did this hour after hour, up to fifteen hours a day. The job was demanding on both the eyes and the intellect. I have never read and processed so much information in my entire life, and I will probably never do so again.

But on the flip side, being immersed in so much data quickly turns a CMO into a subject matter expert and a great resource to collectors, managers, and headquarters staff. CMOs are keenly aware of the CIA's collection strengths and weaknesses in their respective areas. Because CMOs read and process so many reports, we get to know our Areas of Responsibility (AORs) extremely well. You want an update on a region? Ask a CMO. You want to know which sources are doing a good job, which sources are suspect, and which might be fabricators or double agents? Ask a CMO. We know what solid intelligence looks like, what we expect to see from our sources, and what seems too good to be true or never pans out.

Getting out of the office and into the debriefing room not only gave me a great opportunity to give my eyes a rest and put my debriefing skills to work, but it gave me the chance to meet the sources whose work I processed every day. What followed was the world's best schooling in terrorism, because as I quickly discovered, it's one thing to read about terrorists and quite another to meet them face-to-face.

As expected, even after several debriefings, the details surrounding the ambush of the NGO officer remained murky. Although I had some idea which insurgent leadership the perpetrators were linked with, I was never able to confirm my suspicion. Nonetheless, every interview taught us something about the insurgents' modus operandi—and how to protect our troops and Americans working in Baghdad.

I admit it—I was thoroughly intimidated by one of the sources I had to interview during this investigation. That was because Abu Muhammad was not merely an aspiring jihadist. He wasn't a website developer, mujahideen recruiter, or ideologue. He was a fighter. I'd read all about it in the file; the more I read, the more nervous I got. Not only did his jihadist pedigree give me the jitters, but his physical appearance in his file photo was equally striking. For people like him, the end always justifies the means.

I had only been an intelligence officer in the CIA for three years, but I was keenly aware that the relationship with Abu Muhammad was a tricky one. True terrorists don't decide to work with the CIA because they like us. We are the enemy, so their motivations for engaging us are complex. Some are tired of the killing, some feel used by their terrorist cohorts whose ideology and behavior they no longer buy into, and some just need the money. Others seek protection that they think is afforded to them when they partner with the all-knowing and omnipotent CIA. And some choose to work with the agency to take out their competitors and increase their own influence and prestige on the streets.

Abu Muhammad had been a spin-off from another source who had provided valuable counterterrorism intelligence on terrorist leaders in Baghdad. A cold call from the case officer had surprised Abu Muhammad but had resulted in a series of meetings in which he agreed to work with the CIA against al-Qa'ida elements in his section of the city.

In order to get the most out of the relationship, I would have to understand who Abu Muhammad was. I couldn't motivate him unless I "got" him: What kind of personality did he have? What drove his decision making? What were his motivations? What did he like and what did he hate? What made him tick? Working with a terrorist source would require a solid understanding of his unique worldview and ideology. I didn't have to agree with it (and I certainly didn't), but I had to know where he was coming from.

And here's where it really got tricky: I had to befriend the terrorist. I had to find a way to bond with him in order to acquire the intelligence we needed to prevent attacks against Iraqi citizens and Coalition troops. Even when these guys cooperated, they always held something back in order to protect themselves and their interests. The game of intelligence in a war zone required diligent and concerted efforts to get the goods, to be sure the sources were sharing the details I needed to do my job.

When debriefing any jihadist insurgent, most agents have three handicaps: we are Americans (strike 1), "nonbelievers" (strike 2), and CIA officers (strike 3). As I prepared myself to walk in and meet Abu Muhammad for the first time, I knew I had a fourth handicap: I was a woman.

For the majority of these men, I was a complete oddity. I shouldn't have been working outside the home, never mind serving my government in a war zone. I was a woman without the comfort and protection of her family, a foreigner thousands of miles away from home. Just by virtue of "exposing myself" to men who were not a part of my family, I was seen as a loose woman with no faith and no morals, rather than as a US government official.

And in the sexually repressed culture of the Middle East, any opportunity for men to mingle freely with a woman feels illicit and exciting. I was keenly aware of this dynamic and knew that the second I walked in the room and Abu Muhammad laid eyes on me, his head would be in one place—the gutter. And there was nothing I could do about it. This was my life in the Middle East, for better or for worse. I was used to it. I'd been repeatedly propositioned, followed, harassed, touched, groped, and otherwise annoyed by the constant assumption that I was not respectable because of my gender, skin color, and nationality.

Even my last name is suspect. Whenever I travel in the Middle East—Egypt, in particular—I am careful to act the part of the tourist, not someone who speaks Arabic or knows the country. This way, I'm not perceived as a threat. However, whenever airport security sees my last name, I can count on the following interrogation scene to play out every time:

"Are you from the Middle East?"

"No."

"Then why do you have this name?"

"Someone in my family is from the Middle East."

"Who? Your mother? Your father?"

"No, my husband."

"Where is your husband from?"

"He was born in Lebanon."

"He's Lebanese?"

"No, he's Egyptian."

"Have you been to Egypt before?"

"Yes."

"How many times?"

"Uh . . . many."

"Is your name Assad or *Asaad*?"

When a person from the Middle East asks me this question, it is code for "Are you Muslim or Christian?" You see, there are two distinct versions of this name in Arabic. "Assad" means "lion." This is the last name of President Bashar al-Assad of Syria. If you bear this name, then people know that you are probably Muslim. The other version, pronounced "Asaad," is the Christian name, which means "happier."

They ask this because they want to know how to categorize me in their minds. They are sizing me up to figure out how to interact with me.

Because I have had to deal with it so many times, I have become an expert at figuring out how to handle the imbalance, how to establish myself as a respectable human being—despite being a woman, a Christian, *and* a CIA agent.

Granted, it's one thing to strike a balance with an immigration officer at the airport, but this wasn't just *any* Arab male. Abu Muhammad was a terrorist. Bad guys at this level are incredibly intelligent. In fact, they are some of the most street-smart people you will ever meet. They can spot a fraud or a disingenuous personality a mile away. They can sense weakness or insecurity, and they can see right through you unless you are just as perceptive as they are. Their ability to read people is a survival tactic developed over a lifetime to allow them to prosper in the cutthroat world of tribal politics and massively repressive, authoritarian regimes. They come from places where only the strong survive and master manipulators thrive. Respect isn't freely given; it is earned. That's why I was doing my best to calm down in the moments before my meeting with Abu Muhammad. I couldn't afford to let him see my fear.

I stood at the door of the debriefing room straightening my jacket and preparing for the grand entrance. Unlike in the movies, there was no two-way mirror for me to use to catch a glimpse of him before walking through the door. Instead, I closed my eyes and mentally rehearsed everything I knew about him. Finally, I turned off my phone, took out the battery, and shoved it back into my purse to prevent my phone from being used to geolocate the CIA compound or to remotely access the microphone and record the meeting. I tried to exhale slowly, hoping that breathing deeply would help me gain advantage over my shaking hands.

It's okay, I reassured myself. *Be tough. Don't show weakness. You can do this. You've been preparing for this moment your whole life. He may be a terrorist, but he's a human being, too.*

To remind myself how pedestrian Abu Muhammad really was, I thought about the most recent requests he had made to his case officer. The terrorist, who surely had challenges such as ethnic cleansing and sectarian war to deal with, sought help for more personal concerns. It's hard to imagine, but terrorists are real people, too, burdened with their own hang-ups and insecurities.

This made me feel better and more confident in my mission. I told myself, *I can deal with Abu Muhammad. No problem.* And with that, I took a deep breath and opened the door.

In the split second that Abu Muhammad saw me, he did exactly what I thought he would do. His eyes lit up with wonder and excitement. I imagined that in his head, he was high-fiving himself, exclaiming, *Oh yes!*

As John, the case officer, stood up to greet me, Abu Muhammad jumped out of his seat and stood in rapt attention. His eyes followed me intently as I crossed the room.

It's hard to act natural when you know that everything about your appearance and behavior is being carefully catalogued. Nothing gets past these guys. They size you up from every angle. They use every opportunity to take in the very thing that is *haram* (forbidden) in conservative Islam. Here I was—a decent-looking female who was not wrapped up in a black cloak—sent to engage with him. It was his lucky day.

Establishing rapport is one of the most critical parts of any debriefing. The importance of trust cannot be overstated; if a terrorist was going to consider putting his life in my hands by becoming a mole and ratting out other members of his group, he needed to know I had the operational know-how and savvy to protect him and his information. Given the years I'd spent studying, living in, and traveling around the Middle East, I was keenly aware that my gender put me at an immediate disadvantage. In the source's mind, I couldn't protect him because I could never be a player in the dangerous worlds of terrorism and espionage. At this point, I was nothing more than a sexual object.

The best intelligence officers know how others perceive them and understand how to manage these factors. Proper self-assessment is key. Without this, it would be impossible to surmount the obstacles between me and my source and to capitalize on my God-given strengths. How could I connect with or manipulate a source if I didn't understand how he perceived me when I walked into the room? My male colleague who was six feet three and weighed 250 pounds was going to be assessed very differently than I was, standing five feet four with a small frame. Regardless of how distasteful it might be, I had to fully grasp and be prepared to confront this person's stereotypes about me.

Communications specialists say that you have only a few seconds to make a first impression. I believe that in asset meetings, intelligence officers face the same challenge. Once that first impression is made, they have only a few minutes in which to either cement those assumptions or introduce other variables into the equation. I had about a five-minute window in which to establish my bona fides. That's all the time needed for any terrorist to decide whether he would respect me or not. I had seen several officers fail in these first few minutes of assessment and never regain control of the relationship. And intelligence is all about control.

As I read Abu Muhammad's body language and watched him carefully, it became apparent that this hardened terrorist was more focused on flirting than on getting down to business. Therefore, I had to redouble my efforts to exude professionalism and tact, while also being friendly and approachable. To maximize the impact of the introduction, I had to tap into all that I had ever studied about Arabs and the Middle East. If I didn't do this properly, his mind would be forever fixated on me as a female rather than as a professional officer he should trust with his life.

As the case officer was making the introductions, I shook Abu Muhammad's hand. If I'd allowed it, he'd have stood there holding on to me, using the handshake as an excuse to linger a little too long.

(I'm not a fan of the let-me-stand-here-and-caress-her hand-as-long-as-possible trick.) So after the firm shake, I carefully extracted my hand from his grip, and we sat down in our respective chairs. My nervousness began to dissipate as I intensely focused on how to connect with him on my terms.

In my first debriefing with Abu Muhammad, I struggled to strike a balance. The terrorist and I were doing a dance of dominance, and I had a very fine line to walk. I didn't sit too close to him, lest he think I was trying to be inappropriately cozy. But I didn't sit too far away to avoid appearing intimidated or aloof. I looked him carefully in the eyes when I spoke, but I couldn't hold his gaze too long or he would assume I was flirting (eye contact speaks volumes in the Middle East). At the same time, insufficient eye contact would indicate that I was scared or being dodgy. Though still nervous, I squared my shoulders toward him and sat up as straight as I could. My body language exuded the exact opposite of what I was feeling at that moment: confidence.

My friendliness and welcoming demeanor are often mistaken for a lack of sophistication or intelligence. Because of this, I had to front-load the conversation with Abu Muhammad in a way that indicated I was well-read and knowledgeable. He needed to know that I had done my homework; I had read the case file and was fully updated on his background and reporting record. Just as important, he needed to know that I understood the crazy and complicated world that was Iraq and that I got him as a person. If I didn't appeal to his sense of justice (however warped that might be) and his ego, then I would fail.

Therefore, I took an authoritative approach.

"Abu Muhammad," I began in English, "I am so happy to meet you. I have been following your case closely and have been impressed with what you have accomplished in such a short period of time working with John. I very much appreciate your actionable intelligence and your effort to get it to us before attacks were carried out. It is not an easy thing to do, but obviously you are well connected and smart."

I could see the compliments were working. Abu Muhammad was beaming.

He responded in heavily accented English.

"Thank you. It is very nice to meet you, Layla." (Layla was the name I chose to use with Abu Muhammad because it translated nicely in both English and Arabic and was a name he could easily remember.)

I said, "*Shukran, shukran, tasharrafna!*" ("Thank you, thank you, I'm honored to meet you!")

Abu Muhammad was shocked. "*Bititkalami 'Araby?*" ("You speak Arabic?")

"*Na'am, bas ana batkalam 'Araby shwaya bass. Darast fil al-Qa'hira wa lakin la atathakar kitir min al kalimat.*" ("Yes, I speak Arabic, but only a little. I studied in Cairo, but I don't remember many words.")

"*Darast fi Misr?*" ("You studied in Egypt?")

"*Na'am, ana bahab Misr. Darast al-'Arabiyah, al-thaqafah, al-deen, wal-tarikh hinak.*" ("Yes, I love Egypt. I studied Arabic, culture, religion, and history there.")

Abu Muhammad looked at John and chuckled. He could not believe what he was hearing. Although I had forgotten much of the Arabic I'd learned at Georgetown, my pronunciation is pretty good, which gives people the impression that I am far more proficient than I really am. Because of this, Abu Muhammad's head was spinning as I kept changing his impression of the woman who had walked through the door. Now that I'd shocked him with some Arabic, he didn't know how to categorize me.

Understanding this and wanting to keep the meeting flowing in the right direction, I quickly got down to business.

"Abu Muhammad, I'm concerned with what's been happening in the Mansour district of Baghdad with the uptick in sectarian violence and increased attacks against Coalition Forces there. The number of IEDs being deployed in your neighborhood is ridiculous, and they're not just killing our troops, they're killing innocent people. In fact, last week's IEDs mainly injured Sunni civilians, not Coalition Forces."

He nodded his head. Meanwhile, I could see surprise flicker in his eyes with the incredible realization that I actually knew what I was talking about.

I continued. "We need your help now more than ever if we are going to stabilize your neighborhood. The insurgent groups can continue these random and haphazard attacks, but as John noted, your real problems are much bigger than us. Iran's intervention in Iraq is much more harmful to the Sunnis than Coalition Forces are."

He vigorously nodded, and I could sense he was trying to grasp how a Western woman could know all of this and speak intelligently about such topics.

As this revelation hit him, I sensed a sea change in his perception of who I was. He had quickly arrived at the place I needed him to be: He had decided that I was more than a woman, that I was an officer whom he could trust. I had successfully recruited him to be my friend, and now he could think of me as a counterterrorism partner. And what a feeling that was. In that moment, I could sense the release of tension in the room (not least of which was my own). The change was so palpable; the whole atmosphere shifted from sexually charged excitement to respect. We could finally get down to business. When Abu Muhammad was not only eager to work with me but anxious to answer my questions and fulfill my requests, I knew the tide had turned. Abu Muhammad wanted me to understand that he could deliver, that he was "the man."

Without him even realizing it, I'd used Abu Muhammad's flawed assumptions about me to crack him open, and now I would be able to get more intelligence out of him than just about anyone else would. I'd started the meeting from a place of being less than human, but I would be leaving with the information our CIA team had been desperately trying to extract: critical intelligence on the identities of the terrorists who had attacked and killed the US diplomat and her security retinue in Baghdad.

I lived for these moments. Jumping through cultural hoops, confronting stereotypes, and establishing dominance in such a short period of time was a real challenge and an amazing accomplishment. I couldn't help that I was playing with a handicap, but in the face of those challenges, when I was able to accomplish what others could not, success was doubly sweet.

This debriefing marked a turning point in my career. I discovered skills I didn't know I had. In addition to my own surprise, colleagues and managers were fairly shocked. I was such a "nice person," they assumed this meant I wasn't crafty, sophisticated, or capable of rocking it against such challenging targets.

Because of my success in the debriefing room, I was finally recognized for having a solid operational mind, a facility for collecting hard intelligence, and an incredible intuition that helped me untangle tough cases.

Yep, I could finally tell myself. *I've got this.*

CHAPTER 12

TRUTH OR CONSEQUENCES— A TALE OF THREE SOURCES

In the movies, secret agents face their adversaries with guns, weapons, and flashy cars. And they're so proficient in hand-to-hand combat that they can bring enemies to their knees with the right choke hold or take them down with a well-placed aimed shot. As much as I'd like to think I was that cool, in reality, life in the CIA is much more pedantic.

What most people don't know is that the CIA is really a massive sorting agency. Intelligence officers must sift through mountains of data in an effort to determine what is authentic and useful, versus what should be discarded. We must consider the subtleties of language and the nuance of the nonverbal. We must unwind a complicated stream of intelligence by questioning everything. In the counterterrorism realm, this process has to be quick; we have to weed out bad information with alacrity. We can't afford to make mistakes when it comes to the collection, processing, dissemination, and evaluation of terrorism intelligence. As we say in the CIA, "The terrorists only have to get it right once, but we have to be right every time."

Contained in that massive flow is an incredible amount of useless, inaccurate, misleading, or fabricated information. The amount of bad reporting that is peddled, not only to the CIA but to intelligence agencies all over the world, is mind-boggling.

That's precisely why one of the greatest challenges we faced as counterterrorism experts was figuring out who was giving us solid intelligence and who wasn't. And when we were dealing with terrorists, getting it wrong could mean someone's death.

In early 2007 when Iraq was awash with violence, many Iraqis who had formerly counted the United States as the Great Satan for occupying their country switched sides and were willing to work with Coalition Forces against Iraqi terrorists. Brave locals were rebelling against al-Qa'ida's brutal tactics and were doing whatever they could to take back the streets from these thugs. This was a turning point in the war. Our counterterrorism efforts became wildly successful, fueled by accurate and highly actionable intelligence.

In one such case, we were contacted by one of our established sources, who was extremely agitated. Mahmud had come from his village claiming that he had seen something that sent chills down his spine. As Mahmud was driving not far from his home, he saw an unknown person exit a building that one of his cousins owned. The building was supposed to be empty and unoccupied. For reasons Mahmud could not explain, he thought that something bad was going on and that maybe the man he saw was a member of Al-Qa'ida in Iraq (AQI).

Up until this point, Coalition Forces had found Mahmud's information extremely reliable. Of course, they did not know his name or personal details, but they made sure we knew that his information had checked out. They contacted us on numerous occasions to praise us for the source's reporting, explaining that it had allowed them to disarm IEDs and detain insurgents who were causing problems in his village.

Mahmud had a solid track record. But the bits he provided this time were sketchy and lacked sufficient detail. You can't just disseminate intelligence reports saying that a location "feels wrong," "seems wrong," or that some random dude you just saw "looked like a bad guy." That kind of information does not meet the threshold for dissemination by the CIA. In this case, however, the handling case officer and I went against protocol and put the report out.

Within the hour, we were contacted by one of the MNF-I (Multi-National Force–Iraq) units with responsibility for that AOR. They regularly executed counterterrorism operations in that village and wanted to know more about the sourcing. They were interested in taking a look at the abandoned building because they had been trying to locate terrorist safe houses they believed were somewhere in the vicinity of the building mentioned in our report. They had a feeling that nearby safe houses were being used to store large amounts of weaponry and a few had been turned into VBIED (vehicle-borne improvised explosive device) factories. But there was one big problem: Military units had acted on similar intelligence reports before, but the reports had been setups—the alleged safe houses were wired to explode when the soldiers entered.

A spate of these types of explosions had occurred east of Baghdad in Diyala Governorate, and while we had not yet seen this happen out west in al-Anbar Governorate, one could never be too careful. Basically, the military wanted to know: How good is your source? Do you trust him? Do you think he could have turned on you? Could this be a setup?

This was one of the hardest parts of my job. While I had to protect the identity of our sources when passing on intelligence, I had to balance this with the need to share pertinent details that would allow the military to do their job. It was critical to give them appropriate context on the sources, their access, and their reporting records, and to give them a sense of how good the report may or may not be. Given our positive track record with these military units, I knew that they would trust my judgment, and therefore, I needed to get it right. Lives were at stake.

My mind was spinning.

What do I think? Is this a setup? He's usually such a good reporter, but what if someone discovered he was the mole?

Even if Mahmud was "on our side," the insurgents could turn him against us by threatening the lives of his wife and kids. Similar things had happened before. I prayed, "Please, Lord, give me wisdom."

The bottom line was, I didn't know anything for sure, and I told the military commander that. But I also remembered that just the week before, Mahmud had provided a report that MNF-I units said was amazingly accurate regarding the location of an IED in his village. They found the IED and dug it up before the Coalition Humvee rolled over it. So as of then, he was definitely good, and I told the commander that as well.

The next day, the case officer came to my desk and said, "Did you hear?"

"Hear what?"

"Mahmud's information was spot on!"

"Really?" *What a relief,* I thought. "What happened?"

"When the soldiers entered the abandoned building, they found seven Iraqis tied up on the floor, barely clinging to life. It was more than a safe house. It was a torture house. There were piles of dead bodies in the next room."

Mahmud's intuition about the stranger he saw exiting that building had been correct. Something about the unidentified man's behavior or appearance—the look on his face, the posture of his body, the way he walked or the way he dressed—had hit Mahmud as being "off" or "wrong." It turned out that local AQI affiliates had commandeered the building and were using it as a base to terrorize the local population.

My colleague pulled out copies of the military's photographs that captured the unbelievable scene. The first images showed the battered bodies of the young men who had just been saved from certain death. According to the soldiers, when they entered the building and found the prisoners on the floor, the young men were in shock.

Emaciated and trembling, they kept saying, "Thank you. Thank you. Thank you." They could barely stand, so the soldiers steadied them as the young men lifted up their bloodstained shirts for the camera, revealing torsos covered in welts and bruises. If that unit hadn't shown up when they did, those men would have been dead by the next day.

I swallowed hard as I flipped through the photographs of the horrors in the next room, and my eyes welled up with tears. The terrorists had discarded the mutilated bodies of other villagers in the adjacent room, leaving them to rot in a twisted mound. I could hardly accept what I was seeing. It reminded me of Holocaust photos that were so inhumane one could not process the depth of the depravity: men and women . . . battered and bruised . . . lives stolen . . . eyes frozen open in emptiness and horror.

My stomach began to churn, but I made myself look at the pictures. I had to understand what we were fighting for, what our soldiers faced every day. As much as I wanted to dig a hole and stick my head in the sand, I needed to see what was really happening outside our cozy encampment in the Green Zone.

They say war is hell; they don't know the half of it.

G ranted, not every source I dealt with was as reliable—or altruistic—as Mahmud. Take Mansur, for example. Mansur was not your average terrorist. He was the *amir* (leader) of an al-Qa'ida cell in western Baghdad. Even more interesting was the fact that he claimed to have been a member of Fedayeen Saddam prior to the US invasion of Iraq. Fedayeen Saddam can be translated into English as "Saddam's Defenders," or "Saddam's Men of Sacrifice." The root of the word in Arabic, *fedaya*, refers to the willingness to sacrifice yourself for others, even unto death. This is the word used in the Arabic version of the Bible to describe Jesus' willingness to be put to death on the cross for the redemption of humanity.

Fedayeen Saddam was a deeply secretive paramilitary force drawn from the tribes most loyal to Saddam Hussein. These men killed, maimed, and tortured to protect Saddam from his real (and imagined) foes. Having groups like the Fedayeen at his disposal was one of the ways the tyrant maintained an iron grip on the Iraqi people. He employed them much as Iran's revolutionary leadership did with the Basij or as Bashar al-Assad has done with the Shabiha militias in Syria. The group enforced loyalty and maintained control of the population through violence and intimidation.

As a student of human behavior with an insatiable hunger to understand people, I was extremely curious (and a little nervous) to see what a former Fedayeen Saddam looked like—up close and personal.

What makes a guy like that tick? I wondered.

I'll never forget my first impression of Mansur. The driver and I pulled up to the CPU (car pickup) site, and the person who emerged from the shadows was not at all what I expected: Instead of being a stocky and imposing figure, Mansur was skinny as a rail. He appeared so fragile that I thought, *I could take that guy down myself if I had to.* I quickly admonished myself for underestimating this twig of a man.

You know better than that, Michele. Never judge a book by its cover. Give the guy a break. He probably didn't expect to be met by a girl either.

We swung the door open and Mansur climbed into the backseat. He immediately slouched down so no one could see him in the car. I turned around in my seat and was surprised to see fear in his face. I stuck out my hand and greeted him in Arabic.

"*Sabah al-khayr. Ahlan wa sahlan.*" ("Good morning. Welcome.")

Mansur hesitantly shook my hand while muttering the appropriate response.

"*Sabah al-nur.*"

His hand was cold and clammy, and his handshake was limp.

But there was no time for pleasantries or conversation. We needed to get back to the meeting site as quickly as possible. The vehicle dodged in and out of traffic as the driver and I checked the rearview and side mirrors to be sure we were not being followed. We were in the Green Zone, but one could not take safety for granted anywhere in Iraq. We needed to remain attuned to our surroundings—and know what was beside, behind, and in front of us.

Trained to be aware of our vulnerabilities at all times, we drove in a manner that minimized our chances of being ambushed. We also took care not to venture too close to MNF-I Humvees that bore signs warning, "Maintain distance from this vehicle or deadly force will be used." When we reached the meeting site several minutes later, we breathed a collective sigh of relief.

Once we were settled inside the meeting room, Mansur relaxed. He launched into his prepared brief. I madly scribbled notes as Mansur revealed al-Qa'ida's latest plans for an attack in a west Baghdad neighborhood. There was no time to breathe. Mansur was so full of information that I could barely keep up. By the end of the meeting, I had scribbled about ten pages of notes that I'd have to decipher later in the office.

Writing up intelligence reports and operational notes from asset meetings is the least stimulating part of being an intelligence officer, but it is essential. Although the process of typing up the details of a personal meeting is extremely time consuming, as we say in the CIA, "If you don't write it up, it never happened." I had to find a way to communicate the substance and tone of a meeting to the legions of people at headquarters following and assisting with the case.

In addition, I had to be sure to capture all relevant details of planned terrorist operations for the benefit of intelligence consumers. Every detail was important to Coalition Forces and US military analysts and operators who used those reports to stop attacks before they occurred. One thirty-minute debrief could require a day's worth of research and report writing.

Operational meetings are a whirlwind, making three hours feel like five seconds. Because I had to focus on so many things at the same time, it felt like the ultimate juggling act. I had to listen carefully;

take notes; ask appropriate follow-up questions to clarify confusing or incomplete information; be aware of counterintelligence red flags; maintain rapport; be aware of changes in the source's behavior, reporting, or general attitude; review communications plans; conduct training; and prepare for the next meeting.

Because it took so much energy to do all of this, by the time we were finished and had driven Mansur to his drop-off location, I was completely wiped out. All I wanted to do was return to my tiny little trailer and crawl into bed. Instead, I made my way back to the office, knowing I had to not only type up my report but generate several cables to communicate the results of the exchange.

I should have felt a sense of accomplishment for running a safe and productive debrief, but I soon realized that I felt something else—unease. I couldn't understand why. Something was bothering me, and it continued to hang over me like a shadow the rest of the day. I kept trying to shake it, but the weird feeling would not go away. In fact, it nagged me for days. I kept wondering, *What is wrong with me?* Though I didn't want to acknowledge it, something about Mansur disturbed me, *but what?*

That persistent, unshakable feeling of angst was an indication something wasn't right, though I could not articulate what the problem was. I pondered this over the course of a week until the reason for my temporary insanity slowly came into focus. I finally told the handler, "I don't think Mansur is who he says he is."

I felt a bit foolish saying this because I had nothing to back it up. The handler loved Mansur and told me that CMOs and branch leadership back at headquarters had a very positive impression of the source and his production. He further reminded me, "Mansur has done so much for us! He is the reason why al-Qa'ida is no longer in his village. All the intelligence he gave us on the group there checked out."

In discussions with US military colleagues, the handler learned that most al-Qa'ida members in the source's hometown were either detained by Coalition Forces or killed in counterterrorism operations enabled by Mansur's information. This was amazing feedback to get on a case. It doesn't get more solid than that. But for reasons I did not yet understand, I could not suppress the doubt that continued to push its way up like a geyser in my mind.

It certainly would have made my life easier to reject this intuition, but I felt compelled to explore what was driving the sense that something was wrong. Over the next few days, I was able to pull small bits of information out of my subconscious, to slowly reveal what I had "known" in the first few seconds I met him.

This man was not behaving like all the other terrorists I had met. He did not project the persona of a terrorist leader or *amir*. He was terrified to get in the vehicle and shook like a leaf for several minutes after crouching down in the backseat of the armored car. In fact, I remembered thinking, *This guy is about to wet his pants!*

The other terrorists would walk into a room and immediately fill it up. They were some of the most arrogant, ego-driven people I have ever met. They had strong personalities, and Iraqi terrorists, at least, acted as if they didn't fear for their lives in the least (or maybe they just believed they were invincible). They would regularly do things we Americans were certain would get them killed. They acted with a kind of pride that suggested they were either really smart or really stupid, or had a death wish (or some weird combination of all of the above).

One particular Sunni insurgent was the poster boy for bad guys and the perfect example of someone whose ego preceded him. He was turned by the CIA to work against other members of his terrorist group. He provided good insights into their plans and intentions, enabling us to thwart attacks against Coalition Forces soldiers patrolling the streets of Baghdad. For this cooperation, the CIA paid him handsomely.

The only issue was that the bonus he received had to be paid in cash. On one particular day we handed him a bag full of US currency in hundred-dollar-bill increments. Unfortunately, due to a couple of deadly car bombs that rocked the city that day, an early curfew was enforced throughout Baghdad. There were no taxis in sight that he could use to get home. We suggested that we hold on to the money and give it to him at the next meeting when he could arrange for a safer way to transport the cash.

Despite our supplications, the insurgent decided to take his bag of money and walk home, straight through a Shi'a neighborhood. (Remember, this guy was a Sunni insurgent.) To do such a thing was to tempt fate. If an Iraqi accidentally wandered into the wrong Sunni neighborhood with a name on his driver's license that clearly identified him as Shi'a, he would never be seen again, and vice versa. The lines were drawn in the sand, and both sides of the conflict knew which areas to avoid and which ones were safe zones.

But the Sunni insurgent could not be dissuaded. He decided to walk all the way home, right through the middle of his enemies' neighborhood. We weren't sure how, but he arrived home safely and in one piece. Maybe it was his fearless attitude that convinced local residents that he was not out of place. This could possibly be attributed to his swagger and cocky demeanor. His attitude was what kept him safe. Only a few people in the world could get away with such a thing, and he was definitely that guy.

Mansur's behavior had been quite different. He had trembled in the back of my vehicle and nervously fidgeted when I asked him certain questions.

Somehow, my brain had compared Mansur's behavior and personality with the other terrorists I had met and knew instinctively that things weren't adding up. He did not fit the profile. It had taken my cognitive brain several days to unravel the clues that I had processed in the blink of an eye. Once I was able to tease these details out of my subconscious brain and make sense of those jumbled thoughts, I could finally discern what my gut had been trying to tell me.

"I hate to say it," I told my colleagues, "but I think Mansur is a fake."

Now, nobody wants to hear that his or her baby is ugly. And nobody wants to think that he or she has been wrong about a case or has been misled for more than a year. That's why it's important to be able to confirm or deny any misgivings about a case. We had to determine whether this theory was correct (or not). We needed to dig into Mansur's access and position, as those details are the foundation of every operational relationship. We began to review his production and realized that while he had provided actionable intelligence in the first six months of the case, the value of his production over the last year had not been clear.

During the ensuing debriefs, I was attuned to the details of Mansur's stories, which allowed me to spot inconsistencies in his information. In addition, I carefully monitored his nonverbal behavior for clues that he was uncomfortable discussing certain topics. I noticed that he shifted in his seat and appeared very nervous when I asked detailed questions about his position in the group and queried him about group dynamics.

If you are an accountant, you will be able to tell me the details of your daily tasks, such as balancing ledgers and preparing financial records. If you are a teacher, you will be able to spell out in great detail what you teach, where you teach, who your students are, and what the teaching experience is like. If you are an active member of a terrorist cell that plans and executes operations but can't tell me what goes into the operational planning process—i.e., how you choose your targets, who cases the targets and recruits suicide operatives, where you acquire weaponry and build the IEDs, and where you hold planning sessions—then one of two things is occurring: Either you are withholding information, or you are lying and don't have access to the information. And Mansur wasn't just claiming to be a member of the group, but one of its leaders. He should have known the group better than anyone else.

It took us several more meetings to flesh out Mansur's claims, but when all was said and done, we were able to prove that he was definitely not an *amir*. Furthermore, he wasn't even a member of al-Qa'ida.

At the beginning of his relationship with the CIA, Mansur had provided critical pieces of intelligence that significantly advanced the counterterrorism cause in his village. Mansur had done a very honorable thing: He had the courage to contact authorities and offer to reveal the identities of local terrorists and the locations of their safe houses. This provided counterterrorism forces with the intelligence they needed to rid Mansur's village of al-Qa'ida, which had taken control of much of al-Anbar Province in western Iraq.

However, Mansur's access to this intelligence didn't come from being one of the bad guys. The village was small enough that everyone in town knew who the terrorists were. It was no secret. Mansur's five-year-old son could tell you who the al-Qa'ida fighters were and where they lived. In addition, Mansur had never been a member of Fedayeen Saddam. He had initially grabbed the CIA's attention with this tantalizing claim. Mansur had been right: Being approached by an al-Qa'ida cell leader and former Saddam loyalist certainly got our attention. But these were just Mansur's fabrications.

After the village was released from the grip of the terrorists, Mansur wanted to maintain his relationship with the CIA. He didn't want to lose his only source of income. I couldn't blame him. He had many mouths to feed, and in the withering economy of a war zone, he wanted to keep a good thing going. Mansur was the sole breadwinner for his large family. That's a lot of pressure for a young man who had no education and no discernible skills. That's when Mansur started making things up. He parlayed a tiny bit of access into a full-time job working as a source for the CIA. Incredibly, he kept up the ruse for a year.

If I had to feed a family and had no job, I might be making up intelligence to put food on the table too. The point is, it wasn't always easy to figure out who was telling us the truth and who had ulterior motives at play.

Such was the case with Ahmad. Ahmad was one of many people working against AQI. Not only did he provide intelligence to the CIA, but Ahmad's fighters had been battling al-Qa'ida for months to push remnants of the group out of their city. AQI was desperate to take the town back.

For some reason, Ahmad never set right with me. Even though he had been providing information for many months, I did not trust him. Every time I got a report from Ahmad, I combed over it carefully. It's not like he was "worse" or more hard-core ideologically than other sources. Several of the men we dealt with were far scarier than he was, and although I detested their ideology and worldviews, at least I knew *why* they were collaborating with us. The CIA could work with a variety of motivations, but we had to know what they were.

I preferred the straightforward admission of some sources who said, "I hate you, but I will work with you because of X, Y, and Z." Fine. At least they weren't pulling our chains. We knew exactly where they stood and why. But with Ahmad, I didn't know where his loyalties lay or what his justifications were for engaging the Americans.

Ahmad seemed slippery. I kept wondering whose interests he was really serving. I suspected that Ahmad was a gun for hire, a hustler and swindler loyal to nobody but himself. Whoever was the highest bidder, or whoever appeared to provide the best package, was the one whom Ahmad collaborated with that day.

In order to keep AQI at bay, Ahmad's group had erected a checkpoint to control access to the village. Ahmad and his men checked identity cards to ensure that only members of the local community were able to come and go from the town. Ahmad kept asking for more and more resources to hold the checkpoint and to assert the group's control over the area. But his entreaties seemed too demanding. It sounded to me like Ahmad wasn't heading up the neighborhood watch efforts because he hated terrorists or cared about the city, but because he wanted to build up his own resources and street creds.

Is he a good guy or a bad guy? Most of the time I could not tell, and I didn't believe that he was working with us for the benefit of the local community. He knew how to talk the talk, but I didn't buy it. I was even worried that he was shaking the local townspeople down for money to "protect" them from AQI.

Then Ahmad contacted his handler at the CIA with urgent information. He said, "We've just had a major battle at the checkpoint. My fighters have been holding AQI back for days, trying to keep them out of the city. There were explosions everywhere, and I lost many men in the fight. AQI deployed five VBIEDs against us. They also used automatic weapons, killing hundreds of people at the checkpoint. It was really bad, but in the end we were successful, *al-hamdu-lil-allah* [thanks be to God]. My men held the line and prevented the terrorists from coming back into the village."

After relating the details of the villagers' bloody battle with al-Qa'ida, Ahmad requested additional funds to support his counter-terrorism efforts. But something about the story didn't feel right. AQI often attacked villages and towns in this manner, but five VBIEDs at the same time? This seemed like overkill given the size and strategic value of the location they were allegedly fighting over.

Verifying information is supposed to be basic protocol for intelligence officers, but in a war zone, the press of business and the lack of sleep meant that time and energy were precious commodities. They were a luxury most of us did not have. We were pulled in a thousand different directions with caseloads and information management requirements that were untenable.

I could have let it go—that certainly would have been the easier route—but I knew that the more time we spent on bad sources the less time there was to focus on the most pressing business of identifying and disassembling the AQI networks. I racked my brain trying to figure out whether there was a problem with Ahmad's report. I went back through the notes from the meeting and carefully reviewed his description of the bloody battle on the outskirts of that village.

Then it dawned on me: If there was an engagement of this magnitude yesterday at a clearly defined location, then we should have no problem obtaining evidence it had occurred. If Ahmad was telling the truth and he and his friends were risking (and losing) their lives in the war on terror, then we should be able to confirm his account and find ways to help the villagers stave off the enemy.

Thankfully, in war zones, there are a variety of resources that can be used to fact-check information. You just have to know how to summon them, how to talk people into helping when they are just as overloaded with work as you are.

Within the span of twenty-four hours, we were able to deploy a range of assets (human and technical) to take a closer look at the area. And guess what we uncovered? Nothing, nada, *walla haga.* We could find no evidence that anything resembling a battle or even a minor scuffle had occurred at that location. There were no burned-out vehicles, no scrap metal littering the ground, and no scorched earth or post-blast markings where multiple VBIEDs had exploded. Ahmad had said that thousands of rounds were expended in the fight, but there were no shell casings on the ground.

And what about all those dead bodies? In Islam, when someone dies, they must be buried as soon as possible, usually within twenty-four hours. This means that the dead would have been buried within a day or two. But no funeral processions had wound their way through the village streets. There had been no recent activity at the cemetery, no sign of grief-stricken mourners. The morgue wasn't full of unclaimed bodies, and no injured fighters were being treated in local hospitals.

Our conclusion: Ahmad's story was a fabrication, meant to show the CIA how incredible he and his people were at fighting AQI. He wanted money, and he was willing to do whatever he could to trick us into giving him more.

It's funny . . . when I first started working as an officer in the field, I thought that the process of determining what was helpful information and what was misleading or fabricated would be enormously hard. Iraq taught me that this wasn't necessarily the case. Separating truth from fiction was not an impossible task. It just required common sense and a bit of motivation.

That, and the faith to trust my God-given intuition.

In both Ahmad's and Mansur's cases, my internal wiring went crazy telling me that something was wrong. Just because a source was useful in the beginning did not mean he or she would stay that way forever. Things changed (especially in a war zone), people changed, and circumstances changed. I couldn't let my guard down for a minute.

The year I spent in Iraq was—in many respects—hellish. But the experience I gained working with informants was invaluable—not only for the agency, but for me as well. I was finally starting to believe that not only was I good enough, I might actually be pretty skilled at interacting with sources and vetting information. This was a significant realization for me, as I had spent years believing that I wasn't fit for the CIA, that I wasn't really supposed to be there, or that I had somehow slipped through the cracks of the hiring process.

I had always imagined that people hired to be spies were endowed with gifts beyond measure. While I was learning how to drive a car or graduating from high school, they were almost certainly honing their spy craft, learning new languages, and acquiring black belts in the martial arts. I was just an average human who was hardly destined for a life of espionage and intrigue.

Once I got into the CIA, however, I looked around and realized that the officers weren't carbon copies of the slick actors I'd seen playing them in the movies. They were just regular people. But here's the rub: They were significantly different from me in personality and temperament.

When I walked through the halls of the CIA or met people in leadership positions, I felt completely inadequate and, well . . . different. Many of these officers were unfriendly and extremely serious, and they often sported furrowed brows. As a result, I spent the first few years of my career at the CIA trying to change the way I came off to the world. I really wanted to fit in.

Smile less, I told myself. *Look serious. Don't be so friendly or outgoing.* It seemed to me that the more severe and authoritarian people were, the better the chance they'd get promoted. I could never be frosty or truculent, but I figured I could definitely scale back my genial nature and rein in my extroversion.

I have spent much of my life wondering whether I had the necessary talent or skill required to succeed at every new challenge. It didn't matter if I was in elementary school, high school, college, or the CIA: I have always assumed that everyone else was smarter than me, more experienced, and better prepared.

Maybe that's why I was so surprised when Ted, a retired CIA colleague whom I respect greatly, told me that he, too, had been plagued with doubt from a young age. I would never have thought Ted struggled with a lack of confidence. He was so well respected that the whole room stopped talking whenever he spoke. We all wanted to draw from his experience, intelligence, and wisdom. Yet despite all he had achieved, Ted grew up believing he was behind the curve.

It all started in kindergarten. Ted remembers his first day of school like it was yesterday. The school building was being renovated, so classes began at a local agricultural training center. Five-year-old Ted walked into the strange classroom and immediately noticed images on the walls that he called "exploded engines." They were renderings of automobile engines that looked as if they were bursting in order to reveal various engine parts and demonstrate how the components fit together. Ted assumed that the colorful pictures were hung on the walls for the benefit of the new kindergarten students.

Ted sat down at one of the desks and looked around. The other kids were smiling, laughing, and playing with each other. They seemed to be having a jolly good time. But Ted wasn't feeling very celebratory. He looked back up at the exploded engines with great concern. Ted thought to himself, *They must want us to be able to put engines together. Why else would they put these pictures on the wall?* In his mind, the carefree expressions on the other kids' faces meant that they were not concerned and already knew how to assemble an engine.

Poor Ted was worried that he was lagging behind the rest of the kindergarten class because he had no idea how to put an engine together. As Ted contemplated the situation, he told himself, *School is not going to be easy. I'm going to have to work extra hard to keep up with the rest of the class.*

Ted said he never knew how intelligent he was until he learned his SAT scores were extremely high and that he would be graduating high school at the top of his class. He always assumed he was below average academically, but due to his excellent test scores, Ted received a full-tuition scholarship to college. That was a turning point in his life.

Whenever I think about it, Ted's story always gives me a belly laugh because I can't imagine that he was anything other than extraordinary. But how often do we do that to ourselves? We assume everyone else has it all figured out, and we are the only ones who don't. We beat ourselves up as we try to change who we are or be something different.

Up until my Iraq tour, I hesitated to think of myself as an expert. I had hung on to the assumption that "others" knew more about the Middle East and counterterrorism affairs than I did. But after dealing with hundreds of intelligence officers, diplomats, and administration officials in Washington, DC, and the Middle East, I finally realized that I knew more about the region than most of the people I came into contact with.

I wasn't just "good enough"; I was a full-fledged member of the team. While in Iraq, I figured out that I had an ability to understand, assess, and predict changes in the complicated web of interstate relationships, politics, culture, and religion that characterizes the Middle East.

To say that serving in Iraq at the height of the war was my single most difficult challenge is an understatement. It was the most physically, emotionally, and mentally draining experience of my life.

And yet, had I not gone to Iraq, I would not have discovered how resilient I was. I would not have figured out how good I was at interacting with such a broad range of people, from the US military to Iraqi collaborators. Had I not gone to Iraq, I would not have known how skillful I was at debriefing sources. Had I not been overwhelmed by work, I would not have learned to collect, process, and analyze information so quickly and efficiently. Had I not been exposed to so much bad intelligence, I would not have had the opportunity to hone my craft in identifying and exposing fabricators.

The lessons I learned in one year in Iraq far outweigh what I learned in multiple tours in other locations. Without a doubt, I could not have developed this level of expertise anywhere else.

Maybe God knew what he was doing sending me there after all.

CHAPTER 13

NEVER SAY NEVER

The period that Joseph and I served in Iraq, between 2006 and 2007, was the deadliest of the war. The number of persons killed on all sides of the conflict hit a high point in December 2006, with 3,000 deaths in just one month. IED placements peaked in May 2007 with 2,080 explosions. In terms of overall attacks, the summer of 2007 was the worst, with almost 1,600 attacks occurring during a single week in June.[1]

Needless to say, when our tour in Iraq finally drew to a close, Joseph and I vowed that we would never go back. We would also do whatever we could to avoid ending up in the middle of another hardship tour.

Word to the wise—when you say, "I will never [fill in the blank]," watch out because inevitably, you will end up doing that very thing. I am still unsure which of God's laws governs this principle, but after decades' worth of life experience, I realize such statements could also be translated as *Lord, deep down in my soul I can feel you are pulling me in X direction, but it scares me so much I cannot even fathom how I could do it. Please, please don't make me [fill in the blank].* It's as if we can feel the hand of God moving us—on a subconscious level—and we try to steer clear of it at all costs.

Just as I tried to pray my way out of the Iraq assignment, I wanted to avoid one other location like the plague. After serving in both ▓▓▓▓▓▓ and Baghdad, I assumed that this wouldn't be an issue. We had certainly earned the privilege of a nice assignment.

I remember saying to my friends, "You know what? I'm not choosy. I'm flexible about the next posting, but please, please . . . I'll go 'anywhere but Saratoga.'" (For simplicity, I will refer to the country by this name.) We said this phrase so many times through the years, we decided to shorten it to ABS.

Needless to say, guess where we went next? You got it. We were sent to Saratoga! You'd think I'd learn. You'd think I'd wise up a bit. You'd think I'd stop making such declarations. (On a side note, I've now taken to saying things like "I will *never* live in Italy, Portugal, or the Virgin Islands. Please don't make me go there, God!")

It was hard to fathom how our colleagues could get sent to the most beautiful cities in the world while we were repeatedly sent from one danger zone to another. It seemed like we couldn't catch a break. The pattern was demoralizing and made us feel like we kept getting sucker punched. (I can hear the HR people right now saying, "No one wants to go to Saratoga. What are we going to do? I know, let's send Joseph and Michele!")

Every time we sat our families down to reveal the location of our next tour, they would cringe in anticipation of the news. By this point, they were conditioned to expect the worst, which we usually dished out. And they had gotten used to praying for us—a lot.

Outside of Iraq, Saratoga was one of the few places in the world that truly frightened me. I was completely unnerved.

Even worse, I had the added stress of arriving in the new country alone. Unlike other tours where Joseph and I would come and go at the same time, on this tour each of us was replacing a different officer, and their departure schedules were nearly a month apart. That meant I was scheduled to arrive three weeks ahead of Joseph.

Despite flying all over the world and navigating a host of strange and sometimes hostile cultures, I have never been so scared to land in a country before. I didn't know what to expect, and I didn't know how to act. What if I accidentally did something wrong and was chastised by the locals—or worse?

As the plane made the final approach to the airport, my heart rate soared. I could not believe my own reaction. I was shaking.

Truth be told, this wasn't the first time I had been in this country. Several years earlier, while traveling in the Middle East, I ended up on a flight that had a brief layover in Saratoga. Even though my plane was only on the ground for an hour, what I experienced filled me with dread at the thought of actually living in that country full-time.

Uttering a quick prayer, I pushed myself forward in spite of the fear and nervously stepped off the plane and onto the Jetway. The hundred-plus-degree heat of the desert air hit me in the face like a sledgehammer. It was the middle of summer, and despite the fact that it was well past sunset, the hot wind made it feel like high noon.

A few more steps and we were inside the air-conditioned airport heading toward passport control. Having crossed the threshold into conservative Islamic cultures many times, I automatically changed my demeanor, adopting a meeker comportment. I was the only white, Western female in the crowd and didn't want any extra attention. I dropped my eyes and tried not to make eye contact with anyone, especially the men.

As I proceeded through the airport, I prepared myself for long lines in passport control because several planes had landed within minutes of one another. Once I turned the corner, I saw a line of entry booths and hundreds of foreign workers waiting to get into the country. It would take forever to move people through passport control because of the strict requirements governing the entry of foreign laborers and the language barrier that made the process even more complicated. Getting their fingerprints taken and retinal scans completed would not be an easy task.

As I walked to the back of one of the lines, passport control officers saw that I was an unaccompanied female and waved me to the front of the line. The officer summoned me to the counter, where I presented him with my landing card and passport opened up to the visa page. He looked at my photograph and then looked back up at me and said, "Is this your first time in Saratoga?"

"Yes, sir," I said, feigning cheerfulness at the thought.

He scanned the visa page, entered something into the computer, and then stamped the passport and handed it back to me.

With a big smile on his face, he said, "Welcome, Ms. Assad!"

I replied, "Thank you very much," and exited the arrivals hall.

That's all? I thought. *No problems? No interminable wait in long lines? Nobody yelling at me for not wearing a head covering?*

All the anxiety I'd built up in my head about how I'd be treated as a female traveling alone was unnecessary. Instead of having run-ins with security, I ended up having a surprisingly pleasant entry experience. Frankly, I'd had more difficulties with hostile passport control officers in the UK than here. *Maybe this won't be so bad after all.*

After gathering my luggage, I headed for the exit where my male colleague said he'd be waiting. He was a good friend of mine *and* was the person I'd come to replace. We'd worked it out so that our tours would overlap for a couple of weeks and he could show me the ropes. I scanned the crowd looking for him, trying not to acknowledge all the faces staring at me as I walked by.

Relief washed over me as I saw Andrew waiting behind the rope. After greeting each other, Andrew grabbed my luggage and led me out to the waiting SUV.

And so began my adventure of living in an alternate reality, one in which I really struggled to find my footing and feel comfortable. As much as I knew about Saratoga from my travels and studies, nothing could have prepared me to live so far outside the bounds of what was normal in my own culture.

A dmittedly, I felt much more comfortable once Joseph finally arrived. And the compound where we lived and worked—while far from Main Street, USA—was worlds safer than the surrounding city. Truth be told, we were so busy at work that there was very little time to wander around and explore the city. And that may have been a good thing. I'd heard so many horror stories about run-ins with local citizens and police officers that I went out of my way to minimize the amount of time I spent away from our closely guarded compound.

Adding to the general stress level of living in that culture was the knowledge that terrorist cells were operating all over the country. We were constantly on edge because we knew we were considered the ultimate enemy every time we left the safety of the well-guarded compound. After all, we were targets. Need to go to the grocery store? Keep an eye out for surveillance. Need to buy a new pair of shoes? Look for surveillance. Even the simplest of tasks turned into a major operation given the number of terrorists who were attacking and killing foreigners and members of the country's security services.

During that tour, I had the rare opportunity to provide training to a group of counterterrorism officers with whom the United States had worked closely. Normally public speaking is one of my favorite things to do, and this was a special briefing I'd designed and presented to many counterterrorism officers in the past. But standing in front of that group of about fifty officers, I had a sinking feeling. They wore the most hostile looks I had ever seen. I could hear them whispering, "Who is *this*?" to each other in Arabic.

Simply put, they were annoyed that a Western female who clearly didn't know a thing about the Middle East would dare to stand in front of a group of *male* officers as if she had something valuable to say. What could a woman possibly teach *them*? A woman's place was in the home bearing children and taking care of the family. Counterterrorism was a man's game, so what could I possibly say that could be useful to the descendants of desert warriors? None of them were having it.

Much like with the terrorist debriefings I'd done in Iraq, I knew

I had to immediately establish my bona fides (i.e., street cred) or the training session would be a resounding failure. These officers wouldn't give me long before tuning out, so I had to immediately address their assumptions that I was out of my league. I began by introducing myself in Arabic.

"Hi. I'm Michele. I'm very honored to be speaking to such an esteemed group of officers today. Like you, I do counterterrorism work. I have had the opportunity to work in Baghdad, ██████, and ██████ and have traveled to numerous Arab countries. I received a master's degree in Arab studies from Georgetown University and have been traveling to the region for almost twenty years."

Because few foreign officers had ever addressed them in Arabic, their formerly angry faces instantly washed over with shock. *Bet they didn't see* that *coming.*

Giving a quick rundown of where I had traveled and served also played to my advantage. Credentials are extremely important in that part of the world, regardless of gender. Second and more significantly, I knew that the majority of the group had *not* served in those locations, nor—like most—did they want to. While they were proficient in counterterrorism operations in their own country, most avoided service in Iraq and ██████ because of the inherent danger and instability. To be able to say that I had worked in these danger zones helped me establish myself as an expert in the region, and possibly, just possibly, someone worth listening to.

A few muffled rumblings echoed across the room, followed by silence.

I had their attention.

Having spent many years following their counterterrorism fight, I had a good grasp of their strengths and weaknesses. I knew the areas where they were extremely proficient as well as their limitations, which helped me develop an approach to dealing with an otherwise hostile crowd and focus my training on the areas where even they knew they needed help.

What made perhaps the biggest difference was that I was able to use real-life stories to illustrate my points, further establishing my expertise. Of course, I had to change certain details to protect key sources and methods, but the effect was the same. And it was immediate. They sat in rapt attention, raising their hands to answer my questions and engaging in a robust discussion. All of my experience in the school of hard knocks was finally paying dividends.

It's funny. For years, I was envious of the CIA officers who were deployed to cushy countries while a small group of us were repeatedly given hazardous duty. I spent a lot of time whining and complaining about this perceived injustice. *Why does everyone else get to wander in the fields of green while we traipse from one desert to another?* There were even moments when I wanted to give up. But whenever Joseph and I prayed about leaving the CIA, God kept telling us, *Not yet.* Naturally, we obeyed. But believe me, it wasn't easy.

It took me a while, but eventually I realized that while the "lucky officers" were off enjoying classic architecture, world-class dining, and beautiful apartments, I was gaining invaluable experience and learning more about counterintelligence and counterterrorism than they ever would or could. By the time I had reached my midthirties, I had already achieved a far greater level of expertise than any of the officers who had cozied up to senior leaders for those plum assignments.

What's more, the challenges I had faced working in ████, Iraq, and Saratoga had transformed me from a naive young recruit with an inferiority complex to a mature, highly experienced officer capable of succeeding in the most hostile and exacting environments. The assignments I had once perceived as a never-ending string of punishments were actually amazing career builders.

Somewhere along the line, while I was busy doing the grunt work, staying late into the night, serving on weekends and holidays, and going where others refused to go, I had become an expert in my field. I could speak authoritatively on a wide range of topics and experiences the likes of which most in the agency had never even encountered.

Simply put, the struggle to hone my craft and the struggle to triumph over myriad obstacles created the conditions for something beautiful to emerge—a woman fully equipped and completely reliant on God. When the pain was too great or the challenge too overwhelming, I had nothing but faith to get me through. Whenever I could not see over the horizon, I trusted that he could and that he would provide me with whatever tools or insight I needed to succeed. By the grace of God, I discovered that struggle could become a skill builder, pain could become a motivator, and confusion could serve as a clarifier.

Once Joseph and I spent a holiday weekend in Provence, France, where we learned how some of the most exceptional wines are created. The grapevines are planted in skillfully terraced rows, but surprisingly, the fields where they are planted are not luscious and green. In the summer, the sun beats down hard on the vines, and the weather is hot and uncomfortable—hardly the place one would imagine finding world-renowned vineyards. Frankly, it's a wonder that anything so delicious could emerge from the cracked soil and parched earth beneath them. But apparently the harsh conditions are the secret to their success.

In fact, Provence vintners actually ascribe the beauty and complexity of their wines to the difficult circumstances in which the grapes are grown. The harder the vine works to push down into the dry earth to reach water, the better the fruit. Because the vines work so hard to burrow through the soil, they become hardier and more robust. The process of struggle imbues the grapes with a well-rounded, multidimensional character. The challenges those roots encounter establish, shape, and cajole the fruit into a masterful product.

Likewise, the harsher the environments I served in and the more trying the circumstances, the stronger I became. What I had perceived as a hardship was actually a tremendous gift. And as I would soon come to discover, to whom much is given, much is required.

CHAPTER 14

AN UNEXPECTED
MISSION

By July 2010, our fourth tour had come to a close, and Joseph and I were back stateside. It had been a particularly difficult summer. Joseph's father had died, and several other family members were facing significant health problems.

Without question, one of the hardest parts of this job was being taken away from friends and family for months, sometimes years, at a time. Because of the nature of our work, it was so easy to get caught up in the tyranny of the urgent and forget that life was still going on back home without us. Births, graduations, illnesses, deaths—life just had the stubborn nerve to go on while we were half a world away. No amount of training could have prepared us for that.

I was accustomed to dealing with crises every day, but none of them as painful as losing someone I had loved so dearly, or watching others I cared about suffer so much. The death of Joseph's father combined with ten years of serving in one war zone after another had taken a heavy toll on both my husband and me. It had gradually and almost imperceptibly affected our relationship and eroded our ability to care for our families. We no longer had a vision for our future, which left us feeling empty and lost.

As I sat on the couch of our apartment in Virginia on the verge of emotional exhaustion, all I could do was sob. Sometimes I needed a good cry to let all of my emotions out, and this was such a moment— a time when I felt pushed right to the edge and questioned everything. *Why does life have to be so hard? The training, the traveling, the culture clashes, the lackluster leadership, the mounds of paperwork, the dangerous living conditions, sources letting us down and lying to our faces, constantly having to prove and defend myself, the separation from friends and family, the marital strain. God, what has this all been for?*

As I started to calm down, I felt God's Spirit wash over me in a way that words cannot capture. I had cried out to him, and he was there. I felt his presence in a powerful and all-consuming way just when I needed it the most.

When the tears finally subsided, I sat in silence, not really knowing what to do or how to feel. I asked God, *What do I do now?* In the silence, I heard him say, *It's time to share your story.*

I paused for a while, trying to make sense of the idea. And you know what? I couldn't quite grasp this request.

But, God, why me? I asked. *How would my story help others? I'm not well known or well connected.* And finally, *I'm not smart enough to do this.*

With loving tenderness that still brings me to tears, he said, *I choose you because you have been open to me. You have allowed me to shape you. I don't need knowledgeable and well-connected people; I need the empty vessels. I need those who will allow me to direct their steps, to mold them for my purposes.*

Well, what could I say? This wasn't the first time God asked me to do something that was completely intimidating or far outside the scope of my abilities.

Okay, Lord, I conceded. *I'll do whatever you ask.*

I was completely bewildered. And yet somehow, I felt as if God were preparing me for a new assignment, though I wasn't sure what it was.

I hadn't heard an audible or humanlike voice. The messages from God came to me from deep inside, yet they were separate and distinct from my own musings. They were clear. They were direct. They were personal. And they cut through me like a knife. If God wanted me to share my story, then that's what I would do.

As I thought more about what I felt I was being called to do, it occurred to me that God was encouraging me to do much more than just share my story—he was actually leading me away from the CIA. For me to share my story using my actual name, I would have to resign from the agency and request permission to drop my cover. I had no idea whether they'd ever grant such a request due to the sensitivity of our work. It seemed like a scary proposition.

Meanwhile, Joseph was weary of asking the CIA's permission to visit family members who lived outside the United States. Security officers had given him the runaround for attending his father's funeral, even though he had acquired all requisite permissions to do so. In addition, as the only son in a family of Egyptian origin, he had the responsibility of arranging for the care of his mother.

The security officers told him that they could not support his requests to visit his mother, claiming, "It's too dangerous for Americans to travel to many parts of the Middle East right now." At that point, we made a very easy decision: Family was much more important than work. Joseph decided to seek a position elsewhere that would enable him to focus on family obligations. It was becoming quite obvious to both of us that it was time to move on.

Now, contrary to the popular myth that one can never actually leave the CIA, the truth is, agents can walk out the door anytime they like. There are no restrictions regarding either the years of service required or the timing of their departure. What *is* terribly difficult is figuring out what to do after leaving. The longer agents are in—unless they are of retirement age—the harder it is to leave.

Why? Well, imagine trying to find a job when you are in your late thirties and are unable to say what you've accomplished in the last ten years of your life. The language the CIA approves for inclusion in a résumé (based on your *cover job*) says nothing intriguing and would do little (if anything) to help anyone secure a new job. Furthermore, because agents have been sealed off from the world working undercover, it's not as though they have an active Rolodex of contacts to call on for help, or a professional network to lean on to generate job leads. Without a well-connected family or strong preexisting personal networks, it can be difficult to know where to begin. After all, the agency has a policy that they will neither confirm nor deny a person's employment, making it difficult for former agents to prove their experience and expertise—even once they've received permission to drop their cover.

I suddenly understood how challenging it must be for prisoners starting anew after spending a significant amount of their lives behind bars. Freedom and integration are hard for people who have lived in a closely monitored and micromanaged bubble. How would Joseph and I deal with the black cloud of our former lives when no one else could understand what we'd been through? How could we compete with others thoroughly ensconced in the real world? How would we start over?

In addition to those challenges, we needed to figure out what we were qualified to do. How would we market ourselves outside the intelligence bubble? It was like having to figure out all over again what we wanted to do when we grew up.

In retrospect, ours was an adventurous but sheltered life. We kept our relationships to a minimum because the more international friends we had, the harder it would be to get through the polygraph and security reinvestigations that took place every few years. The more friends we had overseas, the more concerned investigators would be that these relationships could be a counterintelligence flag.

In addition, CIA officers are not permitted to have contact with journalists, or with members of Congress or their staff. And even though it wasn't a regulation, Joseph and I also tried to avoid contact with NGO workers, human rights advocates, and clergy, largely because we didn't want our US government affiliation to bring unwanted scrutiny to their activities or taint them if our cover was ever blown. We didn't want to give the enemy any reason to believe that these people were CIA officers or agents as well.

Staying away from people in these professions was not natural for us because in our pre-CIA lives, we were deeply involved in those sectors. Both Joseph and I had worked with humanitarian organizations, human rights groups, and faith-based communities. We were also members of a church and had friends and acquaintances all over Capitol Hill, where we lived when we were in graduate school.

When our careers at the agency commenced, we had to leave it all behind. To almost all of our friends and professional contacts, it appeared that we'd fallen off the face of the earth. Only a few family members and close friends knew where we were and what we were doing. For everyone else, it was a bit of a mystery.

While we were quietly going off the grid, the world was moving in the opposite direction, toward greater exposure and connectivity. While we were withdrawing from society and were being trained to fly under the radar, normal citizens were being coaxed by business and culture to put it all out there: The more people knew about you, the more connections you made on LinkedIn or Twitter, the more Facebook friends you had, the better.

We swam against the current, doing everything possible to fade into the background. In order to reduce our digital footprint, we eschewed social media and limited our web-based activities. We resisted setting up accounts on MySpace, Facebook, Twitter, and Instagram so we didn't give out too much information about our lives. Just like other CIA officers, we would occasionally google ourselves to be sure nothing came up.

In addition to limiting our online presence, we kept social interactions to a minimum and were mindful of the content of our phone conversations and e-mail exchanges. We had to assume that all of our communications were being tracked and analyzed by those we were working against. Therefore, we couldn't take the chance that one of our friends might unwittingly say something that "outed" us or called into question our true affiliation. Even things as seemingly innocuous as photographs could jeopardize our status if the wrong people got access to them and used the electronic time and date stamps to analyze our movements or track our activities. We had to limit our circle of trust to those who could handle the secret.

This cloak-and-dagger existence continued for ten years. The chasm between the arc of our lives and a normal human existence was further widened by the requirements of having to move every year or two. We were in a continuous state of transition, never able to put down roots. We'd come home once or twice a year, but only long enough to catch our breath before heading back out to the field. Our enormous collection of suitcases got a great deal of wear and tear as we spent an inordinate amount of time on planes and trains and in automobiles.

As we began to think through the ramifications of actually leaving the agency, I couldn't help but wonder, *Will it even be possible for Joseph and me to have a "normal" life? And if we do, what will that feel like?*

After a decade of uncertainty and chaos, I desperately wanted to experience some constancy again, but I also wondered whether too much stability would smother rather than free us. Much like the character Brooks in *The Shawshank Redemption*, Joseph and I had become "institutionalized" after ten years with the agency. In the CIA, we were both well-respected experts in our field. We were well traveled, spoke multiple languages, performed well under stress, and had phenomenal people and problem-solving skills. But to the rest of the world . . .

Then there was the question of whether anything on the outside could satisfy us the way that a national security job at the CIA did. The recidivism rate of officers trying to get out and then returning to the CIA deterred a lot of people from taking the risk. Over the years, Joseph and I had seen several colleagues walk out the door only to return a year or two later because nothing on the outside interested them as much as their work in the Directorate of Operations, no matter what challenges came with it.

Even when they had to deal with poor management, a lack of effective leadership, or cutthroat colleagues, many officers found that their identity was inextricably linked to being an intelligence officer and working for the CIA. The idea of not having access to top-secret information, not being the first to know about hot topics, and not having insider knowledge of counterterrorism and foreign affairs issues was too much to bear. Let's face it: The experience of working with a group that helped shape the most interesting headlines in the world was hard to replicate elsewhere.

Joseph and I had both become addicted to serving in positions where we could see the immediate impact of our work and the fruit of our labor. We had also become adrenaline junkies. After we'd spent so much of our careers in hot zones, it would be hard to let go of jobs that put us front and center in the war on terror. Where else would we receive immediate feedback from consumers regarding the quality of our work or the efficacy of our intelligence? Could any other job be as stimulating? Could any other career take us to the edge as the CIA had? Would it be possible to find anything, outside the confines of intelligence, in which we could have such meaning and purpose? How could anything compete with the head-spinning experiences of being undercover officers in the CIA?

In spite of my enthusiasm to follow God's leading, I experienced a moment of self-doubt. *Can we even make it on the outside?*

There was no question that leaving the agency required an enormous leap of faith. On top of everything else, on a more practical level it would also mean letting go of a government job that paid well, took care of our housing costs, and was stable, regardless of political leadership or shifts in the economy.

Thankfully, I'd had sufficient life experience to know that God's plans are always better than mine. His ways may confound me, but they have always been in my best interest and have always taken me where I need to go. I had never questioned God's leading before, and I had no intention of starting now. His urging was clear. It was time for me to leave the agency.

Ironically, just as Joseph began his career with the CIA several months before I did, he also left before I did to see if he could make a go of it. Ten years prior, we had entered into this wild adventure together. Now we were about to embark on another one. And once again, we had no idea what lay ahead.

About a year after I'd heard God's call to tell my story, as I signed the paperwork required to leave the CIA, I swallowed hard. The security officer reminded me that I was legally obligated to continue protecting my cover and all of the secret information I had read, processed, and been involved with over the course of my career.

He also reminded me that if I chose to return to the CIA, I'd have to redo the polygraph and background investigation since it had been years since my last reinvestigation. The very thought of going through all of that again made my head hurt.

Acknowledging the rules and regulations he had laid out, I verbally agreed and noted I had no further questions regarding my security clearances or reactivation requirements. In my mind, I was clear on what was to happen. There was no coming back. This was it. Once I walked away, I would not return.

On my last day, with a heavy heart, I hugged my colleagues good-bye and wished them well. I hated leaving them—they were the iron that sharpens iron, and I felt less of a person without them. Then I grabbed my purse and a small box of personal items and exited the vault, which is what we called our secured work area. As I took the elevator to the main floor and walked toward the turnstiles, I remembered the feeling of awe and wonder I'd had when I first entered this grand hall. I'd had no idea what was in store for me back then. For that matter, I had no idea what was in store for me now.

My final act of separation from this great entity occurred as I exited the turnstiles and turned around to hand my badge to the security officer. It had rested comfortably around my neck for a decade, and I felt naked without it. Quite unceremoniously, I surrendered the identity card that bore the image of my smiling face (yet was curiously lacking in name or agency affiliation). Then the sliding glass doors opened, and I walked out of the CIA forever. The agency that I had risked my life for, that I had defended, and whose identity had become inextricably linked with my own, was now behind me.

Without question, I was a very different person from the woman who had walked through the same doors almost exactly ten years before. It was hard to believe how much I had seen and experienced during that decade. This was the place where I had discovered myself. This was where I'd uncovered my gifts, where I'd figured out what I was really good at. It was the place where I had experienced the depth and breadth of God's grace and provisions through some of the darkest and most difficult moments of my life.

As I walked toward my car, I was flooded with a slew of mixed emotions: sadness at closing this great chapter, relief at having made it this far, and guarded anticipation for my future.

And yet I was confident in my decision. I had heard from God. I knew it was time to go. With a heavy but hopeful heart, I threw up my arms and jumped off the cliff. It was at once terrifying and exhilarating.

Only God knew where I would land.

CHAPTER 15

NOW WHAT?

After ten years of having our entire lives mapped out for us, Joseph and I now faced the daunting task of figuring out our next move—*on our own*. Sadly, we could count on one hand the number of professional (non-CIA) contacts we had kept up with throughout the years. As it happens, one of the few people with whom we were able to maintain a relationship was a former boss of Joseph's. A highly respected human rights attorney, she quickly connected us with another attorney, who then connected us with a former US government contractor named David. He was looking for "security experts" to do freelance consulting work.

Having worked in the counterterrorism world himself, David understood how hard it is for people to come out after having served so long undercover. And because he had an intimate understanding of the intelligence sector, he didn't require cleared résumés or detailed summaries of our personal accomplishments. He understood where we were coming from and believed in us from the start. Once again, God was looking out for us.

David provided the perfect platform for us to pivot out from the shadows and into the civilian world. He threw numerous projects our way and referred potential clients to us, and before long, we were doing freelance work for a variety of organizations.

As security consultants, we put our intelligence officer skills to use conducting due diligence investigations, giving personal security training, leading corporate fraud investigations, assisting with logistics needs in dangerous parts of the world, providing infrastructure security evaluations, and offering terrorism assessments. We also helped law firms investigate complex cases in the Arab world, compiled risk assessments for multinational corporations looking to expand their operations in potentially hostile areas, and designed plans to rescue employees trapped in hostage situations.

Every project was different. Some were interesting and gave us a deep sense of satisfaction, while others were demanding and difficult—largely due to clients levying unrealistic or impossible objectives on us. Because of our background, a few clients labored under the gross misconception that Joseph and I had a secret bevy of superpowers that we could use on their behalf. Still other clients—no matter how many times we told them that we were no longer employed by the US government—falsely assumed that we had "special connections" we could use to help them out. They thought we were capable of executing all kinds of voodoo to advance their cause. Imagine their disappointment when they came to discover that Joseph and I were not, in fact, Mr. and Mrs. Smith, superspies, but instead just Joseph and Michele Assad, hardworking everyday Joes.

As we established a track record of success, our client base increased. It wasn't easy and it didn't come quickly, but it was nice to actually have a "normal" life again. We had been so used to living within the confines of a CIA existence that we had forgotten what it felt like to be on our own. And contrary to my fear that I would desperately miss the excitement of the CIA, I was happy to finally relax. Ten years of living and working in war zones had taken their toll. We needed to decompress from working long hours, weekends, and holidays. We needed to breathe.

Granted, it wasn't a deep breath. Not long after leaving the CIA, Joseph and I were hired by a consulting firm in Abu Dhabi that served the security interests of large multinational corporations, small businesses, and individual clients in Asia, Europe, Africa, and . . . the Middle East. That's right—the Assads were headed back to the Middle East.

We spent the next four years living and working in Abu Dhabi in the United Arab Emirates (UAE). Located on the eastern side of the Arabian Peninsula on a little piece of land that juts out into the Persian Gulf, the tip of the UAE is less than a hundred miles from Iran. The tiny country shares a border with Saudi Arabia and Oman, and because of its location, the UAE serves as a crossroads to the world's great capitals in Africa, Asia, and Europe. A natural transit point for continent-jumping businesspeople, it was the perfect place for us to set up shop.

Rising majestically like a mirage in the sands, its skylines glistening in the sunlight against the backdrop of a desert landscape and the dazzling turquoise waters of the Persian Gulf, the UAE was by far the most comfortable, in terms of living standards and culture, of all the places I've lived in the Middle East.

While Dubai grabs the most attention from the media, Abu Dhabi is, in fact, the capital of the UAE. It heads up a federation of seven emirates or city-states that also include Dubai, Sharjah, Ajman, Fujairah, Umm al-Quwain, and Ras al-Khaimah. Each emirate is led by a different *shaykh* and has its own unique character. While the UAE is modern in terms of its infrastructure, the UAE's business, commerce, and political cultures are governed by a complicated web of tribal allegiances and family relationships. It is very difficult for foreigners to understand these relationships and the decision-making processes that govern the UAE's affairs.

The UAE is a young country, having been established by the late president Shaykh Zayed bin Sultan al-Nahyan in 1971. Shaykh

Zayed encouraged the small, underdeveloped emirates to establish a federation. The tribal leaders of each emirate agreed to move forward together, realizing they were stronger as a unified nation than they would be on their own. Shaykh Zayed had a strong vision for the UAE's future, investing extensively in education and infrastructure.

Though the UAE is about the size of Scotland or the state of Maine, its proven oil reserves are the eighth largest in the world, and its proven natural gas reserves are the seventh largest.[1]

The UAE is a feast for the senses: highways abuzz with fast cars, the world's most innovative architecture, world-class restaurants, and hotels with cutting-edge design. For many, the UAE is the height of luxury.

Of course, Joseph and I enjoyed having a front seat to the ritziness and the glamour. Still, I couldn't shake the feeling of emptiness that seemed to envelop me while living there. I missed my family and friends. I missed my country and my culture.

Business was doing well, but it felt like something was off. During our time in the Emirates, I wasn't entirely sure where Joseph and I were headed. While praying about it and asking God why he had us in the UAE, I felt him impress this on me: *You asked me for a break, and I've given you one. You asked me for time to catch your breath—and here it is. I've brought you to the desert—literally and figuratively—to prepare you for your future. Use this downtime to connect with me. I will fill up the places where you feel empty. Don't worry about your future; just focus on me.*

From that moment on, I went out of my way to concentrate on God, and to reach out to him in the middle of that desert. Even though I missed home, I was full of gratitude for his love and provision. I was thankful for the time he'd given us to heal and to be restored after ten years of living at the speed of light. I'd been so used to fighting: fighting the clock, fighting the burden of an overwhelming amount of work, fighting the bureaucracy, fighting exhaustion, fighting my own fears, and fighting to stay alive.

We had finally emerged from a career that broke many officers and split families due to the immense stress of working in the intelligence sector. We'd been set free from ten years of immersion in the war on terror. We'd come out into the light and were beginning to live again. I might not have been home in the United States, but I could finally relax.

As Joseph and I continued to build our clientele, we explored how our unique skill sets could be used in a variety of contexts that we had not previously considered.

Naturally, my presence in meetings continued to surprise male interlocutors who often assumed I was the note taker or secretary before finding out I was one of the firm's consultants. I even participated in meetings held in offices with no restrooms for women because the company's entire workforce was male. And because it was the Middle East, after I'd been served coffee and tea all morning, I ended up having to use the men's restroom while the male CEO stood out in the hall to make sure nobody else walked in. That wasn't embarrassing . . . at all.

Just as during my time in the CIA, a handful of people in the security industry underestimated me because I was a woman. And once again, I was able to use that to my advantage. My favorite example of this was during a dinner with friends in March 2014.

A Polish businessman named Aleksy invited us to dinner in Dubai, requesting a special favor of us. In addition to a few other friends, Aleksy had asked a business contact named Sunny to join us. Sunny was the representative of a private investment firm based out of Bahrain. He boasted of obtaining a 2.5 percent monthly return for his clients over the course of seventeen years, and now he had pitched Aleksy about a timely investment opportunity. Apparently, a rare block of investments had opened up, and the firm was willing to take $300 million for a special fund focused on emerging markets in Asia. Aleksy was tempted to place a little money in the fund but wasn't quite sure whether the claims of such steady returns were possible, so he wanted our assessment of Sunny and the company he represented.

The whole group was in on our little secret. I knew it was going to be fun when Sunny pranced into the room with an ego the size of a float in the Macy's Thanksgiving Day Parade. He acted like he was a regular at the restaurant, winking at the hostess, who flashed him an annoyed expression that said, *Ew. Creep. You're not a regular. I don't know you.* He was loud and obnoxious, greeting everyone like he was their favorite uncle.

When I saw *that* much ego, *that* quickly, I knew he was going to be a talker. If you put me in front of a talker, I can elicit all kinds of goodies—and thank goodness, because my substantive expertise is *not* in international investments or emerging markets. Just as with Mansur and Ahmad back in Iraq, I would have to rely on basic common sense and my ability to read nonverbal cues to figure out whether Sunny and his investment opportunity were legit.

After initial introductions, we all sat down in the swanky bar atop Dubai's Grosvenor House Hotel. Aleksy introduced Sunny to the group, which included a Polish couple, two Czech citizens, one Indian, and two Americans (me and Joseph). Sunny wasn't given any details about our backgrounds or experience. He just knew we were casual acquaintances of his potential client, originally from the United States.

Sunny got off to a good start. He pulled out his cell phone and flashed a picture of a gorgeous motorcycle gleaming with chrome that he said he'd just bought at Bike Week in Daytona Beach, Florida. He told everybody how he'd dropped a hundred grand on this Harley, clearly working hard to impress his audience with his spending power and "cool factor." He obviously had no idea that of all the places in the world, Joseph and I were from central Florida and had a home in the Daytona Beach area. He really could not have imagined that he'd picked a topic about which these two random Americans had a great deal of knowledge. In order to keep Sunny talking, we played along, oohing and aahing at the images of the bike (none of which actually included him).

Then we asked, "What kind of Harley is that?"

Sunny looked a little surprised before he replied, "It's something like a Fat Boy." And there it was: the first verbal indication that Mr. Sunny was probably lying about the bike. He used a key qualifier that indicated he wasn't sure of his answer: "something like." He spent that much money on a bike but couldn't specify the model? Anybody who buys expensive bikes or cool cars immediately tells you the make and model because that's what everyone wants to know. It's important when you're assessing someone to listen very carefully to his or her words. A lot of clues to someone's veracity can be buried in one response.

Then we asked, "Where did you buy this incredible Harley?"

He responded, "At the Harley dealership."

We said, "There are so many Harley dealerships in the area; which one was it?"

If you live in central Florida and you care about motorcycles, then you will know where all the Harley dealerships are (which we do). And if someone had just paid $100,000 for a motorcycle, might that person remember the specific dealership where he'd made this major purchase? Our query was followed by a pregnant pause. Sunny didn't expect that question.

Sunny looked surprised. He asked, "Why, do you know the area?"

"Yes," we conceded, "we've been there a few times."

He stumbled a bit before answering the question, saying, "Ah, you know, the main one . . . on the main strip."

He then backtracked a little, saying he'd bought the Harley but left it behind at the dealership, and he couldn't remember the exact location. He tugged at his collar, looking as if it had suddenly gotten very tight around his neck—classic nonverbal behavior called the "hangman's noose" that suggests extreme discomfort with the line of questioning.

Over the next hour or so, I elicited an incredible amount of damning information from Sunny. Every time he opened his mouth, he dug himself into a deeper hole. He was not able to talk about his wildly successful private equity firm for more than a minute without running into a wall and being unable to answer extremely basic questions. And my questions were not sophisticated by any measure. I know next to nothing about private equity firms, the structure of investments, or expected rates of return. But I did find it a stretch that a money manager with no Internet profile or online presence had allegedly obtained a return for all of his clients at the rate of 2.5 percent per month—for seventeen years, despite several downturns in the economy.

When asked what kind of fund he was raising monies for, Sunny responded, "Emerging markets."

I asked, "Emerging markets where?"

His nonverbal behavior showed increased stress as he shifted uncomfortably in his seat and responded, "Asia."

"Where in Asia?"

"All over, but primarily China."

I kept digging. "What type of emerging markets or industries in China?"

"Ah, I really don't know," he said. "That's why I bring in the bankers to answer those kinds of questions."

This was a major red flag. This was not a trick question. If you're raising hundreds of millions of dollars for an investment, you'll be able to tell potential clients some very basic things about the focus of the fund and the types of industries that you are investing in.

I queried, "So who is the fund manager?"

He said, "Denzel Pierson."

When I acted like I knew Mr. Pierson, Sunny got very nervous. He fidgeted again in his seat, as if the chair had suddenly gotten too hot to sit in. Then I said I didn't actually know Mr. Pierson, but that I was curious and was definitely going to check him out. I wanted to know who he was if he was *that* successful.

Sunny cleared his throat and said, "You won't find anything about him online. There's nothing there."

I decided to get a little confrontational with Sunny. This is so far outside my normal personality; I am actually uncomfortable challenging others in such an open and forthright manner. But when I'm after information and I smell a rat, it's a hoot to assume a bolder and more forceful persona. I sat back in my chair, looked at Sunny with a furrowed brow, and said, "Well, that's disturbing."

Sunny displayed significant agitation and said, "Why is that disturbing?"

I said, "Because in this day and age, if you are running a private equity firm of this magnitude, earning this rate of return for seventeen straight years, then your name is going to be out there. For sure."

He said again, "Well, you won't find anything."

I was really having fun now. I shook my head and offered a one-word response: "Disturbing."

As I dug for more details, beads of sweat appeared on Sunny's forehead. He tore off the sweater he was wearing as the temperature in the room seemed to soar. Sweat rings had developed under his arms. He was doing such a poor job of holding his own that I actually felt bad for him, so I changed the topic of conversation, intending to return to business issues at a later time.

Personal questions are simple to discuss if you are being honest about yourself and your background. This part of the conversation should have been pleasant and easy for Sunny, but it didn't take long to figure out that not only was he short on details about the high-value business deals that he was drumming up on behalf of "Denzel Pierson," he was short on details regarding his own life.

When I asked Sunny about his background, he claimed to have been "US Special Forces." When I asked which group, he said, "I was an Army Ranger and Green Beret."

I found this claim hard to believe, and I seriously doubted its validity. Someone referring to himself as a Green Beret is suspicious because that is not the group's official title, nor is it how a member of one of the US Army Special Forces (Airborne) units normally refers to himself.

When I mentioned having also served the US government and told him that I'd worked in multiple war zones, he got quiet. He looked at me with a cautious expression on his face, possibly trying to figure out if I was joking. I guess I didn't look (to him) like the kind of person who'd really know anything about such dicey parts of the world. When I asked him where he served in the field, he couldn't name any main operating bases or forward operating bases in Iraq or Afghanistan. And while he claimed to be an adviser to the Afghan government, he didn't know a thing about Afghanistan, and he couldn't tell me which Afghan ministry he worked with.

Then Sunny let me in on a big secret. "I also get a paycheck from Langley," he said with a wink and a nod. I guess he was going to cover up his lack of information about his own life with the explanation "Well, I can't tell you that; it's secret."

Sunny didn't realize that he was telling a former undercover CIA officer who specializes in vetting people and information that he was a super-secret agent. I almost spit the pita and hummus out of my mouth. It was all I could do not to laugh. Sunny was setting his own traps and then happily walking right into them, not knowing what a spectacle this was turning out to be. His overzealous attempts to impress his audience were turning him into a caricature as he laid claim to the coolest references he could think of.

Sunny had concocted quite the legend. He was a member of the Special Forces, a CIA intelligence officer, a private equity fund representative, a college graduate, and the CEO of his own military and logistics consulting firm based out of Houston—all at the same time. I ran the calculations, taking into account the amount of time he would have spent in college and the years he would have spent training for two separate special operations forces, the CIA's clandestine training program, and the amount of time he'd worked for the investment firm. Having looked at Sunny's LinkedIn profile, I calculated that if these claims were true, Sunny would have had to begin his illustrious career at the age of twelve. And this didn't take into account the additional work experience he listed in his profile, which would have meant that Sunny had entered the workforce at the tender age of seven.

But before I'd even run the numbers, Sunny's terminology gave him away. CIA officers don't actually refer to their employer as Langley, just as members of Army Special Forces don't call themselves Green Berets. If he'd had any idea whom he was telling these tales to, he would have felt anything but cool.

Sunny was a rookie liar, but he has probably made off with millions of dollars of other people's money anyway. (Surprisingly, he admitted to me that he was "wanted" in Kuwait because of a bad business deal. I could only imagine how much money that might have involved.)

For fun, I drew up a five-page assessment of Sunny and all of his claims (most of which I was able to debunk or seriously call into question). Aleksy was amused and grateful that Joseph and I were able to provide such a comprehensive assessment in such a short period of time. He obviously chose not to invest in Sunny's fund but enjoyed allowing Sunny to pay for dinner, drinks, and the concert tickets he'd promised the potential investors.

Like many imposters, Sunny was not particularly intelligent, so he relied on his charming personality and impressive persona to win people over. His methodology was that of a typical fabricator. First of all, he would overwhelm people with so much information that they didn't have time to process or analyze it all. This is why scam artists are often referred to as fast talkers.

Second, he relied on buzzwords, such as "Special Forces," "Langley," "Harley-Davidson," and "emerging markets," to grab and hold people's interest. Next, he tried to make up for a lack of substance by projecting a certain appearance—that of a successful businessman.

Sunny wore fancy designer clothes, threw around a lot of cash, and flitted around the Middle East on a private jet. Last but not least, Sunny tried to make people think they were joining an exclusive club and he was doing them a huge favor by allowing them to be a part of the wildly successful fund (i.e., the Bernie Madoff strategy).

Sunny could have taken a few lessons from the CIA playbook. You must be able to defend your cover. If you make something up, you should keep it as close to real life as possible so you can remember the details of the legend you've created. It is important to be comfortable with your cover, as you may need to answer questions about it while under stress.

And if people see sweat rings under your arms and beads of sweat on your brow, they may not buy what you're selling. Some of Sunny's best giveaways were his massive amounts of perspiration and his desperate attempts to redirect the conversation when asked questions of any depth about himself or his fund. It seems Sunny hadn't gotten schooled in cover very well during his alleged stint at the CIA.

I have to admit, I had a blast that evening. Granted, it wasn't the high-stakes, life-or-death counterintelligence work I was used to, but it *was* fun to flex my behavioral analysis muscles again.

I guess it just goes to show you, you can take the girl out of the CIA, but . . .

CHAPTER 16

YOU CAN'T GO HOME AGAIN

In April 2015, while working on our taxes and taking stock of our financial situation, Joseph and I had a sudden realization: We'd made such good progress in our careers as security consultants that we could probably work from anywhere in the world.

As long as we were close to an airport, we could serve the interests of the consultancy, flying as needed to meet with clients, conduct investigations, and execute contracts. After we discussed this option with the UAE-based company, they agreed that we could spend more of our time in the United States and attempt to work from there.

We couldn't believe it. We had lived a nomadic life for almost fifteen years and could hardly conceive of the idea of putting down roots. I was in such shock at the possibility of living and working out of the United States, I could barely function for two days. Were we finally going home? Would we be able to live near family and friends?

Despite my emotions, I didn't want to do anything if it wasn't part of the plan for our lives. We prayed for God's direction, and much to our delight, we felt an overwhelming sense that this was what we were supposed to do.

By June, we'd packed up our household effects and returned to Florida. We joked that although we'd had a home in central Florida since 2004, we'd only vacationed in it; we'd never actually lived full-time in the house since we had ping-ponged from one government assignment to another. That lifestyle had required an incredible amount of flexibility because we were in a continuous state of change, adaptation, and assimilation.

Once we were home, I couldn't believe how easy life was. Struggle had been such a big part of my existence, I had forgotten what it was like to fit in. I was used to being the foreigner, the infidel, or the only woman in the room. Now I could assimilate back to life in America and become an active member of my family again. We could celebrate birthdays and holidays together, something I'd missed for much of my adult life.

Finally, we were going to be "normal."

And then . . .

One afternoon while sitting in my living room folding clothes, I began to sing along to worship music. As I did, the following message popped into my head: *Joseph, God's going to use you to help save your people.*

The strange words obviously weren't mine. I had no idea what God was telling us, but the words bubbled up inside of me and felt like they had to come out.

It's really weird to deliver a message that you don't understand, that makes no sense to you. But I couldn't hold it back. The words were meant to be spoken out loud. So I gave voice to the message.

"Joseph, God's going to use you to help save your people."

Joseph turned to look at me and said something like "What?"

I let the words roll off my tongue again. "God's going to use you to help save your people." Then I gave him a look that basically screamed, *I have no idea what I just said or what that means.*

I really didn't.

But we both knew this wasn't a joke. It had to be a "God thing," but we weren't sure what he was directing us to do. We did agree on this: God's call to Joseph felt very personal.

Walking alongside other Middle Eastern believers might be considered part of Joseph's birthright, since his family traces its Christian lineage back to the first few centuries AD. His father was a pastor, and from a young age, Joseph was exposed to his parents' humanitarian and ministry work with orphans and widows. He also learned how difficult it is to serve other people in a country where many such activities are considered illegal.

As a child, he endured taunts and threats from classmates. Later, the Egyptian government made it painfully clear to him that he was not entitled to the same rights as Muslims under Shari'a law.

After graduating high school, Joseph spent a year crisscrossing the United States with nine other international students through a program called Missionaries to America. As a high school senior, he had completed the national exam used to determine students' course of study. Based on his good test scores and English proficiency, Joseph planned to enroll in the country's well-respected College of Tourism when he returned from the tour.

Yet when he and his father attempted to register him for classes, they were told that when he deferred his college entrance by a year, his paperwork had been sent to another university. After going from office to office in multiple institutions and governorates throughout Egypt, they were referred to the Ministry of Education's student placement office in Cairo. Frustrated at the tangled mess, Joseph said to the administrator, "I don't understand what's going on here. Why won't you let me register in any of these universities?" With a grimace, the administrator finally said what no one else would: "You don't understand, *Joseph George Assad*?"

By referencing Joseph's three-part name, which clearly reflects a Christian heritage, the administrator was indirectly informing Joseph and his father that the treatment he was receiving was due to his religious identity.

Joseph pushed back, asking, "Is it because I'm a Christian?"

The unfriendly administrator curtly responded, "Well, I didn't say it; you did."

Desperate to enroll Joseph in university, his parents started looking into private institutions. But even those colleges were unable to obtain the requisite paperwork from Cairo in order to consider his application. The central office from which Joseph and his father received the verbal rejection had stamped Joseph's education file with the words *Gher maqbul,* which means "not to be admitted" or "rejected."

The shock of being denied admission to the university sent Joseph reeling. What had he done to deserve this? What would happen next? Education was everything in Egypt, and without it, he had no future.

The answer came from an unlikely place. A youth pastor in central Florida had met Joseph when he visited her church, and had stayed in touch with him. When she discovered he'd been unable to register at university, she felt compelled to act. She reached out to the president of Palm Beach Atlantic College (now Palm Beach Atlantic University), the school her sons had attended, and explained Joseph's predicament. She included a video she had shot of Joseph telling his story when he was in Florida. She asked the college president a bold question: Would PBA consider giving Joseph a scholarship so he could come to the United States to get his education?

Her entreaty paid off, and Joseph was offered a full-tuition scholarship to attend the college. The youth pastor's church rallied around him too, providing money for airfare, books, and living expenses until Joseph could begin to support himself. He had never forgotten the church's generosity.

Not surprisingly, given his parents' example and the assistance he himself had received, Joseph and I had helped several Middle Eastern

Christians over the years with financial support, educational scholarships, and advice. We'd helped desperate converts find refuge before their families could kill them for "rejecting" Islam. (According to the Pew Research Center, as of 2014, fourteen out of twenty countries in the Middle East and North Africa criminalized apostasy, or abandoning one's faith.[1] Eighty-eight percent of Muslims in Egypt and 62 percent of Muslims in Pakistan supported the death penalty for people who leave Islam. A majority of Muslims in Malaysia, Jordan, and the Palestinian territories share this view.[2])

We also tried to help Christians who were under pressure to become Muslims. In one case, Muslim neighbors were trying to force a Christian family to convert to Islam. When the family refused, the neighbors beat the husband to death. We provided financial support to the mother and her four children, who were taken in and protected by a local Christian ministry.

Joseph and I had promoted philanthropy that advanced the legal, cultural, and economic positions of Christian minorities in the Muslim world. We'd designed microeconomic projects to promote food security and economic stability among Christian farmers and agriculturists in North Africa. But none of these projects were on the scale that the message I'd received seemed to suggest. We'd just have to wait and see what God had in mind for us. As it turned out, we didn't have to wait long.

About a month after returning to Florida, I felt a strong urge for Joseph to contact a friend with whom he had worked in the human rights and religious freedom sector. He had kept in occasional contact with her through the years.

Weeks went by and we got busy. Joseph forgot to call. Yet the "feeling" that we needed to make this connection grew stronger each time it popped into my head. It got to the point that it was driving me a little batty. I told him, "Please, Joseph, contact your friend. You *need* to speak with her now."

Joseph finally sent her an e-mail in mid-July. We quickly discovered that the urgency I felt to make this connection must have been spurred on by the Holy Spirit.

She responded to Joseph, saying, "You could not have contacted me at a more critical time." She had just been brought into a special project by Hollywood producer Mark Burnett. Mark had been seeking ways that he and his wife, actress and producer Roma Downey, could support persecuted Christians in the Middle East. They began by funding projects to support families displaced by ISIS. But soon it came to their attention that some Iraqi Christians felt they could no longer remain in the Middle East. Several groups asked for help finding countries willing to give them refuge from the genocide.

Mark and Roma assembled a small team to support this work. They didn't create a company or an NGO; it was simply an ad hoc group of people with shared passions and "get it done" attitudes, people specializing in advocacy, education, marketing, and fund-raising.

Mark's goal was to airlift groups of Syrian and Iraqi Christians away from ISIS-controlled territory. It was a bold idea, a daunting task. But taking on enormous challenges is nothing new for Mark and Roma.

Mark is a veteran risk taker. He came to the United States from Britain at the age of twenty-two, and after scaling one challenge after the other, he became the insanely successful producer of *Survivor*, *The Voice*, *Shark Tank*, and *Celebrity Apprentice*. Acknowledging that moving groups of Christians out of a war zone was no easy task, Mark said that he'd never stepped into any of his projects knowing with 100 percent certainty how it would all work out. But that never stopped him from moving forward when he had an instinct to do so.

Given the logistical and security challenges involved in such an operation, the group needed someone extremely familiar with the region, someone who knew how to navigate the complexities of the Middle East. That's where we came in.

After speaking with Joseph, Mark asked him to manage the evacuation. He and Roma generously committed the funds to make this effort possible.

Joseph was more than happy to forgo other job opportunities because this wasn't a job to him—it was deeply personal. It was a matter of the heart. God was allowing Joseph to use his background and expertise to help other persecuted Christians find places of refuge, just as the church had done for him so many years ago.

Eager to contribute in any way I could, I volunteered to help Joseph conceptualize the project and plot a way forward. It was not going to be easy. If ever there were a good time to find countries willing to take persecuted Christians, this was definitely not it.

It was the summer of the great migration. ISIS had swept through Syria and was pushing east into Iraq. After taking Mosul in June 2014, they turned their attention to Christian villages southeast of the city. They began to threaten the residents of the Hamdaniyah district, which included Qaraqosh and other small villages, warning them that they would soon overrun the Christian-majority region. In an attempt to starve the inhabitants out, ISIS initiated a blockade of vital supplies by setting up checkpoints on the outskirts of the city. They cut off the flow of water, fuel, and electricity and threatened Muslim neighbors not to do business with the Christians.

As time progressed, the Christians felt a building sense of fear and unease, wondering when their rations would run out. They watched ISIS destroy neighboring Yazidi towns and speculated when they also would be attacked. Meanwhile, the villagers survived on nonpotable water, which caused the spread of skin rashes and disease. Without fuel, cars and other transportation became useless, making it difficult for residents to obtain supplies, go to work, and function as they had before. They struggled to survive.

Then on August 6, 2014, ISIS initiated a full-on assault and began shelling Qaraqosh. That day, a rocket killed two children and one adult in the community. After having held ISIS at bay for so long, the Peshmerga (Kurdish forces) commander assigned to Qaraqosh informed the town's archbishop that Kurdish forces were abandoning their posts. They couldn't (or wouldn't) hold ISIS back any longer.

That was the moment when church officials made a most painful decision. The church bells rang out, the agreed-upon signal indicating that ISIS was coming and it was time to leave. Those who had access to telephones spread the word quickly, and others went door-to-door to be sure everyone had gotten the message. Within the space of a few hours, the panicked residents had packed as many family members as they could into every working vehicle and fled toward the city of Erbil.

Almost all of the Christians fled that evening, many with just the clothes on their backs, their identification documents, and a handful of prized possessions such as the family Bible. Against the protestations of family members, a few older residents stayed behind, mostly parents and grandparents in their eighties and nineties who couldn't bear to leave their ancestral home. Many were never heard from again.

Because so many people fled Qaraqosh and other small villages at the same time, the short trip to the Kurdistan region became a long, hot journey. The roads were so clogged that the one-hour drive took up to twelve hours. Many families had to complete the last few miles of the journey on foot because the Peshmerga closed the checkpoints and blocked vehicles from entering the city.

Overnight, a humanitarian crisis of epic proportions was thrust unexpectedly on churches, NGOs, and Kurdish authorities. Erbil overflowed with people in need of basic provisions such as food, water, and toilet facilities. Many made their way to local churches to seek assistance. They claimed little patches of space on the ground, on sidewalks, and in abandoned buildings, as well as in and around church sanctuaries.

In the midst of all the chaos, hundreds of displaced families huddled in the courtyard of Mar Elia Church in Ankawa, a north-western suburb of Erbil.

Like many of the people who flocked to his sanctuary that summer, Father Douglas al-Bazi understood what it meant to stare death in the face, to be tortured for one's faith.

In November 2006, when Father Douglas was serving as the vicar of a Chaldean Catholic church in Baghdad, he was kidnapped by members of a Shi'a militia. Held for nine days, he endured beatings and the stress associated with not knowing whether he would live through the experience. Father Douglas was well aware that most people did not survive kidnappings—even when their family or church members paid a ransom.

After withholding water from him for four days, his captors placed a bottle of water in front of the parched priest and said, "Just say the *shahada* and it will all go away." (The shahada is the Islamic confession of faith, which states, "There is no God but Allah, and Mohammed is his Messenger.") Father Douglas refused.

His persecutors continued to torture and taunt him. They broke his nose, knocked out his teeth with a hammer, and fractured his vertebrae. Father Douglas woke up each morning wondering whether that would be the day he died.

Even though his captors threatened to cut his head off and replace it with a dog's head, the symbol of an infidel, he refused to convert.

Then, with a boldness that I cannot imagine, Father Douglas told the militants, "Go ahead and just kill me now, but at least tell my congregation I'm dead, so they don't have to wonder."

Weirdly enough, in between the abuse meted out to him each evening, his captors would ask for his advice on personal matters, and even—at times—forgiveness for their actions.

Much to his surprise, Father Douglas was eventually released after a ransom was paid. But that wasn't the end of it. Father Douglas endured yet another kidnapping and release, as well as an attack on his church, where he was shot with an AK-47. In fact, the bullet is still lodged in his leg.

Prior to the war, more than two thousand families belonged to the Baghdad-based parish, and by 2013, fewer than three hundred families were left.

Having lost so much of the community he served in Baghdad, Father Douglas left the capital in July 2013, relocating to Erbil, where he was placed in charge of the Mar Elia Church.

Now within the span of a couple of days (August 6 and 7, 2014), approximately two hundred thousand Christians from the Nineveh plains had fled to Erbil to escape the clutches of ISIS. Overnight, Father Douglas's sanctuary and its dirt compound filled up with hundreds of traumatized men, women, and children. They were in shock and unable to process the enormity of what had just occurred, but Father Douglas understood. He tended to their physical needs, he tended to their spiritual needs, and he tended to their emotional needs. He provided leadership at the most critical time, when these people were raw, depressed, and extremely vulnerable.

As time progressed and the IDPs (internally displaced persons) were unable to return to their homes, Father Douglas tried to give them hope. He didn't speak of faith and redemption from an empty space, but from a place of knowing. He didn't speak of forgiveness in theory, but after having repeatedly wrestled with the notion and having found the strength to express it to his tormentors. He didn't speak of courage and endurance as popular Christian and humanistic concepts, but as principles that he had been able to manifest in the darkest of hours.

God doesn't thrust afflictions upon us, *but* when they occur, he uses them to make us stronger and more effective than before. God knows that we can minister in more real and authentic ways when we've been there . . . when we've struggled through similar situations. Because we can speak from firsthand experience, our words carry more power, our actions more meaning. That is why God does not require perfection. That is why wounded people serve so well as his hands and his feet. Ministry is giving others what you yourself needed and received.

Father Douglas knew well the struggles of these persecuted Christians. He had personally experienced the worst kind of persecution, having stared death in the face time after time. But against all odds, he lived. God had preserved his life. Now it was clear why.

When Joseph's friend heard about the situation at Mar Elia, she reached out to Burnett, who in turn reached out to Joseph. Within a matter of days, the mission began to take shape. The problem was simple, yet complex. We had to find a way to get the displaced Christians out of Erbil and into a safe country. Of course, given the current immigration crisis, that was going to be easier said than done.

Desperate people from Africa, the Middle East, and Asia had been pushing onto the shores of Europe, pouring over its borders from every direction, including the sea. The crisis hit a fever pitch in 2015, when more than a million migrants flooded into Europe. In comparison, only 280,000 people had crossed illegally into Europe in 2014.

The human tidal wave of migration was the result of two separate factors. The first was a significant psychological shift in which victims of the conflict realized they could not go back to their homes or continue to live in such desperate circumstances. They had slowly come to appreciate the intractable nature of the conflicts. Desperate Syrian families had prayed that the war would subside. That didn't happen. Iraqis who fled the clutches of ISIS when terrorists took over Mosul and the Nineveh plains had held out hope that the international community would push ISIS back out of the villages or out of Iraq. But that didn't happen either.

The status of both conflicts had not changed, and nothing on the horizon suggested that they were anywhere closer to resolution. Refugees and IDPs became less and less hopeful that they would be able to return to their homes or resume their former lives. With heavy hearts, they began to search for a brighter future elsewhere.

The second major factor responsible for pushing a million people into Europe was the increased presence and activity of people smugglers. These heartless and greedy "fixers" became quite proficient at funneling desperate refugees onto the continent from North Africa, the Middle East, and Asia.

Unfortunately, affected countries had not considered solutions for stemming the illegal flow before refugees arrived on the shores of a woefully unprepared Europe. The human smuggling pipelines required the kind of strategic response we tend to reserve for national security and terrorism issues.

Fortunately, Joseph and I had experience in both—not that that made our work any easier. In addition to the fact that countries around the world were overwhelmed with asylum seekers, finding countries willing to take *Christians* posed a significant bureaucratic challenge as well.

Most countries' immigration policies are tied to the process set forth by the United Nations High Commissioner for Refugees (UNHCR). We, however, would not be working through the UNHCR or utilizing that process for several reasons.

The first was due to the timing. The UNHCR process takes many years to accomplish. After UNHCR registers and prioritizes refugee applicants, receiving countries have to complete their own internal administrative processes and vetting procedures. Waiting five years for resettlement is not unusual, if candidates are resettled at all. In fact, only a small percentage of refugees and asylum seekers are resettled globally. For example, in 2014 alone, 866,000 asylum applications were submitted to the UNHCR.[3] Out of those, 103,890 were submitted by the UNHCR to potential receiving countries, resulting in the resettlement of a total of 73,331 individuals.[4] That's less than 10 percent.

Second, the UNHCR process does not service IDPs. In order to seek resettlement in a new country through UNHCR, people must first leave their country of origin and become refugees instead of IDPs. This puts IDPs in a tough spot because many of them live in camps within their own country but are just as desperate as those classified as refugees.

The other significant reason that we did not want to utilize the UNHCR process was because most Christians do not seek refuge in UNHCR camps. Far from being filled with only innocent victims, many camps are a microcosm of the conflicts from which they emerge. Some unwittingly house former fighters, insurgents, and even members of terrorist groups, who carry out anti-Christian activities and other crimes in the camps. Because of this underreported and incredibly harsh reality, Christians, Yazidis, and other non-Muslim minorities mostly choose not to go through the UNHCR process to avoid facing the same persecution from which they just fled.

Opting to go around the UNHCR process meant that the responsibility fell solely on us, not only to find a country willing to accept the Mar Elia refugees, but to provide solid assurance to those countries that none of the refugees we evacuated were in fact ISIS members or insurgents perpetrating a ruse to gain access to their countries.

It was a formidable undertaking, but given that we had spent the past fifteen years determining the authenticity of sources in terrorist-ridden countries, we had the perfect backgrounds for it. Simply put, it was a mission Joseph and I had been preparing for our entire lives.

CHAPTER 17

BACK TO IRAQ

Our first task was to find a host nation that would be willing to accept the asylum seekers from Mar Elia. Of course, given the current political climate, ours wasn't the most popular cause to bring before world leaders. We knew the odds were against us.

Because we were intimately aware of their immigration policies, we immediately crossed off several potential countries, including the United States. This was hard to accept—especially because we were keenly aware that there were many Americans who were more than willing to open their doors, their hearts, and their wallets to help this group. It's not as though we would be asking the US government to give the Iraqis special treatment or to add more people to the welfare rolls. However, we knew that our government clung to the falsity that Christians in the Middle East were honored as "People of the Book" (as they are referred to in the Qur'an). Therefore, the administration reasoned that Christians could not be experiencing difficulty, persecution, or genocide.[1] As much as it broke our hearts, we removed the United States from the list and continued to look elsewhere.

Then on August 19, as Joseph and I were sitting in the kitchen having coffee and reading the paper, Joseph stumbled across an article in the *Washington Post* that said Slovakia was willing to take in two hundred Syrian refugees, but . . . they *had* to be Christian.[2]

It was a sign from God.

"That's where we need to go," Joseph exclaimed. "Slovakia!"

After skimming the article over his shoulder, I sat down across from him. "Yes! That's exactly what we need to do! Now who do we know in Slovakia?"

Crickets chirped in the background as we sat in silence, both of us aware that we had absolutely no contacts or experience there. We quietly sipped our coffee and pondered which of our acquaintances might have a contact in this tiny Eastern European country. A few minutes later, it hit me.

"I know! Aron—Aron Shaviv—he's done some senior-level consulting work in Slovakia, right?"

"Yes, Aron!" Joseph beamed. "That's right. I think he *does* have some good contacts there."

"Can you call him? E-mail him? See if he can help?" I was on a roll. "We need to get in at a very senior level, like the president, prime minister, or minister of interior."

Within fifteen minutes, Joseph had reached Aron, who confirmed that he did, in fact, have good connections in Slovakia and could probably help us out. As anticipated, Aron was a godsend and *exactly* what we needed in that very moment. But this was just the first step. We still had so much work to do to move the initiative forward.

Because we had so much experience with government bureaucracies, we knew that the decision to work outside the UNHCR process would require a top-down approach. We needed to make our plea to the most senior government officials we could get in front of. Furthermore, we'd need to help them figure out how to organize such a project and how to work their own bureaucracies—provided they were amenable to our cause.

Joseph and I knew that getting the Slovakian officials to reach such a decision would not be easy or quick. Political leadership would need to obtain the support of their security and intelligence agencies. We knew firsthand how slow and burdensome the coordination process was when multiple government agencies were involved in a task. But if we could prove, in the very beginning, that we were trustworthy and capable of ensuring that none of the people we were helping were members of insurgent or terrorist groups, then this would significantly speed up the logistics and cut down on any potential intragovernment political squabbling.

We quickly discovered how integral our experience was going to be in figuring out how to make this work. A decision to take a group of Christians wouldn't be made by one person, but through the buy-in of multiple actors throughout the government.

To get the ball rolling, we decided to front-load our communications with information that would immediately address the concerns of a wide variety of agencies. Instead of focusing on the group of Iraqi IDPs, we decided we would first establish our bona fides as former US government officials and then explain the comprehensive steps we planned to take to identify and vet the applicants.

If we were going to have any chance of convincing the Slovakian government (or any other government, for that matter) to accept these families, they would have to be comfortable that any asylum candidates we put forward would not pose a security threat to their country. There was only one way we could make this promise: We would have to go to Iraq.

We would need to meet with, vet, and gather documentation for each of the asylum candidates individually. This way, we could give potential governments very specific information about the people we wanted to help. We wanted to be able to speak authoritatively to the various officials who would most certainly ask questions about the vetting process as well as the stories of the people we were representing.

While Joseph made travel plans, I reviewed the UNHCR registration applications and asylum process. We wanted our system to be as airtight as possible. No method is perfect, of course, but if we were putting our names and reputations behind the effort, we wanted ours to be as foolproof as we could make it. And it was. By applying vetting strategy and tools that we'd used as intelligence officers in the CIA, Joseph and I came up with a vetting program that was even stronger and more comprehensive than anything used by the UNHCR or the United States.

First, every Iraqi applicant over the age of eighteen would fill out the comprehensive application forms we'd designed, which requested full biographical details, work experience, and education. Second, each applicant would need to provide as many identity documents as possible. Third, we would work to confirm that the documents we collected were valid. This effort included reviewing papers, comparing them with others from the same issuing authority, and, when possible, checking with the issuing authority to confirm their authenticity.

Knowing how important documentation is in the Arab world and the care and attention people give to those documents, we knew that most people would have carried the papers with them when fleeing their homes—even those who left in a hurry. That's why when many arriving refugees told European officials that they had no documentation, it should have been an immediate red flag. Birth documents, identity cards, driver's licenses, and religious certificates are even more essential to everyday life in the Middle East than they are in the United States. So if people pitched their docs, that meant that either they were legitimately running from ISIS (and should have a good story to tell to explain the lack of documentation) or they were trying to hide something.

Last but not least, we planned to interview each family, asking about their identities, backgrounds, job history, educational level, and reasons for wanting to leave Iraq. As seasoned intelligence officers, we knew how to identify verbal and nonverbal responses that required additional attention and investigation, and because we were so familiar with the culture, we'd recognize whether the stories we were being told were logical and fit stories from other sources. In short, we could easily figure out whether the answers were culturally, historically, and geographically accurate.

Once our plan was in place and our flights booked, Joseph and I set off for Erbil in September.

I have to admit, I *never* imagined I'd be returning to Iraq. When we finished our respective tours and left the country back in 2007, I was so relieved to get on that plane—to leave the killing fields—I vowed I'd never go back. But as I said earlier, never say never.

Complicating matters even further, we knew that this time around, we would be significant targets for many of the groups we had worked against while in Baghdad, including AQI and ISIS. More important, we were concerned about being targeted by Iranian-backed militant groups and their associated government ministries. We were almost certainly on a list of US government employees who had served in the war zone, and there was no doubt we remained on an Iranian intelligence target list. Just as we assumed that ISIS had sympathizers and even operatives in Kurdistan, so did Iran, and they were a much bigger threat to us than ISIS at that time. We were concerned about being thrown into the back of a car or stuffed in a trunk and being driven across the Iranian border, never to be heard from again. The Iranian regime has targeted some of its enemies in this way, kidnapping them out of neighboring countries.

We decided to return to Iraq anyway. We needed to be aware of our surroundings and take appropriate precautions, but how could we not go? Everything we had done up to this point in our lives had led us to this moment. For years, I had been asking God what it all was for—the hardship, the frustration, the danger, the separation from family and friends—and now he had answered. This is what we had been training for. This is what we had been called to do.

Mar Elia Chaldean Catholic Church served as the temporary home of 560 Iraqis, and between September 6 and 12, Joseph and I interviewed the four hundred IDPs there who wanted to seek asylum in another country. The single-wide trailer that had served as a library and occasional classroom to the camp's children had been transformed into a makeshift interview room, as had Father Douglas's small office. Books, crayons, and small toys lay next to piles of applications. We interviewed small families, big families, and everything in between. We collected a huge amount of documentation for each person, and by the end of our trip, we had enough paperwork to fill a suitcase.

To say that it was exhausting is an understatement. We worked from about nine in the morning until about nine at night, taking a two-hour break for lunch. It was an enormous undertaking, requiring a team of ten young people to help candidates fill out extensive application forms, make copies of their documents, take photographs of each applicant as well as their larger family grouping, and schedule the interviews.

And since my Arabic is not sufficient to capture the details of such important discussions, several people on the team served as Arabic and Aramaic translators for me. We could not have accomplished this task without the tireless efforts of every person involved, as well as Father Douglas's assistants, who kept the interview line filled with anxious hopefuls.

The interviews were complicated and required a great deal of energy because we had a lot of information to cover. We explained to the IDPs that we represented a group of Americans who cared deeply about them and wanted to help them find a place of refuge, if that was what they wanted. We were forthright and honest, making clear that we had not identified any countries, we couldn't promise anything, and that if we did find a place, it would be because God opened the door. The last thing we wanted to do to people who had lost their homes and livelihood was to make empty promises or get their hopes too high.

Knowing how difficult it would be for these people to leave their home country and resettle in a new place, we repeatedly warned them, "It doesn't matter what you are running from. Even if you are fleeing ISIS, the most difficult thing in the world is learning to live in a new country. It will require great struggle and sacrifice, and it might even be more difficult than remaining here in Iraq."

They looked at us like we were crazy. They could not comprehend how difficult it would be to establish new lives elsewhere, but we had to tell them anyway.

Then, we asked them to explain to us, in detail, why they wanted to leave Iraq. Their stories were heartbreaking. The majority of the IDPs were from Hamdaniyah, located near Mosul in northern Iraq. Hamdaniyah is about twenty miles southeast of the city of Mosul and thirty-seven miles west of Erbil, close to the ancient Assyrian cities of Nimrud and Nineveh. The vast majority of its inhabitants were ethnically Assyrians, people who still speak Aramaic, the language of Jesus. They have carried the torch of the Christian faith through the ages, never imagining they'd one day be displaced from their homeland.

After arriving in Erbil, many of them had received death threats via phone calls and text messages. The callers demanded that the Christian families return to their homes and said that they had to convert or their spouses and children would be beheaded. The most disconcerting part of it was that the terrorists mentioned family members by name. It was clear that many of those threats were issued while the terrorists were in the Christians' homes riffling through documents bearing the families' personal information: names, phone numbers, and other personal data.

Other IDPs were contacted by Muslim neighbors who said that they should pay the *jizya* (tax) if they wished to return to their already looted homes and businesses. Other callers gave this warning: "If you return to Hamdaniyah and you do not convert, we will burn your house to the ground—with you and your whole family inside of it."

This is the story we heard repeatedly from the families we interviewed. However, the last interview we conducted on the evening of September 11 was one that I'll never forget. It was the interview that reminded us of the staggering losses these people had experienced, the human toll of ISIS's violence and destruction.

With heads hanging down and expressions of profound pain on their faces, a husband and wife, holding tightly to their two children, told us their story.

Once church leadership gave the signal to leave the city, they— like everyone else—gathered their extended family members together, preparing to leave as quickly as possible. In the confusion, they were separated from the wife's sister and brother-in-law, who were in a separate vehicle. The sister and her husband were unsure which path to take out of town and must have taken a wrong turn. That was the last time this family saw them, because the next thing they found out was that ISIS had captured the couple.

ISIS called the family and informed them that they had the sister. They demanded $2,500 for her release. The family paid the ransom but never received any instructions about how to retrieve the young woman. They were soon contacted again, allegedly by the kidnappers, who now demanded $30,000. The family had nowhere near the resources to provide such a sum, so they approached their bishop and asked for help.

Even though it was against church policy, religious leaders agreed to provide the funds to buy back the sister. They paid the first $15,000 and told the kidnappers they would provide the remaining amount upon delivery of the sister to her family. The money was taken, but the sister was never released.

Tears trickled down from the wife's eyes as she told this painful story, while rocking her sleeping baby on the couch in front of us.

She and her husband think that her sister became an ISIS bride (sex slave). I could not imagine carrying on with life, knowing the hell she was enduring. I didn't know how I could go on living if I knew my sister were in such circumstances, but I doubt this family felt any differently. They were probably taking one day at a time, doing their best to carry on despite the extreme pain of this life-altering tragedy.

When we inquired about their brother-in-law, the room became very quiet. Several painful seconds went by, until the husband explained that their brother-in-law had worked for Coalition Forces during the war and it was likely that ISIS learned this early on in the kidnapping. He added for clarification, "We don't think he's here any longer." Our hearts dropped. We understood what he was suggesting.

As if they hadn't suffered enough, the family mentioned that one of their young cousins had also been taken captive by ISIS during the takeover—she was only fourteen. The family had been repeatedly told that she was also married off to an ISIS fighter, as a spoil of war.

We spoke with another gentleman, Yohanna (John), a journalist who lived with his wife and two children in Mosul. When ISIS spilled over the Syrian border and took control of Mosul, they threatened all of the journalists, demanding that they write and release only ISIS-approved stories. Any departure from these narratives would cost them their lives. Indeed, scores of journalists were killed after they secretly passed on information to Reuters or other news agencies and were somehow identified as the sources.

After being warned by ISIS over his cell phone that he was next on the hit list and that the group planned to slit the throats of his two children, Yohanna and his family fled Mosul for a majority-Christian village east of the city. They found refuge there for a short period of time before ISIS invaded those villages, sending them packing once again.

When Yohanna related his story, he didn't do so with the affect of a confident journalist. Rather, he sat in front of us with his six-year-old daughter on his lap and his head hung low. He spoke softly, almost in whispers, as a man who had been repeatedly beaten down, as a man overcome with frustration that he could not do more for his family, that he could not shield them from this tragedy.

Because he did not come off as poised or self-assured, I wondered if he really was a journalist. Then he pulled out a folder that contained extensive credentials and copies of several of his articles.

As we thumbed through the remnants of his former life, we commented on how impressed we were by the file. I think he needed to hear that.

Yohanna had lost his job and his livelihood, and his family had now been displaced twice by terrorists. Sitting in front of us was a man emptied of life and expression, emasculated by being unable to provide for the physical, emotional, and mental well-being of his family.

The eyes are the window to the soul, and Yohanna's eyes revealed a deep well of sadness. They lacked any sparkle; they lacked life. Instead, they reflected the scars of repeated emotional trauma that had emptied them of hope.

Several hours after reading the sorrow in Yohanna's face, I was taken aback by the cold look of another man—Hamad, the fiancé of Danial's daughter, Miriam.

CHAPTER 18

DECISION TIME

After a brief glance, Hamad wouldn't look me or Joseph in the eyes again.

When he entered the trailer with Miriam, he gave us weak handshakes and quickly sat down. Given the trauma so many men had been through, his slouched posture and downcast eyes weren't an immediate cause for alarm. But it was clear that he didn't want to be there. Unlike all of the nervous applicants who had actively engaged with the people they hoped could help them escape such desperate circumstances, Hamad seemed almost bored. That made no sense. *If he is risking so much, why does he seem so blasé about meeting with us and having this conversation?*

"As I'm sure Miriam told you," I began, "when we met with her family today, she asked that you be added to the list with them since you are a recent convert to Christianity. We need to speak personally with each person interested in leaving Iraq, so we thank you for coming in."

He gave barely a grunt, so I continued.

"So, Hamad, why did you convert?"

"Ah, well . . . I always had leanings toward Christianity, and one day I just decided that since I lean more toward Christianity than Islam, I should just convert."

Wait . . . wait . . . wait. That makes no sense! In a culture where rejecting Islam is punishable by death, that was a very unimpressive justification for conversion. This is not a wishy-washy choice or one that's made haphazardly. It is a life-and-death decision.

Joseph and I exchanged a look. *Is this guy kidding?*

Joseph pressed for more details, and Hamad gave him the name of the priest he said had baptized him. Next, we asked Hamad to tell us more about donating his kidney, and he pulled up his shirt to show us a long scar he said he'd gotten from the surgery.

Something still seemed off.

"Tell me, Hamad, what you think of Jesus," I asked.

Hamad's body language immediately changed. As he shifted in his seat, his knee began bouncing up and down. Seemingly unsure of what to say, Hamad paused for several seconds and then offered, "Well, Jesus was a good man. I really respect him."

Boom. There it is. This man was no convert. Muslims respect Jesus as a man and as a prophet, but if you have converted to Christianity, Jesus is no longer just a man; he is your Savior. He is the reason why you are willing to put your life on the line. Hamad was using the language of a Muslim—*not* a convert.

Joseph moved closer to Hamad, looked him straight in the eyes and, using religious terminology only a true Christian convert would understand, asked, "Hamad, what did Jesus do for you on the cross?"

At that, Hamad sat up straight in his seat and pushed his chair back from us. His eyes glossed over and his entire countenance changed. It was almost as though he had been taken over by something—or *someone*—beyond his control. It was downright creepy.

Next to him, a noticeably anxious Miriam tugged at his sleeve. "Well, Hamad, answer him!"

Silence. He did not so much as blink.

Suddenly, a strange, highly inappropriate smirk began to spread over Hamad's face. I felt a chill run down my spine.

"Hamad, answer him!" urged Miriam.

He just sat there, motionless, glaring at Joseph, seeming not even to breathe.

"Hamad," a near-hysterical Miriam slapped him on the arm and pleaded, "why can't you answer the question? Hamad? Hamad! . . . *Hamad*!"

Despite Miriam's pleas, Hamad could not or would not address this question. That was it. The meeting was over. The interview had confirmed what Joseph and I intuitively believed was going on— Hamad was not telling the truth about his conversion or the reason he wanted to leave Iraq. He was using this poor girl. Hamad could not be trusted.

By the next day, Joseph was able to confirm that the priest who allegedly baptized Hamad never had. Furthermore, Hamad could not prove that he had ever given a kidney or any money to ISIS. We learned, however, that he had been in a bad car accident; the scar on his abdomen was a result of injuries he'd sustained when his car rolled over.

The next time Joseph met with Miriam, he informed her, "I hope you can understand what's been happening here. Hamad has been trying to take advantage of you. He is no good. You and your parents must know that Hamad does not have your best interests in mind and has been lying to you about the kidney, the ISIS ransom, and his conversion. I suggest you break off the engagement and stay as far away from him as possible."

Was Hamad simply a liar who wanted asylum abroad for economic reasons . . . or had we uncovered the one extremist in the group posing as a Christian convert?

Either way, Joseph and I had done our job.

Hamad was off the list.

E ven though Father Douglas and his staff tried to keep our project on the down low and asked those we interviewed not to tell other people about the project, word spread like wildfire all over Ankawa. Consequently, the church was bombarded with hundreds of people asking to get on the list to be resettled in another country.

We often felt like we were in charge of the *Titanic* lifeboats, being asked by desperate people in the sinking ship to let them climb in—panicked that they would be left behind. Except we weren't even sure we had a lifeboat. It was a horrible position to be in.

One evening Father Douglas brought us into his office and told us about another family who wanted to meet us. We went out into the reception area, and there stood a mother and her two daughters, fourteen and twelve. The surprisingly young mother said, "Please, I need your help." She took the hand of her older daughter and pressed her toward us, saying, "My daughter is blind. She needs an eye surgery. Please, please help us."

My eyes filled with tears. I hugged the beautiful girl and then held on to her outstretched hands.

The young mother continued. "We are so desperate in the other camp. It's not good there. We share space with another family, only separated by a sheet to give us privacy. But the other family has two teenage sons, and my husband is no longer in the picture. He doesn't care about us, so we're alone. And we feel very vulnerable. And I worry about my daughters in the camp. I worry about rape and I worry about their safety. I worry about their futures. I want them to be able to finish school, go to college. But nothing, nothing can happen for my daughter if she's blind. Please, can you help us?"

I had been able to control myself all week, strongly focused on the tasks we had to accomplish. But for some reason, I could not do so at that moment. Tears streamed down my face. It was as if the emotions of the entire week were threatening to burst forth, like a dam that could no longer hold back the flood. How we wished we could bring them back to America with us. How we wished we had the time and resources to secure medical treatment and make their lives so much brighter and better than they were now. But we didn't know how to do that.

When Joseph asked her about her family circumstances, the mother explained, "My husband and I are not divorced. He is violent and abusive, but every time I have inquired about obtaining a divorce, I am told I cannot. As you know, it is hard for women to obtain such things in Iraq. I have begged my husband to let us go, but he refuses." Without her husband's support, this woman would have a very difficult time gaining additional assistance for herself and her daughters.

Joseph told the woman that we weren't sure we could help, but we could carefully consider the case. At a minimum, he told her we would share her story with others, in hope that we could find some way to assist her.

I moved forward to give her a tight hug. She held on to me, crying in my arms, a woman overwhelmed by the worst of what life has to offer. It seemed she was doing her best, finding her way over to Mar Elia Church to plead her case to the foreigners. I imagined that had I been in her position, I would have done the same thing.

We felt so guilty going back to our hotel that night. We weren't staying in a five-star hotel, but we had privacy, running water, a bed. Overall, we had a great life. We had an amazing and comfortable home. We had everything and more than we would ever need. But there was nothing we could do for that family at that moment. Nothing. And we could not have felt worse.

After fitting in as many interviews as we possibly could, Joseph and I departed Erbil for Dubai. From there, I was to catch a flight back to the United States, while Joseph continued on to Slovakia and another country to meet with government representatives and church officials. Aron had set up meetings with Ministry of Interior representatives to explore whether either country might be amenable to accepting IDPs from Father Douglas's camp.

Instead of hauling the suitcase full of applications home to continue the process of checking documentation, devising the best way to organize the files, matching photographs with applications, scanning the paperwork, and organizing the electronic version of the physical files, Joseph decided to take the documents with him to Europe. He thought that by showing the government officials the people's original photographs and documents, he could quickly move the discussion out of the theoretical realm. Numbers and statistics mean so little, but seeing the Iraqis' pictures and connecting them with real stories . . . that would be much harder to downplay or ignore.

Given its contents, I was concerned about surrendering control of the suitcase to the airlines as checked baggage. That blue suitcase held documentation representing the lives of four hundred precious people and a week's worth of sweat and toil by a large team. We could not afford to lose it or have it damaged in any way.

So I did something a little unconventional. I placed my hands on the bag, lifted my eyes to heaven, and said, "Lord, please send your angels to protect this bag, to ensure it gets where it needs to go."

The next day, I took the fifteen-hour flight back to the United States and tried to recover from the intensity of that trip, while Joseph continued on to Europe. Since Joseph had all the paperwork with him, I didn't know what to do with myself. I spent a great deal of time in prayer. For some people, prayer seems like a chore, but I love to pray. I love the intimacy of talking to God, so that's what I did.

Over the next few days, I felt a sweeping power wash over me when I prayed for the persecuted Christians and asked for wisdom and guidance as we moved forward. As I meditated on God and the grand project set before us, I felt overcome with faith for the outcome.

That week, Hillsong United's "Oceans (Where Feet May Fail)" became my special prayer for everything related to the project.

As I prayed that the Spirit would "lead me where my trust is without borders,"[1] I was reminded of God's sovereignty over every nation—and the life of every person we'd interviewed. The words of that song represent the prayer of my life—asking God for the grace to move forward in spite of my fears and misgivings, to have the courage to walk into the waves, no matter how high or how threatening they may appear. Songs like this focused my mind on what really mattered, and this, in turn, increased my faith as I prayed over the lives of the people we were trying to help.

Meanwhile, on the other side of the ocean, Joseph and the suitcase had arrived safely at their destination after a long flight to Vienna, Austria, and a taxi ride to Bratislava, Slovakia. When Joseph reached the location of his first meeting, he had to drag that enormous blue suitcase up two flights of stairs. Several Slovak officials tried to save him from the strain, asking, "Can I store that for you down here on the first floor? There's no need for you to take your luggage with you all the way up to the conference room."

"No, thank you," he responded politely. "I need it with me."

It looked more than a little strange for Joseph to haul around a piece of luggage to senior-level meetings. But there was a method to his madness, so he awkwardly pulled the bag into the room and carefully placed it near his chair.

After general introductions, Joseph revealed key pieces of his background, focusing on the fact that he himself had been a persecuted Christian from the Middle East who was denied an education in his native land. He said that he had been extremely fortunate to have been welcomed into the United States, where he obtained his education, and then later to have acquired citizenship there. He further explained that not only had he thrived in the United States, he had had the privilege of serving his country as a counterterrorism officer. After sharing these personal details, Joseph carefully laid out his role in the project, describing all those involved and their efforts to identify safe havens for persecuted Iraqi and Syrian Christians.

Joseph was quite shocked at what came next. The officials

explained that his visit was well timed. Two months prior to this meeting, the Slovak government had told the office that handled asylum and immigration cases, the Office of Migration, to start preparing to receive Christians from the Middle East. They had even established an NGO to support the project. They had only one major issue—two months had gone by, and they had not identified one single Christian to help.

Joseph smiled, placed his hand on the suitcase, and said, "Well, I've got your Christians right here."

They glanced at him and then at the mysterious suitcase with puzzled looks, and he continued.

"I just came from Iraq. My wife, Michele, and I interviewed, photographed, and gathered documentation for about forty extended families and four hundred people total. They see no future for themselves in Iraq and want to seek asylum abroad." He explained that they had found a temporary safe haven in the courtyard at Mar Elia Chaldean Catholic Church.

As Joseph unzipped the bag and took out a folder to show government officials the work we'd just completed, they got out of their seats and walked over to the suitcase. They hovered over him to get a closer look at what was in the bag. As the group thumbed through the files, they were amazed to see how much documentation we had for each person and each family.

"This took you only a week?" they asked, flabbergasted.

"Yes," Joseph replied. "It was a long week, but we did it."

They were at a complete loss.

"What you just did in a week would have taken us about a year to accomplish."

That was the point. We knew how long it would take for governments to do all of this. They'd need numerous meetings to decide which refugee group to work with, which applications to use, and the best methodology for interviews. Then, after deciding which employees would help applicants complete the applications, conduct interviews, and process all the data, they would have to plan a trip to Iraq. In the best-case scenario, this process could take up to a year. Joseph and I were trying to make it as easy as possible for a government to work with our group. We were happy to do all of the legwork if it meant speeding up their decision-making process.

Our unique approach, combined with our intimate understanding of internal government politics and procedures, was what separated our effort from all the other organizations looking to resettle persecuted Christians, Yazidis, and other desperate IDPs.

The truth is, most well-intentioned groups get tripped up because they work with only one government agency while ignoring other key decision makers such as the security and intelligence services. This shortsighted approach focuses on the humanitarian aspect of the decision, while ignoring the national security issue that now looms so large.

Having worked for the US government for so long, we knew we would have to help interested governments work within their own bureaucracies. A political decision to resettle special groups of people outside the UN process would need to be agreed upon by numerous government agencies in order for us to move forward with speed and efficiency.

Security services couldn't sign on to the project without being fully briefed on the effort and provided with specifics on the applicants and the procedures used to vet them. Politicians, government officials, and security professionals had to be absolutely certain that ISIS or other extremists weren't parading as Christians, nor political insurgents masquerading as moderates. Therefore, every single ministry we interacted with was given a comprehensive data sheet on our backgrounds and expertise, as well as details of the vetting program we had implemented.

The other major difference in our approach was our ability to anticipate a country's administrative requirements. We did everything we could to collect the data they would need to conduct meaningful traces, run cursory background checks, and prepare for the integration process. In addition to their biodata, we had obtained passport-size photographs of every applicant and extensive personal information such as education level, degrees, and work history. We did more than any other petitioning organization had ever done before. Now it was up to the Slovakian government. While we awaited their decision, we did what we had been doing all along—we prayed.

Over the course of the next few weeks, thousands of prayers were lifted up to God as the Slovakian government considered our request. Joseph had brought all of the Iraqis' applications and photos home with him, and we spent four weeks scanning and digitizing all the documents, which we sent electronically to the Slovakian government.

As they waited for Slovakia's decision, Joseph and some of the other team members continued to explore other avenues, trying to identify other countries willing to accept Christian IDPs. They traveled throughout the United States and all over the world, initiating hundreds of telephone calls and holding scores of meetings. It was a nonstop effort.

Then one morning, as I was asking God to intervene in the situation, I sensed him say, *I'm not doing you a favor by helping out. These are my people, and this is my project.*

I suddenly realized that God wasn't just *in* the project; he was *driving* it. We were simply the tools he was using to accomplish his will.

This realization turned my desperate pleas into powerful, faith-filled, mountain-moving kinds of prayers. What happened next was one of the most amazing experiences of my life.

It took several weeks, but we finally received a positive response from senior government leaders in Slovakia. The initial approval granted, we then spent months helping their officials move our request through the appropriate channels, and we worked hard to encourage open communication with various government agencies, which helped the Ministry of Interior obtain responses quickly. Once they received all necessary ministry approvals, the request went back up to the senior levels of government for final consideration.

Weeks later, the message we had been waiting for arrived. On November 12, Slovakia's prime minister, Robert Fico, formally approved the plan for Slovakia to accept a group of our IDPs. No other country had said yes to our request.

The evacuation was set for December 7. Slovakia agreed to take 150 people in the first group. Joseph and I had vetted 400 people but didn't want the responsibility of choosing which 150 would evacuate to Slovakia. Fortunately, Father Douglas, who knew the people much better than we did, made those decisions. If it all went smoothly and the Slovakian government was able to move the people efficiently through the asylum and integration processes, then the government would consider taking additional families.

We took this as a challenge to prove that such an evacuation could be accomplished quickly and efficiently—if the right people with the right set of skills and expertise were involved. Our hope was that if this proof of concept worked, other countries would gain confidence and follow suit, opening their doors to people displaced by ISIS in Iraq and Syria.

But even that wasn't the most amazing part.

On November 17, Joseph and I heard from a good friend, Adam Ciralsky, a television producer and journalist whom we hadn't seen or spoken with in many months. He happened to be in Florida and wanted to catch up with us for a day or two. When Adam arrived that evening and learned about the project, he asked, "Do you have media?"

"Media?"

"Have you arranged for media coverage of the evacuation?" he asked.

We weren't sure how to respond. Frankly, obtaining media coverage of the event had never even occurred to us. We were too worried about the basics—namely, whether we'd be able to pull this whole thing off. There were a million and one details to consider, to manage, to plan for, and media wasn't one of them.

"Do you mind if I contact a friend of mine who works at ABC News and see if she might be interested in the story?" he asked.

Joseph and I glanced at each other, eyebrows raised, and responded, "No, we don't mind. Feel free."

Adam immediately texted his friend. As expected, she asked numerous questions about the project. She wanted to know who we were, what we were trying to accomplish, and the identities and roles of each person involved.

The next day we had a follow-up phone call in which we answered even more questions. As the call wrapped up, ABC offered to cover the entire evacuation, from start to finish. They wanted to send their *20/20* investigative team to Iraq to follow the last-minute planning efforts all the way through to the group's arrival in Slovakia.

We were stunned. Just like that, the media coverage piece had dropped right into our laps—a mere ten days before our departure to Iraq. And we hadn't even been looking for it.

Now all we had to do was, well . . . everything.

CHAPTER 19

ESCAPE

The last few days of November were jam-packed with phone calls, e-mails, and a thousand logistical details. We had to coordinate every piece of the planning puzzle with numerous entities, which was a communications challenge since we were dealing with people in at least four different time zones. Joseph slept only a few hours each night, waking up at 3 and 4 a.m. to connect with Slovak officials, who were six hours ahead of Eastern Standard Time (EST), and Father Douglas and his team in Iraq, who were eight hours ahead of us.

I woke up the morning of November 28 filled with anticipation for our departure from Orlando International Airport to begin the final chapter of this massive project. That anticipation was dashed when I learned from Joseph, who had been awake for hours, that all flights into Erbil had been canceled. Apparently, Russia had informed Iraqi officials that it would be launching missiles across Iraqi airspace to hit ISIS targets in Syria, and as a precaution, Iraqi officials canceled all flights in and around the affected airspace. They anticipated that flights would be disrupted for at least forty-eight hours, after which authorities would reassess the situation based on further input from Russia.

This extremely unfortunate development foreshadowed what

would turn out to be the most difficult challenges we faced since the inception of the project, as there is no logistical challenge greater than trying to plan a huge event involving hundreds of people in an active war zone.

When discussing when we might be able to get into Iraq to prepare for and then execute the mission, the company we'd chartered to provide the evacuation aircraft noted, "Every carrier has told us that their policy on flying into Erbil is a moving target at best. We are staying on top of it, but there is always the possibility of last-minute surprises. As one carrier put it, 'You can't make us guarantee service in an uncertain environment.' We will keep you in the loop as things progress."

Over the next two days, flights were booked, flights were canceled, flights were rebooked, and then flights were canceled again. We weren't able to depart Orlando until November 30, pushing our landing in Erbil back to December 2.

The next few days were a blur, which we would not have remembered had we not had a full camera crew capturing the lunacy of so many political, cultural, security, and logistical challenges.

The film crew didn't capture every challenge we faced. On December 4, Joseph and I were eating a late dinner at our hotel. The restaurant was empty—until a group of diplomats sat down at the table right behind us. They didn't waste any time with small talk; they dove straight into business. They spoke in concerned tones about "the threat issued today" and "ISIS plans to attack."

After exchanging an alarmed look, Joseph and I carefully leaned back in our chairs, straining to catch as much of the conversation as possible. We quickly realized that this party included European and American diplomats, along with a local Iraqi bishop.

Having been on the collector's end of this scenario hundreds of times, we knew exactly what was happening. An intelligence service had obtained a clearly identifiable threat and had alerted all potentially affected parties because of their *duty to warn*.

They had just learned of a credible—but frustratingly vague—threat from the Kurdish authorities. ISIS intended to attack targets in Erbil with a VBIED, aka a car bomb. Collectors had no knowledge of the time frame or specific methodology of the attack, or that information would have been shared in the threat warning.

Joseph and I immediately realized the significance of the threat to our project. We were working with the priest in charge of Mar Elia, which was located on the edge of town, in the section of Erbil closest to the front lines with ISIS.

We embodied all the targets ISIS loves to hit: We were a significant grouping of former American officials and media representatives, hanging around the courtyard of a notable Iraqi church whose compound served as a temporary shelter to more than five hundred internally displaced Iraqi Christians. The church building, administration trailers, and living quarters were not set back from the surrounding streets, which made them vulnerable to attack. There was minimal security around the compound—just a simple fence in the front and a small concrete wall that stretched around the back perimeter. We couldn't have been a bigger and more obvious target. One well-placed car bomb could take us all out.

Furthermore, we were preparing for the historic airlift and relocation of 150 of those displaced Iraqi Christians to Europe, something that all of Erbil seemed to know about because so many Christians were inquiring how they could get on "the list" to leave.

Joseph and I were used to dealing with threats as counterterrorism officers, but this was different. Along with Father Douglas, we were responsible for the well-being of hundreds of persecuted Christians who had already been severely traumatized. Many had lost family members to the terrorists, as well as their homes, businesses, possessions, and entire livelihoods. The last thing they needed was to feel vulnerable again, to think that ISIS was coming to Erbil.

We shared this information with Father Douglas, but as it turned out, he had heard about it that day through his own channels. It seemed that much of Erbil was aware of the heightened threat situation. For Joseph and me, it added to the stress of needing to get the evacuation accomplished as quickly and efficiently as possible.

Finally, December 6 arrived. Our flight was scheduled for the morning of December 7, which meant that this was the last full day before the first group of IDPs left Iraq for new lives abroad.

Naturally, we had carefully choreographed the events of those two days, including a full program of activities leading up to the boarding of the aircraft, as well as activities closely coordinated with the Slovak government following the IDPs' arrival on the seventh. Given how long it would take to get everyone and their luggage onto the buses for the move to the airport, we planned to start loading buses early, around 3 a.m.

Nervous anticipation built throughout the evening of the sixth as members of the group said their last good-byes to friends and extended family members who would remain in Iraq. That evening, Father Douglas performed a mass in Mar Elia Church to bless the evacuation and pray for all those heading to new homes. He prayed for those trying to rebuild their lives in Erbil and for those displaced all over the country.

After the service, hundreds of people would come together for a special dinner in the Mar Elia courtyard to mark the group's last night in Iraq. We would begin loading the buses just a few hours later, and most families decided to stay awake until then. Things were finally going according to plan.

Then in the middle of the mass, Joseph started receiving strange texts claiming that Erbil International Airport would shut down at 10 p.m. Apparently, Russia wasn't finished with Iraq's airspace yet.

By the time people sat down to eat dinner, official word started trickling in, confirming our greatest fear—the evacuation would not begin in a few hours after all. Every detail, every plan, every preparation came to a grinding halt. We all went into shock, unsure what to do.

This was more than just your average delay. We had reserved the plane only for the seventh. Since that plane would not be able to land in Erbil, we would have to scuttle to find a replacement—and fast. Considering all the hoops Joseph had to jump through to get the first plane, we had plenty of reason for concern.

Informing Father Douglas about the airport closure was one of the most difficult things Joseph had to do. After they spoke, Father Douglas looked dazed and confused.

Over the next few painful days, Joseph and his logistics team worked nonstop to figure out when the airport would reopen. It was almost impossible to book an aircraft when nobody knew when flights would be permitted to resume or how insurance companies would feel about covering flights into and out of what the industry described as "an active war zone." Joseph could barely eat or sleep, worried about how he was going to get the group to Slovakia in a timely manner.

Even though the delay was out of our control, we knew that any major hiccups could result in Slovakia opting to refuse a second round of refugees. We needed this to go smoothly to build the government's confidence that such missions were not as problematic as they had believed.

Having tentatively scheduled a flight out of Erbil on December 9, we decided to collect everyone's luggage the evening of the eighth.

I quickly texted my prayer group, which was comprised of my dad, Art; my stepmom, Crystal; my sister, Julie; my cousins Jenna and Nerina; my aunt Mary; my grandma Nerina; and my close friends, Stephanie and Cher.

We are collecting and weighing all bags now in faith.
December 8, 6:54 p.m. / 10:54 a.m. EST

I had promised to keep them informed as the mission unfolded, and in turn, they promised to pray for whatever help we might need.

And we needed it. Just collecting and organizing the luggage was a massive undertaking. Of course, it didn't help that the temperature outside was hovering near the freezing mark.

We brought the travelers into the courtyard in waves to avoid being overwhelmed with too many people and too many bags at the same time. Eager to avoid any unnecessary drama at the airport, we had gathered, weighed, and color coded the luggage before setting it aside in a special room for placement in the luggage trucks the following day. It took three hours to process all the bags.

No sooner had we finished weighing and moving the last bag than Joseph called me over and told me the bad news. He had just received word that the flight we had booked for the ninth had just been canceled. I could not believe it. It was one setback after the other.

Once again, I texted the group.

> The charter company just changed their mind. We don't know what that means or why. But looks like it's off again.
>
> December 8, 9:11 p.m. / 1:11 p.m. EST

Joseph and his logistics team were in discussions with multiple companies trying to identify which one was able to meet our short-fused requirement. Unfortunately, given the security circumstances, it was tough to pin any of them down. We were told "yes" when they meant "maybe." Or they would agree in order to secure our business and then be forced to admit that they did not have a plane on the ground and were uncertain when they could pre-position an aircraft in Erbil for our requested departure. Others wanted to help but weren't as adept at making necessary flight arrangements for Iraqi airspace.

Every time we told the travelers the trip was back on, the aircraft would slip through our fingers. Those poor people. They had already been through so much. No doubt many of them were beginning to wonder if we actually *were* going to get them out. They had been conditioned by events in their lives to expect the worst.

It was an emotional roller coaster.

And they weren't the only ones beginning to lose hope. That evening Joseph and I hit the wall as well. Between jet lag, all of the frantic last-minute preparations, and trying to buoy the spirits of all the travelers, we were physically and emotionally spent. Even worse, I felt spiritually empty. I had felt like such a spiritual warrior for the past four months, with faith-filled prayers easily rolling off my lips. But now . . . To make matters worse, I was starting to get sick, possibly from being in the cold for so long while helping with the luggage. I don't know how Joseph kept going physically. Clearly (and thankfully) his immune system was better than mine.

As I lay in bed with a massive headache, a raging sinus infection, an aching body, and my mind numb at the continued negative turn of events, I lost my ability to pray. I summoned a teeny bit of energy to text my family and friends, telling them how very exhausted and washed out we felt. The next text I sent reflected this frustration:

I will not bother you guys again with any updates until I can send one that says "wheels up." You must be sick of me—I AM sick of me . . . giving updates. Sheesh.

December 8, 10:01 p.m. / 2:01 p.m. EST

Immediately, my family texted back saying that they wanted as many updates as we could give—no matter the circumstances. They asked that we keep them informed so that they could continue praying for us. The outpouring of love and positivity warmed my heart and provided the encouragement I needed.

Joseph and his travel assistant worked late into the night trying to find alternative aircraft.

After hours of fruitless phone calls, Joseph thought he had found a local carrier willing to work with us. Because they were based out of Kurdistan, they were much more capable of operating in the volatile airspace. Unfortunately, this particular company couldn't fly us out of Erbil until December 12 or 13. Those dates were not going to work. The Slovak government was anxiously awaiting our arrival. They were managing numerous logistics requirements on their end, which included working with various ministries, airport staff, church officials, and logistics companies to receive our large group. Every delay on our end caused problems on theirs.

Plus, because we had already weighed and stowed all of the evacuees' personal belongings, each extra day we spent in Iraq was a hardship for the families, who were now limited to the clothes on their backs and were essentially living day-to-day off the generosity of others for food, formula, diapers, and other basic necessities. We really needed an earlier departure.

One of our contacts in Dubai suggested that Joseph meet directly with the airline's CEO at his headquarters in Erbil first thing the next morning. We needed help in appealing to him and currying favor for an earlier flight out of Iraq—if the airspace reopened. To that end, Joseph called another friend of ours, a political consultant in Washington, DC, who had high-level government contacts in Kurdistan. Joseph explained our situation and asked if there was anything he could do to reach company executives. Our friend said he couldn't make any promises, but he'd try.

That morning, in a desperate bid to nail something down, Joseph left the hotel for the company's headquarters. He carried a massive burden, and there was little, if anything, I could do to help. I lay in bed in a sick stupor, which compounded my emotional and spiritual fatigue.

That afternoon (and his morning), my dad sent the following text:

Psalm 28:7-9: The LORD is my strength and my shield; my heart trusted in Him, and I am helped. Therefore my heart greatly rejoices, and with my song I will praise Him. The LORD is their strength, and He is the saving refuge of His anointed. Save your people and bless your inheritance; shepherd them also and bear them up forever.

December 9, 2:13 p.m. / 6:13 a.m. EST

A couple of hours later, he lovingly informed me that he was stepping in to do what I could not.

Praying for the aircraft.
December 9, 4:56 p.m. / 8:56 a.m. EST

I thanked my dad for that prayer. In the middle of our operational fog, he and others came through. Their lips lifted up the prayers that we, emptied of energy after fighting so hard and so long, could not. They prayed for wisdom, they prayed for strength, and my dad prayed for a plane—the aircraft that seemed to be so elusive, and the only remaining requirement to complete the puzzle.

Meanwhile my sister, Julie, texted me.

What's the news today? Did the airport open?
December 9, 4:50 p.m. / 8:50 a.m. EST

Although I had not heard from Joseph all day and had no idea what was happening on his end of things, I passed on what I knew.

The airport is open but the charter companies have been slow to agree to restart immediately. J and our logs guy spent all day trying to nail down another aircraft. In this part of the world where nothing is for sure, it's been hard to read between the lines. Meanwhile, the group waits patiently (not sure how—we have all of their luggage).
December 9, 5:15 p.m. / 9:15 a.m. EST

In the ensuing texts, everyone made it clear that they had been praying hard for a miracle. What we did not know was that a miracle was in the making.

About ten minutes after Joseph arrived at the airline's administrative office, the CEO stepped into the reception room where Joseph was waiting. He looked distraught. "What is this about Slovakia?"

he demanded. "I had to shut down my phone because I received 170 phone calls about this last night. I had to turn my phone off so I could sleep!"

Joseph was just as surprised as he was. "I have no idea who made all those phone calls."

"I don't even have a contract with you, Mr. Assad," the CEO snapped, "so I don't know what's going on here. What is it that you want?" Judging by his tone, Joseph didn't hold out much hope that the man was willing to jump through any hoops for us. Joseph said, "Sir, I really need a flight from Erbil to Slovakia as soon as possible."

Despite his surly attitude, the CEO surprised Joseph by calling his air traffic manager into the office to review flight schedules.

"When do you want this flight?" the CEO asked.

"Today," Joseph responded.

"That's impossible," the traffic manager said. "We don't have an aircraft prepositioned to do that."

More employees were called in to deliberate on the matter, discussing aircraft availability and flight schedules. The CEO finally turned to Joseph and said, "I am willing to cancel an existing passenger flight in order to accommodate your request. We can schedule your flight for tomorrow, December 10, but we need to quickly execute a contract in order to file flight plans, obtain flight clearances, and move forward."

Joseph was more than happy to comply. It seemed that God had indeed provided a plane.

Joseph spent the rest of the day running around Erbil completing contract requirements and conferring with airport authorities to ensure there would be no unforeseen challenges to our travel the next day. He returned from the airport not feeling particularly secure about it all. He'd met with various security officers but did not get the sense that he was making any headway. Joseph had done everything humanly possible to grease the skids, but this was the Middle East, where problems in communication and hierarchical structure caused unnecessary complications, no matter what steps you took to avoid them.

Once we received the fully executed contract for the aircraft on the morning of December 10, we started to think that this might actually happen. Father Douglas notified everyone in Mar Elia, and the people—once again—prepared themselves for the great departure that was to occur—God willing—that evening.

The flight was scheduled to leave between 8 and 10 p.m., but just like everything in this evacuation, the exact timing was hard to pin down. The departure time kept slipping as the company worked to obtain flight permissions from air authorities in Erbil and Košice, Slovakia. Regardless, we planned to begin the loading process around 2:30 p.m.

The continuous changes required daily (and hourly) updates of the master schedule, passenger manifests, checklists, and information sheets. We had to ensure that everyone was on the same page and knew where they needed to be and what they needed to do. The next few hours would require us to be as organized as possible, but as with all complex operations, it was impossible to anticipate every contingency.

For example, as group one began to assemble in the courtyard, one of Father Douglas's assistants realized that everyone's passports were still in the safe. They should have been passed back out that morning, but in the press of business, we forgot to confirm that they'd been distributed. The next forty minutes were a mad rush to get those passports into the right hands. And that was time that had not been built into the schedule.

Then once the luggage trucks and minibuses began to arrive at Mar Elia around 2:30, we realized that the logistics company we'd paid to handle local transport requirements had provided smaller minibuses than those we'd reserved. This meant our group would have to squeeze tightly into three vehicles that were far too small for the number of people we were transporting. Typical Middle Eastern bait and switch. You pay for one thing and get another.

Despite the passport snafu and the tiny buses, I was so excited to finally be heading for the airport that I couldn't resist snapping a few pictures and texting them to my prayer group. After all, their prayers had gotten us to this moment.

[Image sent: Photo of travelers gathering in Mar Elia courtyard]
December 10, 3:20 p.m. / 7:20 a.m. EST

[Image sent: Photo of luggage being loaded onto a truck]
December 10, 3:21 p.m. / 7:21 a.m. EST

As soon as she received the pics, my aunt Mary responded.

Is today the day?
December 10, 3:22 p.m. / 7:22 a.m. EST

With renewed optimism, I replied.

Yes, I feel so emotional.
December 10, 3:22 p.m. / 7:22 a.m. EST

Then I sent her a picture of the families saying good-bye to one another, and of a little girl clutching her doll. The looks on their faces said it all.

[Image sent: Photo of people bidding farewell to each other. Those left behind are crowded behind the courtyard fence, watching the travelers get in line to board the buses.]
December 10, 3:38 p.m. / 7:38 a.m. EST

[Image sent: Photo of little girl holding her baby doll, ready to leave Erbil]
December 10, 3:38 p.m. / 7:38 a.m. EST

A little more than an hour later, I sent the text I'd been waiting to send for four days.

On our way to airport now

December 10, 4:53 p.m. / 8:53 a.m. EST

The fact that we had made it to this point was a miracle. But despite the progress of the last twenty-four hours, we were still cognizant of the remaining obstacles we faced, any of which could throw off the evacuation. The journey was not over yet.

CHAPTER 20

THE FINAL PUSH

The families boarded the three passenger buses swiftly and systematically, even though the vehicles were smaller than the ones we'd reserved. As I glanced at Joseph and Father Douglas, their faces showed focus, determination . . . and sheer stress as they hurried from bus to bus to ensure that all 149 passengers were accounted for and that the luggage trucks were lined up and ready to depart the compound.

To the members of our group, the looming evacuation was a fait accompli. On one bus, the Iraqis were singing, clapping their hands, and doing all they could to lessen the emotional impact of leaving their homeland. On the other buses, group members were more pensive, the expressions on their faces reflecting a mix of sadness, relief, and cautious optimism.

But Father Douglas, Joseph, and I couldn't relax yet. There were too many unknowns, too many trip wires that needed to be cleared before the plane lifted off the runway. If living and working in the Middle East had taught us anything, it was to expect the unexpected. And we were significantly behind schedule, which rendered us more vulnerable to the potential obstacles ahead.

I climbed back to the third row of the SUV. Joseph and our logistics support person sat in front of me. Father Douglas was in the passenger seat, next to the driver. Though I might have appeared stoic as our vehicle pulled out of the compound, my mind was spinning, my hands were shaking, and my heart was racing as I wondered whether we would clear the airport's security system in time.

Because Iraq is considered an active war zone and the Erbil airport is within thirty kilometers of the front lines with ISIS, the airport is classified as a high-threat area. Therefore, the airport's security is one of the tightest in the world. To prevent car bombs from being detonated against such an essential facility, passengers are not permitted to drive up to or park at the airport, so we had to clear multiple layers of security before we could reach the terminal. The entire evacuation was riding on our ability to pass through these final checkpoints quickly. At any point while on the airport property we could be questioned, delayed, or turned away, thus threatening the success of the entire operation.

The first checkpoint is where initial security screening of travelers takes place. All passengers are stopped there and waved into a screening area. Vehicles and luggage are searched by officers with police dogs specially trained to identify explosives and explosive precursors. Once passengers clear the first checkpoint, they are permitted to drive to the second security perimeter. This checkpoint funnels ticketed passengers into a special loading zone located about a mile away from the airport. The passengers are dropped off by loved ones or allowed to park their cars here in a fenced-off and carefully contained area. Passengers then go through additional screening before their luggage is loaded onto official airport transit buses, which then take passengers and their luggage to the airport, depositing them at the main entrance. It is a lengthy and time-consuming process under any condition, but because we were trying to transport 149 extremely edgy, highly emotional people and were already running behind schedule, let's just say the tension was ratcheted up a few extra notches.

Bottom line, we needed to avoid any unnecessary scrutiny by airport officials. We didn't want to give anyone a chance to question the purpose of our travel or to hold up the group. We weren't doing anything wrong, but this was the Middle East, so it didn't matter. If officers didn't like the way you looked or the way you answered a question, they could ask you to step aside for extra scrutiny. We couldn't afford to run into either a difficult security officer, who might take pleasure in thwarting our evacuation, or a confused one, who might simply ask too many probing questions.

Because most of the people in our group had never traveled and were feeling the extreme stress of leaving their homeland behind, they had a hard time remembering to identify themselves as IDPs rather than refugees. People do not become refugees until they leave their country of origin. Technically, then, our group was composed not of refugees but of IDPs, who are free to travel anywhere, as long as they have the appropriate travel documents and valid visas. The travel of refugees, on the other hand, can be halted.

When we had playacted with the Iraqis to be sure they answered questions correctly while going through immigration and security lines, several tripped up. When we said, "Are you a refugee?" they accidentally answered yes. They didn't understand the technical or legal difference between a refugee and an IDP, but if they answered incorrectly when questioned by authorities, it could throw off the entire evacuation.

The fewer opportunities there were to answer these questions, the better.

No security officer wants to be the person responsible for something going wrong, and most would rather be safe than sorry. In this type of bureaucracy, everyone wants someone else to make the decision, which relieves them of any responsibility (and eventual blame) if something goes awry.

Joseph and I had attempted to do an end run around these obstacles. Before we'd arrived in Iraq, Joseph had obtained the name of

Erbil International Airport's chief of security and put Father Douglas in touch with him to ask if he would be willing to help us out. Now Father Douglas did not have a preexisting relationship with the senior ranking military official, and since he wasn't being introduced to him by a trusted intermediary, the odds of the general's agreeing to our request were not great. But once again, God had provided, and the general agreed to allow Father Douglas's convoy to bypass both checkpoints and drop off passengers directly at the airport terminal.

Father Douglas provided the general with details of the convoy, including vehicle descriptions and license plate numbers. The general told Father Douglas that our convoy needed to arrive at the checkpoints no later than 4 p.m., and he would advise the guards on that shift to expect us. He had given them instructions to let our vehicles drive straight up to the terminal to unload. He stressed the importance of arriving on time because there would be a shift change at 4 p.m., and the general could not ensure that his instructions would be shared with the next set of soldiers and security officers.

Getting this kind of permission was no small miracle. The general really had to trust the priest, whom he had met only over the phone. He had to be absolutely certain that no one in the eleven-vehicle convoy posed a threat to Kurdish authorities or to the airport. That's a lot of trust in a part of the world where people rarely confer trust on others—especially ones they've never met. The general responded to Father Douglas's request with such enthusiasm it surprised us. It almost sounded too good to be true.

Unfortunately, thanks to the passport snafu, we had fallen more than an hour behind schedule. On top of everything else, we had run headlong into rush-hour traffic. As our convoy moved slowly through the streets now clogged with cars, minibuses, motorcycles, and pedestrians and as our vehicles became separated by the snarled traffic, our anxiety increased. The tension was palpable. But then, so was the energy of our prayer warriors back home.

Even though we were in Iraq, thanks to the wonders of cell phone and Internet connectivity, we were firmly tethered to family, friends, and people we had never met, who were bathing our every move in prayer. As our mission unfolded, my direct contacts had passed on word of our progress to their friends, family members, coworkers, well-wishers, Sunday school classes, churches, home groups, and intercessory prayer partners, so that they, in turn, could pray for us in real time. Many of these people, a group of about seventy, had volunteered to pray for the project since its inception and had seen it through from the beginning when we had no idea what was possible.

I'm not one to overspiritualize things, but if ever I sensed that actions on earth were being deeply affected by what was going on in the spiritual realm, this was the time. What I felt that day was stronger and more real than anything I could see. What happened in the heavens was directly impacting what we were experiencing on the ground.

Once the lead vehicles pulled out of the busy city streets and merged onto the massive highway that would take us toward the airport, we pulled over on the side of the road in order to regroup. We had to wait five minutes for the remaining minibuses and luggage trucks to catch up and for the convoy to get back into alignment. Once we got the thumbs-up that every member of the convoy was accounted for and the final security vehicle had taken up the rear, we slowly pulled out for the final leg of the move to the airport.

What happened once the eleven-vehicle convoy approached the outer perimeter of the airport seemed to occur in slow motion. Each member of the ridiculously long convoy turned—one by one—off the highway and onto Airport Road. In stark contrast to the intense stress we were feeling, the sun was setting peacefully beside the airport, illuminating the darkened horizon with washes of red, pink, purple, and orange. It offered a serene backdrop to the drama unfolding in our midst.

Our vehicles bounced along the road, moving slowly toward the historic event, which up until this moment had seemed so elusive.

The burden to bring this evacuation to its conclusion weighed heavily on our shoulders. We had the hopes and dreams of 149 precious souls pinned on our ability to navigate these final moments with wisdom and clarity.

As we approached the first checkpoint, it was strangely silent in our SUV. We were concentrating so intently that nobody said a word to one another. I think everyone was praying, asking God to remove any remaining obstacles, to make the path straight. At this point, there was nothing more we could do to affect the outcome of the situation. Our final move to the airport was squarely in the hands of God.

We had choreographed and rehearsed our movements to be sure we had the timing down and the logistics thoroughly thought out, and we had tried to consider every contingency. But despite our best efforts, we had arrived at the first checkpoint late—much too late—and we all knew it.

I t was 5:25 p.m. when we came to a halt at the first checkpoint. The driver rolled down the windows, and Father Douglas, sitting forward in the passenger seat, identified himself to the military officer. We all held our collective breath. *Has the change in guard already occurred? Will this officer know who we were? Will the general's promise stand?*

Anticipation hung in the air like a thick fog. I couldn't breathe. I couldn't move. *Please, God, please, Lord . . . please let us through . . .*

The officer smiled and motioned for us to turn into the security check area. *Oh no! No, no, no!* There *had* been a shift change, and this officer had *not* gotten the memo. Joseph quickly interrupted. "Sir, we're on the list. We have special permission from General ███ to go straight to the terminal."

The look on the officer's face was unmistakable. He had no idea who we were. Not breaking eye contact with Joseph, he picked up his secure radio and called in to find out if we had, indeed, been given special permission to proceed.

Tension continued to build as a line of cars accumulated behind us, held up by our massive convoy. Frustrated that we were blocking airport traffic, a second officer standing in front of our vehicle started to wave at us, directing our driver to turn right into the security zone.

We knew that once we entered that area, we could be stuck there for a while trying to sort out the mess. We couldn't afford to give anyone a chance to second-guess the wisdom of permitting wholesale access of the airport to a convoy big enough to bring the Ringling Bros. and Barnum & Bailey Circus to town. It's one thing to hear that there will be eleven vehicles, but it's another to actually see that many SUVs, minibuses, and small trucks headed toward one of the biggest targets in Kurdistan—with a full camera crew, no less. We couldn't afford for these guys to grow impatient or suspicious, change their minds, and rescind the special arrangement we'd worked out with the general.

Our hearts were pounding. Were we going to be sidelined, or would God intervene? As our vehicle slowly rolled forward and our driver reluctantly began to turn the wheel to comply with the officer's instructions, the gentleman on the radio turned and gave the other officer a thumbs-up. Joseph quickly yelled at the driver, "Go straight! Go straight!"

Seeing the thumbs-up, the second officer stepped aside and motioned for us to go straight, allowing us to skip the checkpoint that would have required a thorough K9 check of all 150-plus people *and* their luggage. By the grace of God and the skin of our teeth, we had cleared the first major hurdle.

But we hadn't crossed the finish line yet. The second checkpoint was the most critical. It was the official airport loading zone that relied on airport buses to take travelers to the main terminal. We knew the general had cleared us with the first checkpoint, but what about the second? What if that guard had changed too?

Once again, we held our breath, the vehicle full of desperate prayers and nervous energy. We approached the stop sign slowly with our windows rolled down, ready to explain who we were, but instead of asking questions, the officers waved us right through. We were in shock. Everyone in the van let out a collective sigh of relief. We didn't know how or when they got word that our convoy had been given special permission to drive directly to the terminal, but the biggest remaining obstacle—and the one that had the greatest chance of throwing off the evacuation—was now behind us.

My hands still shaking, I texted,

This is huge—they let us through this massive security perimeter where most can't go!
December 10, 5:27 p.m. / 9:27 a.m. EST

Granted, this was the Middle East. We may have made it through both checkpoints, but there was always a chance that something could still go wrong. Not wanting to draw undue attention to our group and to mitigate concerns other security officers might have if they saw a throng of vehicles idling at the entrance, Joseph decided to have three vehicles unload at a time. The rest would wait in a nearby employee parking lot until Joseph called them up. By the grace of God, we had made it this far. We weren't taking any chances.

Father Douglas and I were deposited at the unloading zone to help the travelers disembark from the vans and check in. Father Douglas was stationed near the curb. He helped members of our group exit the microbuses, claim their luggage from the corresponding truck, place their bags on luggage carts, and head into the terminal. My job was to interface with airport officials and employees at the airline's check-in counter and answer questions as families lined up. Most of the people in our group had never flown before or been inside an airport, so they had no idea how things were supposed to work.

Accompanied by the first few families, I walked inside to find the appropriate check-in counter. We walked past several lines before my eyes caught a glimpse of the word I was looking for. There it was:

MICHELE RIGBY ASSAD

A monitor hung over the last airline counter with the name of our final destination: *Košice*. That's when it hit me. The evacuation was no longer a vague possibility. It was real; it was happening. My eyes filled with tears, but I quickly blinked them back, trying to keep it together. The word *Košice* might as well have been *Freedom* or *Deliverance*, it represented so much to these travelers.

Who knew when we started this process four months earlier that this was where we would end up? It was clear that something much bigger than us had made this all possible. A powerful God had intervened in the affairs of humans to demonstrate how very much his people mattered to him.

As our families queued up, one of the managers in charge of the counter started pummeling me with questions. "Who are these people? Why are they traveling? Where are they going? Why are Americans helping them? Are these people refugees? Are you sure they plan to return to Iraq?"

I kept answering his questions, doing my best to alleviate his concerns and ingratiate myself with him and the other airline employees.

"These are religious travelers from the church taking some holiday in Slovakia," I explained. "We have been asked to facilitate this travel and to ensure they have a good holiday. No, they are not refugees."

He kept returning to the same question: "Are you absolutely certain these people are not refugees?"

"Nope! Not refugees," I answered confidently with a smile.

I felt like I was back in the CIA again, working hard to keep authorities from becoming too curious. I knew that I had to stay on my toes and apply my best interpersonal skills to ensure that the manager did not call in more senior officials to question me. I was also hoping he wouldn't engage the passengers. If he started asking them a thousand questions, things could unravel quickly, given how nervous and unsure of themselves our group members were.

The last thing I wanted was for the manager to decide that he didn't like us or to become suspicious of our travelers. As long as he

I

remained focused on me, we would be all right. So I smiled a lot. I made jokes, and I chatted away with him about all kinds of inconsequential things. And do you know what? It worked. He calmed down, and despite his intuition that these people weren't your normal, everyday kind of travelers, he decided not to make an issue of it. An extensive background in counterterrorism is a wonderful thing, but it also never hurts to be polite.

After the last passenger checked in, the manager muttered, "I have a feeling that this is the last time we are going to see these people in Iraq." We did not respond. We just smiled and thanked him for his outstanding assistance.

My next few texts were short, but they were packed with emotion.

All checked in

Going through final security [check] now

It's happening!!!

Boarding.
December 10, 8:35 p.m. / 12:35 p.m. EST

[Image sent: Photo from inside the plane showing our group finding their seats and getting ready for takeoff]

Boarded!
December 10, 8:55 p.m. / 12:55 p.m. EST

And then I sent the text that elicited grateful tears from people praying for us all over the world, the text I'd dreamed of sending all week long:

Wheels-up!

At approximately 9:15 p.m. local time, our aircraft lifted off the runway and into the air, and expressions of joy rang out as we ascended into the darkened sky. That was it. We were on our way to Košice, Slovakia, where we would be met by church officials, immigration officers, airport authorities, Ministry of Interior representatives, and the Slovak press corps.

A little more than two hours later, I sent the final text of the evening:

We arrived!!! We're in Slovakia! They [the group] all clapped and cheered when we took off and when we just hit the ground
December 10, 11:24 p.m. / 4:24 p.m. EST

He did it. Despite all of the challenges, obstructions, delays, and cancellations, God made the evacuation happen after all. We had witnessed a miracle.

How else can you explain an Egyptian immigrant, a former homecoming queen, a British television producer, an Iraqi priest, and others coming together to help liberate hundreds of persecuted Christians from the hands of ISIS?

Had I not experienced it firsthand, I don't know that even I would have believed it. But our mission is proof positive that God not only moves in strange and remarkable ways, but he can—and will—move heaven and earth to help his people. And he will pull anyone he needs into the equation as he goes, weaving what look like unrelated threads into sophisticated tapestries, demonstrating that the haphazard jungle of knots and loose ends that make up the apparently unorganized chaos of our lives is not so random after all.

Until we can view it on the flip side, the complete picture is difficult to imagine. But when we see the final product, we can appreciate the virtuosity of his grand design.

Looking back, there is so much I couldn't see clearly—until now. From the very beginning, God had been guiding my every step, all with this end in mind. He instilled in me the gifts of empathy, intuition, and the ability to read human behavior that would be necessary not only to excel in counterterrorism, but more importantly, to discern the Hamads amidst a sea of Christian converts in Erbil. He introduced me to Joseph, who—in turn—introduced me to Egypt, the launching pad for my infatuation with the Middle East. It was God who brought me to the library that fateful day in 1999 to hear a team of recruiters describe an extraordinary, seemingly unattainable career in international espionage. And it was God who gave me the courage to reapply, even after I had already been rejected. For that matter, it was God who kept me from going into the wrong CIA directorate in the first place. He has been firmly in control all along—directing my footsteps and speaking his desires into my heart. All I had to do was listen and obey.

Until quite recently, I thought that God's grand design for me was all about joining the CIA to fight the war on terror. But now I realize that the CIA was not the end goal at all—it was just another step on the journey, one that God used to further refine me and the skills I would need to fight an even bigger war. Everything Joseph and I had done for the past fifteen years had been leading us to this moment, when 149 devoted followers of Christ were set free from an unholy terror that threatened everything they held dear, including their own lives. When I think about it today, it still gives me chills.

As for God's unusual request—the catalyst that led me away from the CIA and into the sanctuary at Mar Elia—I realize now that God wasn't asking me to share my experiences as a counterterrorism specialist to distract me from the pain and confusion I was suffering at the time. He was asking me to tell my story so that people, myself included, could learn that God doesn't require well-connected or influential people to do his work here on earth. Nor does he require impressive résumés, high IQs, brute strength, or superpowers. What he does need are men and women who are completely open to him, people who don't put conditions on their commitment. He needs people who are willing to do what others will not . . . those who will go the extra mile, even when it costs them personally to do so . . . those willing to surge forward when they are exhausted and everyone else has folded . . . those who look pain in the eye and still muster the motivation to keep going . . . those who are willing to wrestle with a problem until it's solved . . . those who allow failure and rejection to make them something better than they were before. God isn't looking for perfection. He is seeking men and women with faith greater than fear.

The course of my life was not wrought by my own design, but by the grace and leadership of a great God. Despite my having a host of flaws that included self-limiting ideas and behavior, he was patient and ensured I got where I needed to go. Though trepidation has haunted me every step of this journey, I have trusted a force that I cannot see.

Have I feared? Almost always.

Have I doubted? Yes, often.

Have I worried that I was intellectually deficient and behind the curve? Every day of my life.

Have I wandered off course? Several times.

Have I failed? Terribly.

Serving God isn't easy. It is gut-wrenching, difficult work. It is not for the faint of heart. But if you listen for his voice, are open to his leading, and obey his will, you will experience adventures beyond your wildest imagination and climb mountains you never dreamed possible. God had a grand design in mind when he created me, and he has a grand design for you as well. It's not always easy to see. But it's always there.

And my prayer moving forward—for me and for you—is that we might always have the patience, the endurance, and the faith to allow him to weave the disparate pieces of our lives together in the service of his grand design.

EPILOGUE

★ ★ ★

As a child, I never dreamed of becoming a spy. I never dreamed of traveling abroad, of living in active war zones, of fighting terrorists, or of helping persecuted Christians escape Islamic extremists.

Back when I was a little girl flipping through the pages of *National Geographic*, marveling at the vast array of strange and exotic cultures, I caught a glimpse of how radically different life could be for other little girls. But I never imagined how dark, how hard, how hopeless it could be.

When Joseph and I were interviewing the families at Mar Elia, I met two young sisters, aged five and six. I'd met plenty of children by then, but something about those two little girls—maybe it was their sweet, shy smiles and quiet mannerisms—stirred my soul. The first time I saw them, they sat quietly on a bench, holding hands while their parents filled out application forms before getting in line to be interviewed by Joseph or me. They looked so much alike that they were hard to tell apart. That's when it hit me: With their cute little curls and dimpled cheeks, Sara and Katherin were the spitting image of me and Julie at that age. They were likely unaware of the threats they faced and the herculean efforts their parents made to shield them from the turmoil.

I felt such a connection to them that I was thrilled when I learned their family was among the 149 chosen for evacuation to Slovakia. Not only was the project a godsend for their parents, who were on an ISIS hit list because of their involvement in a Christian ministry, but Sara and Katherin would now grow up in a safe place where they would have to make no apologies for being ambitious young ladies or committed Christians.

Once we landed in Slovakia, I wanted to scoop the sisters up in my arms, hug them tight, and say, "You have no idea what's possible! Dream big, girls!"

Since that historic arrival, the girls' family has adjusted well. Of course, they struggled with enormous changes, but they are motivated to work hard to assimilate into Europe. They—and other families like them—are beyond grateful for the support they have received.

Unfortunately, a few in the group did not fare as well. For them, the transition was too hard, and the support they received on the ground was insufficient. Learning a new language has been one of the most daunting tasks. Without a solid grasp of Slovak, everything—from meeting new neighbors to shopping for groceries to applying for and gaining employment—is more challenging. In addition, the Iraqis have had to adapt to new political systems, social programs, cultural expectations, living conditions, food, weather . . . the list is endless. Before leaving Mar Elia, we'd often remind the group that, no matter what they were running from (even ISIS), it would be incredibly difficult to start their lives from scratch in a new country.

Faced with that reality, a few families have returned to Erbil. Despite not knowing how they would rebuild their lives, they preferred the difficult situation they knew and understood in Iraq to the unknowns of life in Slovakia, particularly when they were unable to find jobs to support their families there.

Throughout Europe, governments continue to grapple with how best to manage the migrant crisis and assimilate those who have already made it to their shores. After the group of Iraqi IDPs arrived in Slovakia, the project was turned over to a Slovak NGO formed by the Slovak Catholic Church, which has served as the liaison between the group and government agencies and supports the families' integration into their new country. The Slovakian government and the NGO have asked Joseph and me to provide cross-cultural advice and counsel to social workers who work directly with the Iraqis on integration issues. Slovakia has decided against taking additional IDPs and refugees until they feel confident that they can assimilate these newcomers into their society.

Joseph and I continue to do whatever we can, on an individual and personal basis, to see that Middle Eastern Christians can thrive in their ancestral homelands or, when that is impossible, find safe havens elsewhere. Professionally, we continue to work as international security consultants for government leaders and multinational corporations, and we offer training on personal security, terror threats, and the acquisition, vetting, and validation of intelligence. Although we still travel a lot and shuttle between the Middle East, Florida, and Washington, DC, the difference from our decade with the CIA is that we now have the freedom to choose our assignments and to make our family a top priority.

Such personal freedom remains elusive in Iraq. Since late 2016, Iraqi and other international forces have been battling to liberate Mosul and villages across northern Iraq from ISIS. Whether or not they will be able to push out the extremists and hold this area is a key question, as ISIS continues to operate out of Syria, where it holds significant territory. Unfortunately, the push into Mosul has increased the number of IDPs, though most now are Sunni Muslims desperate to escape the ISIS forces, which have no qualms about using them as human shields. While a handful of families have returned to Qaraqosh, it is unclear when it will be safe enough for residents of the cities and villages in northern Iraq to return to their homes and rebuild their lives. ISIS rendered much of the territory uninhabitable by destroying homes, businesses, and other infrastructure and setting up explosive booby traps.

In mid-2016, Father Douglas al-Bazi accepted an assignment to New Zealand, where he is the priest of St. Addai Chaldean Catholic Church. Shortly before that, he went on a speaking tour throughout the United States, which included a stop at the United Nations. Everywhere he goes, he reminds people of Christianity's deep roots in Iraq and urges them to recognize the continuing genocide in his country.

Most of all, Father Douglas doesn't want us to forget his people. When he learned that American Christians were praying for their fellow believers in Iraq, he was overwhelmed with gratitude. "This makes us realize that we are not alone. We know that we have not been forgotten."[1] Somehow prayer unites our hearts with theirs, and in some inexplicable way, God works through our petitions to bring about change.

We can also support Christians throughout the Middle East by validating their suffering. They have spent much of their lives being treated differently for their faith; at the same time, their own leaders, as well as those in Europe and the United States, often promote a narrative that largely ignores their experience of inequality and suffering in Muslim-majority countries.

Finally, we can help refugees (of all backgrounds) who come to the West. We should listen to their stories, determine their needs, and find ways to help newcomers rebuild their lives and assimilate into our great, multicultural society.

We hear so often about how divided our country has become, and social media certainly feeds into those fears. We are bombarded with warnings of economic difficulties, political challenges, religious and ethnic conflicts, acts of terrorism, and environmental disasters.

But rather than being fearful, this is the moment when we need to kick it into high gear. Instead of seeking isolation, let's seek powerful engagement. It takes no special training to welcome a stranger with a smile, to help furnish a refugee family's apartment, or to pray for the Iraqis in Erbil who still live in church courtyards as they wait to see if they'll ever be able to return to their homes in nearby villages.

If the evacuation taught me anything, it's that my thinking has been too small, too limited. Far from being powerless, we have been given everything we need to positively impact our families, communities, and the nations. If you are passionate about refugees, consider partnering with a local church or community organization that supports new immigrants. If you are passionate about education, partner with a community group that provides mentorship opportunities and scholarships. If you are passionate about protecting animals or the environment, then reach out to an NGO dedicated to improving a cause close to your heart and see what you can do to help.

Because God's "power is made perfect in weakness" (2 Corinthians 12:9), the key is not to focus on ourselves or the problems, but to focus on him. The answers will come, and they will come in unexpected ways and from unexpected sources.

Never forget: You've got this!

Right before this manuscript went to print, Joseph and I learned that a close friend and former colleague passed away in the line of duty. We were the same age and had similar backgrounds in terms of faith, education, and passion. Our hearts are broken, but full of gratitude for his willingness to risk everything to make this a better world. In May 2017, a star was added to the CIA's Memorial Wall in his honor.

Much that happened in this book would not have been possible without him.

Enjoy heaven, brother.

ACKNOWLEDGMENTS

★ ★ ★

First, I must thank Joseph, without whom none of this great adventure would have occurred. The night we met in Tavares, I was smitten and knew that I wanted to marry somebody "just like you." You are the most generous, capable, and courageous person I know. Your eagerness to help others is a beautiful testimony to the legacy of your parents. They would be proud of who you are and all you have accomplished. Your unparalleled operational expertise and incredible grasp of international affairs have taught me more than any books or degrees. Your love and encouragement empowered me to do things I never thought possible. Now that rockets, bunkers, and war zones are behind us, I can't wait to see what happens next!

To Julie Clow: Words cannot describe how much I love you, my little sister. To have another human being share so much of your DNA and mirror your thought patterns, assumptions, drive, and personality is a rare gift and one that I don't take for granted. I'm so proud of all you have accomplished. I admire your intellect and incredible determination. Thank you for mentoring me through the seven long years it took to bring the book to fruition. You were the cheerleader I needed to keep moving forward despite numerous setbacks. From the trailer park to Google, Chanel, and the CIA—we've come a long way, baby!

I will be forever grateful for the love and sacrifice of my parents: Judy Morris and Art and Crystal Rigby. Mom, you raised me to love learning and to be a winner. I am who I am because of you; thank you for pushing me to dream bigger and shoot higher. Thank you for providing the financial means and emotional support for my first overseas trips to Egypt, Russia, and Ukraine. I know it was scary letting me go, but thank you for enabling me to follow *the call.*

Dad and Crystal, you have been supportive of every assignment, international move, and major change in our lives. I can't begin to list the many ways you managed our affairs when Joseph and I were abroad. You made it possible for us to keep our heads above water. Thank you for holding us up in prayer and talking us through the moments when we thought we could not endure "one more day" in a war zone. Your daily intercessions for strength and physical protection are what we have valued above all else.

To my beautiful mother- and father-in-law in heaven, we miss you so much. Your faithfulness to God serves as an inspiration for all that Joseph and I do. Your legacy continues to ripple through time and impact thousands of lives—all the people whom you selflessly served. Thank you for the sweet compliments on my writing and entreaties for me to do more. I think this book would make you smile, which gives me great joy.

Thank you to my beautiful sisters-in-law for being such a critical support to us through these years. No matter how far apart we are, you are always on our minds and in our hearts.

Thank you to family and friends who told me I had an important story to tell, even when I didn't believe them: Dad and Crystal, my late mother-in-law, my late grandma Gayle, aunt Jane, aunt Mary, cousins Jenna and Nerina, grandma Nerina, niece Danielle Clow, Phil and Jennifer D., godparents Burney and Karen, and my best friend, Stephanie. You were long-suffering and prayerful for us throughout our CIA tenure as well as the development of this manuscript.

There is no way I would have gotten through ten years at the

CIA without the camaraderie of my colleagues. To "the ladies in Baghdad": I couldn't have endured the insanity of that year without the benefit of your humor and wit. I can't imagine working that hard ever again: running from rockets, jumping into bunkers, waking up in the middle of the night to deal with threat reporting, and drinking from a fire hose of emergencies every hour of the day. You will always hold a special place in my heart.

To the last two groups with whom I served, you were some of the most operationally proficient and emotionally intelligent officers with whom I've ever collaborated. Thank you for teaching me how to honor my intuition and use it to deconstruct the toughest cases. I wish more people could know about your work. You are superstars.

Thanks to "David" for taking a chance on Joseph and me and enabling our transition to the civilian world. Without your generosity, I'm not sure where we would be right now. Your strategic thinking continues to inspire us to find unique ways to solve thorny problems.

I am so grateful for the early supporters of this book: media guru Adam Ciralsky, editor extraordinaire Miriam Shaviv, Julie Anderson, and Marla Carlton. Thank you for believing in me and helping me find ways to push this message forward.

Thank you to Mark Burnett and Roma Downey, without whom there would have been no evacuation. It was your vision that set the evacuation on course. Aron Shaviv and Adam Ciralsky, your assistance to the Iraq evacuation effort was invaluable. Thank you for helping us at such a critical (and stressful) time. You were godsends.

Maria Ribas, you were the first one in the industry to catch the vision for this book. Your advocacy for the earlier version of the manuscript meant so much to me. Julie Clow, Jenny Blake, and Graham Segroves, thank you for supporting me when I heard the calling to write the book but couldn't wrap my head around it. Your coaching enabled me to move forward as I strove to conceptualize the next critical steps of my life.

A special thanks goes out to several people who have been longtime friends and incredible supporters of the book as well as our careers: Bill and Pam Fleming, Dr. John Calhoun, and our alma mater, Palm Beach Atlantic University.

There would be no book without the vision of Esther Fedorkevich, founder and CEO of The Fedd Agency. Esther, you recognized that what I lacked in a platform I made up for in substance and experience. When I was about to relinquish my publishing dream, you agreed to take me on. A special thanks goes out to the entire Fedd team who believed in this project from the beginning: Whitney Gossett, Misty Williams, Christian Rea, and Lisa Schmidt, you each brought your special touches to this project.

Tyndale Momentum, I can't thank you enough for investing in this message of hope and inspiration. I prayed that the manuscript would come to rest with the perfect team, the kind of people who aren't scared to "get off the 'X.'" Sarah Atkinson, I am grateful that you gave this book a chance. Your enthusiasm for this project was such a gift. Thank you for shepherding the manuscript from start to finish, ensuring it received the care and attention it needed at every step. Carol Traver and Kim Miller, your excitement for this book made the editorial process so much easier as you used your incredible skills to transform a rough stone into a shiny pearl . . . in record time, I might add. Dean Renninger, you took a difficult charge and delivered an extraordinary book cover. It is beyond words! Big hugs also go to Sharon Leavitt, Katie Dodillet, Cassidy Gage, and Jillian Schlossberg.

At the beginning and the end of the day, the book is about you, the readers. If my experiences provide the spark and the courage you need to pursue opportunities that seem beyond reach, then all the effort that went into the book will be worth it. Get off the "X" and go get 'em!

ENDNOTES

★ ★ ★

CHAPTER 1: THE SPY NEXT DOOR

1. "How to Become a Leadership Analyst with the Central Intelligence Agency," http://www.ciaagentedu.org/leadership-analyst/.

CHAPTER 4: A MODEL SPY

1. "Not Bad for a Girl from Baltimore: The Story of Virginia Hall," State Department library, http://photos.state.gov/libraries/estonia/99874/History%20stories/Not-Bad -for-a-Girl-from-Baltimore.pdf.

2. Cate Lineberry, "Wanted: The Limping Lady," *Smithsonian*, February 1, 2007, http://www.smithsonianmag.com/history/wanted-the-limping-lady-146541513/.

3. Sarah Helm, *A Life in Secrets: Vera Atkins and the Missing Agents of WWII* (New York: Anchor Books, 2007), 15.

CHAPTER 9: CAUGHT BETWEEN IRAQ AND A HARD PLACE

1. Erik Prince, *Civilian Warriors* (New York: Penguin, 2013), 166.

CHAPTER 13: NEVER SAY NEVER

1. "Large Bombings Claim Ever More Lives," *Iraq Body Count*, October 4, 2007; Bill Roggio, "Iraq by the Numbers: Graphing the Decrease in Violence," *FDD's Long War Journal*, December 12, 2008.

CHAPTER 15: NOW WHAT?

1. "Country Comparison: Crude Oil—Proved Reserves" and "Country Comparison: Natural Gas—Proved Reserves," *The World Factbook*, Central Intelligence Agency, https://www.cia.gov/library/publications/the-world-factbook/rankorder/2244rank .html and https://www.cia.gov/library/publications/the-world-factbook/rankorder /2253rank.html.

CHAPTER 16: YOU CAN'T GO HOME AGAIN

1. Angelina E. Theodorou, "Which Countries Still Outlaw Apostasy and Blasphemy?" Pew Research Center, July 29, 2016, http://www.pewresearch.org/fact-tank/2016/07 /29/which-countries-still-outlaw-apostasy-and-blasphemy/.

2. Max Fisher, "Majorities of Muslims in Egypt and Pakistan Support the Death Penalty for Leaving Islam," May 1, 2013, *Washington Post*, https://www.washingtonpost.com /news/worldviews/wp/2013/05/01/64-percent-of-muslims-in-egypt-and-pakistan -support-the-death-penalty-for-leaving-islam/.
3. "UNHCR Asylum Trends 2014," UNHCR, March 26, 2015, http://www.unhcr.org /551128679.pdf.
4. "UNHCR Global Resettlement Statistical Report 2014," UNHCR, http://www.unhcr .org/52693bd09.pdf.

CHAPTER 17: BACK TO IRAQ
1. After much lobbying by the human rights community and pressure from lawmakers, the State Department finally declared on March 17, 2016, that the Islamic State's attacks on Christians and other minorities in Syria and Iraq constituted genocide. See https://2009-2017.state.gov/secretary/remarks/2016/03/254782.htm.
2. Ishaan Tharoor, "Slovakia Will Take in 200 Syrian Refugees, but They Have to Be Christian," *Washington Post*, August 19, 2015, https://www.washingtonpost.com/news /worldviews/wp/2015/08/19/slovakia-will-take-in-200-syrian-refugees-but-they-have -to-be-christian/?utm_term=.8c7d0d69f460.

CHAPTER 18: DECISION TIME
1. Matt Crocker, Joel Houston, and Salomon Lightelm, "Oceans (Where Feet May Fail)," copyright © 2013 by Hillsong Music Publishing.

EPILOGUE
1. Kathryn Jean Lopez, "Iraqi Priest Embodies Love in the Face of Hate," *Crux*, May 4, 2016, https://cruxnow.com/church/2016/05/04/iraqi-priest-embodies-love-in-the -face-of-hate/.

ABOUT THE AUTHOR

★ ★ ★

Michele Rigby Assad began her career in the government relations department of an international relief and development organization in Washington, DC, in 1995. She joined the CIA in January 2002 to work as an intelligence officer in the Directorate of Operations, the covert arm of the agency. Specializing in counterterrorism and counterintelligence issues, Michele worked in several hot spots, including Iraq during the height of the war. To date, Michele has lived in six countries in the Near East region and traveled to more than forty others.

After a decade of government service, Michele left the undercover life to serve as a public speaker, trainer, and international security consultant focused on the Middle East, Europe, North Africa, and Asia. She and her husband, Joseph, live in Florida.

Michele holds a master's degree in contemporary Arab studies from Georgetown University's School of Foreign Service and a political science degree from Palm Beach Atlantic University.

Michele credits student-led mission trips to Egypt, Russia, and Ukraine and a study abroad program in Egypt, Israel, and the West Bank as being the catalysts to her passion for foreign cultures and international travel. The year she spent studying in the Middle East changed the course of her life, taking her from rural central Florida to the front lines of the war on terror. Michele is motivated to use her unique platform to educate and inspire, showing how critical courage is to living a life of impact and purpose.

Michele writes about her many passions at www.michelerigbyassad.com, where she features articles on counterterrorism, personal security, the Middle East, faith, and inspiration. Connect with her there, as well as on Facebook (Michele Rigby Assad) and Twitter @MicheleRigAssad.

Online Discussion *guide*

TAKE *your* TYNDALE READING EXPERIENCE *to the* NEXT LEVEL

A FREE discussion guide for this book is available at bookclubhub.net, perfect for sparking conversations in your book group or for digging deeper into the text on your own.

www.bookclubhub.net

You'll also find free discussion guides for other Tyndale books, e-newsletters, e-mail devotionals, virtual book tours, and more!